SPIES ON TRIAL

SPIES ON TRIAL

TRUE TALES OF ESPIONAGE IN THE COURTROOM

Cecil C. Kuhne III

ROWMAN & LITTLEFIELD
Lanham • Boulder • New York • London

Published by Rowman & Littlefield
An imprint of The Rowman & Littlefield Publishing Group, Inc.
4501 Forbes Boulevard, Suite 200, Lanham, Maryland 20706
www.rowman.com

6 Tinworth Street, London SE11 5AL, United Kingdom

British Library Cataloguing in Publication Information Available

Library of Congress Cataloging-in-Publication Data

Names: Kuhne, Cecil C., III, 1952- author.
Title: Spies on trial : true tales of espionage in the courtroom / Cecil C.
  Kuhne III.
Description: Lanham : Rowman & Littlefield, 2019. | "Appendices include:
  Espionage Act, National Security Act, Foreign Intelligence Surveillance
  Act, Economic Espionage Act, Freedom of Information Act." | Includes
  bibliographical references and index. |
Identifiers: LCCN 2019011962 (print) | LCCN 2019020103 (ebook) | ISBN
  9781538131350 (electronic) | ISBN 9781538131343 (cloth : alk. paper)
Subjects: LCSH: Trials (Espionage)—United States—History—20th century.
Classification: LCC KF221.E87 (ebook) | LCC KF221.E87 K84 2019 (print) | DDC
  345.73/0231—dc23
LC record available at https://lccn.loc.gov/2019011962

To Clare

It had all the earmarks of a CIA operation; the bomb killed everybody in the room except the intended target.

—William F. Buckley Jr.

CONTENTS

INTRODUCTION

The spy business is, and always has been, an unpredictable one, and sometimes the dark shadows of the clandestine backroom are suddenly exchanged for the bright lights of the open courtroom.

The factual situations and legal issues that judges and juries face in dealing with the adjudication of espionage cases are typically more unusual, complex, and diverse than one could possibly imagine. This book is a collection of courtroom stories—many of which reached the U.S. Supreme Court—concerning the activities of spies who were abruptly apprehended while pursuing the fruits of their livelihood.

For example, in a very unusual case that occurred in 1938, a dry cleaning establishment found in the pocket of a coat belonging to Mihail Gorin an envelope containing a sheet of paper with reference to spy activities. The dry cleaner gave the notes to the police department that then turned it over to the FBI.

Gorin turned out to be a Soviet intelligence agent who had bought classified data from Hafis Salich, a Georgian immigrant and civilian employee of the Office of Naval Intelligence. Salich had access to ONI's files on activities among Japanese-Americans, as well as the covert operations of Japanese consular officials. Salich needed cash to cover his gambling habit, so he sold the information to Gorin. Both Gorin and Salich were convicted for their crimes, and their case went all the way to the U.S. Supreme Court with no success on their part.

In 1951, in what is surely the most famous espionage case of all time, a grand jury indicted three Americans of Russian ancestry—Julius and Ethel Rosenberg and Morton Sobell—for sending top-secret U.S. national defense documents to the Soviet Union. Ethel's brother, David Greenglass, was stationed at the Los

Alamos atomic experimental station, and Ethel and her husband Julius urged David to gather classified data. Julius and a former college classmate, Morton Sobell, also solicited Max Elitcher, a Navy Department engineer, to obtain anti-aircraft and other secrets for Russia.

When he was caught, Greenglass pled guilty to the charges, while the Rosenbergs and Sobell were tried for espionage and treason. Julius and Ethel took the stand and denied any involvement. Morton pled not guilty, but did not testify. The jury found the three guilty as charged. The trial judge sentenced Julius and Ethel to death, and Morton to thirty years' imprisonment. On June 19, 1952, at eight o'clock in the evening, the Rosenbergs were sent to the electric chair to die together.

Five years later—in May of 1957— a Soviet lieutenant named Reino Hayhanen walked through the doors of the American embassy in Paris and announced to the officials gathered there that for years he had been a Soviet spy working in the United States. Hayhanen proved to be a wealth of information, and it was largely through his testimony that American authorities learned of the activities of a notorious spy named Rudolph Ivanovich Abel, who was convicted for espionage but eventually returned to the Soviet Union in a spy exchange for the American U-2 pilot Francis Gary Powers.

Another intriguing espionage case involved a collection of spies—known as "The Cuban Five"—employed by the primary Cuban intelligence agency. These individuals were extremely active in South Florida, collecting information about U.S. military facilities, U.S. law enforcement activities, and U.S. organizations that supported a dismantling of the Castro regime in Cuba. American officials discovered the handiwork of these spies and eventually brought them to trial. They were all found guilty and served lengthy prison terms.

Also captivating was the prosecution that ensued years later when U.S. intelligence agencies learned that Vietnamese spy David Truong was transmitting highly classified documents to Paris. The government was anxious to locate his inside source. Without obtaining a search warrant, they tapped his phone and bugged his apartment for nine months in an attempt to find out who was providing him with this top-secret information. Truong denied being a spy, but the jury thought otherwise and sentenced him to fifteen years.

In what became known as "The Suitcase Scandal," involving large transfers of cash in South America, an individual named Franklin Duran, who failed to register as a foreign agent in the United States, was indicted in federal court for serving as an agent of Venezuela. Duran was caught transferring $800,000 in cash from the Venezuelan intelligence agency in order to influence the presidential election in Argentina. He was sentenced to four years in prison and fined $175,000.

In another case, the Soviet spy game was in full play when Richard Miller, a former FBI agent assigned to the Soviet Foreign Counter-Intelligence Unit, was found guilty of delivering to a Soviet agent a number of classified documents in exchange for $15,000 in cash and $50,000 in gold. Miller claimed that he was actually acting as a double agent and soon planned to inform U.S. government officials of that fact. The jury failed to buy his story.

In a fascinating espionage case dealing with military secrets, Dongfan "Greg" Chung, a former Boeing engineer, was convicted of transmitting vast amounts of sensitive information to the Chinese government in violation of the Economic Espionage Act. The federal agents who searched Chung's home found hundreds of thousands of Boeing and Rockwell documents dealing with the space shuttle, Delta IV rocket, F-15 fighter, B-52 bomber, and Chinook helicopter. In fairly short order, Chung was found guilty and sentenced to 15 years and eight months in prison.

The courts have recently dealt with the activities of the National Security Administration as they monitored telephone communications in their valiant effort to detect terrorist organizations. The NSA requested the Foreign Intelligence Surveillance Agency Court to order Verizon Communications to hand over voluminous records showing not only telephone numbers but call location, time, and duration. The NSA argued that because the data was technically classified as "metadata," the Patriot Act did not require the issuance of a search warrant.

The exposure of the project occurred after the now-exiled Edward Snowden—who as a government contractor—leaked classified documents to the press. These files revealed an extensive system of global surveillance by the NSA and its international partners. The American Civil Liberties Union filed a lawsuit against the U.S. government challenging the program. The appellate court eventually agreed with the ACLU and put an end to it.

As interesting as these cases are, the book before you is not only about spies caught in the acts of espionage. It is also about the "commercial" aspects of espionage. In a unique case concerning the sale of surveillance devices to the general public—an activity that is strictly prohibited by federal law—four individuals who smuggled these listening devices into the country were arrested for selling them to those who were not law-enforcement officers. A sting operation eventually led to their arrest and conviction. In another case—this one involving libel—an individual named Ilya Wolston sued the author and publisher of a book which declared that Wolston was a Soviet spy. The author had plenty of evidence to support his statement: Wolston had been identified as a Soviet agent in an FBI report published by the U.S. Senate, and he had refused to testify in a grand jury hearing involving his uncle and aunt, Jack and Myra Soble, who had pled guilty to charges of espionage.

Then there was the issue of the enforceability of covert agreements. When a high-ranking foreign diplomat expressed an interest in defecting to the United States, the CIA persuaded him to continue his activities, promising that it would ensure him "financial and personal security for life." When this double-agent later landed a lucrative job in the private sector, the CIA stopped providing financial assistance. He sued to enforce the agreement, but was unsuccessful.

Another prosecution involved travel restrictions imposed on a former American spy in the name of national security. Philip Agee, who previously worked for the CIA, travelled extensively abroad, where he frequently criticized American intelligence efforts and revealed the identities of CIA agents. The Department of State deemed Agee's activities harmful in light of the recent Iranian crisis, and they revoked his passport. Agee cried foul in his lawsuit, and he sued to recover his passport.

Naturally, the First Amendment sometimes comes into play when dealing with restrictions on spies. Ralph McGehee was a former CIA officer who signed the typical agreement barring him from revealing any classified information without prior approval. After the CIA censored portions of his manuscript, he claimed the agency violated his First Amendment rights. His book was published with redactions and revisions, but he remained critical of the agency for the rest of his life.

Another case involved a massive project of the CIA code-named MKUL-TRA, which funded the research and development of "chemical, biological, and radiological materials capable of employment in clandestine operations to control human behavior." MKULTRA was established to counter Soviet and Chinese advances in brainwashing and interrogation techniques. The wide-ranging program consisted of almost 150 subprojects which the CIA contracted out to scores of universities, research foundations, and private researchers.

In 1977, several individuals of the public filed a request with the CIA seeking certain further information about MKULTRA through the Freedom of Information Act. The CIA refused to provide the names of the institutions or individuals; claiming it was a matter of national security. After lengthy litigation, the court largely agreed with the CIA.

Another unusual case involved the payment by an individual—who claimed he worked for the CIA—for classified military documents stolen by a long-time friend that worked for a large defense contractor. The documents were delivered to the Soviet Union at its embassy in Mexico City. The seller of these secrets then used the funds to engage in drug deals. It tuned out that the so-called spy did not work for the CIA, and he spent the next six years in a federal penitentiary.

Truth, they say, is stranger than fiction, and that admonition is certainly borne out in these judicial decisions. The courtroom scenes described here are as suspenseful as any spy novel, but the cases and individuals are real. My hope is that you will find this sampling of espionage law to be a memorable one that appeals to the Agent 007 impulses in virtually all of us.

I

APPREHENDING
SECRET AGENTS

1

PRELUDE TO
PEARL HARBOR

This is a very unusual story about a spy that came into the light of day after a random piece of paper containing handwritten notes was left in the pocket of a coat sent to the dry cleaners.

It all began when a Russian named Mihail Gorin came to the United States in 1936 to operate the Los Angeles office of the Soviet tourist agency, Intourist. It just so happened that he was also a Soviet intelligence agent.

A year later, Gorin approached Hafis Salich—a Georgian immigrant and civilian employee of the Office of Naval Intelligence (ONI) in San Pedro, California—about buying classified information concerning Japanese activity in the states. As an ONI employee, Salich had access to classified files on pro-Japan activities among Japanese-Americans, as well as the covert activities of Japanese consular officials. Coincidentally, Salich also had a bad marriage and a voracious gambling habit, and he needed cash to cover the expenses of both.

Salich received some $1,700 from Gorin for the information that Salich supplied. Salich would later testify that the money was a loan. In return, Salich provided Gorin with the substance of the classified information contained in some 43 ONI reports relating to U.S. monitoring of Japanese officials and certain Japanese-American citizens and resident aliens. Salich justified his treacherous actions on the grounds that Japan was, after all, a "common enemy" of the Soviet Union and the United States.

Gorin and Salich were apprehended by the U.S. authorities in late 1938, when Gorin left a $50 bill and a suspicious set of notes describing the Communist proclivities of certain Japanese individuals in San Diego in a coat sent for dry cleaning. The cleaners routinely checked the pockets of the clothes it received. They immediately contacted the police. The book *Secret Missions: The Story of an Intelligence Officer* revealed:

> After the Hollywood police had made their copies, the driver returned to the shop with the original material as directed. Together with the manager and all of Gorin's clothes in his arms, he proceeded to the front office where Gorin and his wife were rapidly reaching the hysterical stage. As the driver handed the clothes to Gorin, he almost snatched them from him, so great was his anxiety to search the inside pocket of one of the coats. Much to his relief he found the envelope just as he had left it with all the papers intact and he and his wife departed.

The police contacted Ralph Van Deman, a former head of Army intelligence. Van Deman in turn informed the FBI, which began to investigate Gorin and Salich.

On December 10, 1938, several agents of the FBI went to Salich's apartment and told him he was under investigation. Salich immediately confessed and readily identified the reports that he had given to Gorin. Salich provided a written statement explaining that, "Conscientiously and honestly I did not think that my actions, aside from being highly unethical, were inimical to the best interests of the United States, to which country I am extremely grateful for what it did for me and which country's citizenship I value," and "I sincerely state that at no time did I furnish Gorin any information which in my opinion would harm this country; on the contrary, I saw some reason to Gorin's argument that we had common cause, and by helping them I would also be indirectly helping our own cause."

The reports provided by Salich consisted principally of the movements of certain Japanese from one location to another and their activities along the way. Several reports dealt with Japanese activities in Mexico and Central America, and a few concerned alleged Communists and their activities. None of the reports contained any information regarding the armed services or their equipment, munitions, or supplies. One report named a number of Japanese "suspected" of being interested in intelligence work. Most of the reports appeared innocuous on their face, but there was no way for an outsider to connect them with other material which the Naval Intelligence may have possessed.

One interesting report contained information regarding the activities of Japanese fishing boats, and an acid said to have been deposited in salt water, causing the steel hull of ships to be corroded through chemical action. Practically everything contained in the report later appeared in a publication.

The indictment against Gorin and Salich was filed on January 11, 1939. The first count charged Gorin and Salich with "copying, taking, making, and obtaining documents, writings, and notes of matters connected with the national defense." The second count charged defendants with "communicating, delivering, and transmitting to Gorin as a representative of the Soviet Union writings, notes, instruments, and information relating to the national defense." The third count charged that the defendants conspired to "communicate, deliver, and transmit to the Soviet Union documents, writings, plans, notes, instruments, and information relating to the national defense."

Gorin and Salich pleaded not guilty, arguing primarily that the Espionage Act of 1917 was too vague in its description of what information was considered illegal, and therefore the act violated the due process clause of the Fifth Amendment and the right "to be informed of the nature and cause of the accusation" provided in the Sixth Amendment.

Gorin and Salich also argued that the "innocuous" nature of the documents meant there was no intent to harm the United States or to aid a foreign nation, and the information acquired by the defendant was not related to the national defense. Furthermore, asserted the defendants, the courts, not juries, should decide whether information is "connected or related" to national defense, noting that some of the information was later published and therefore not secret.

The jury rejected the defendants' arguments and convicted Gorin and Salich on all three counts. Gorin received six years and Salich, four years, and both were fined $10,000. The case was appealed to the Ninth Circuit Court of Appeals in April of 1940. The appellate court summarily rejected all of defense counsel's arguments. The case then moved to the U.S. Supreme Court, which agreed with the Court of Appeals.

The case turned largely on the adequacy of the jury instructions. The trial court's instructions were comprehensive. As to the first count, the trial court instructed the jury that there were four elements to the crime therein charged: (1) the fact of taking or obtaining must be established, (2) there must be a purpose of obtaining information respecting the national defense, (3) there must be an intent or reason to believe that the information so obtained was to be used to the injury of the United States or to the advantage of the Soviet Union, and (4) the information so taken must, in fact, relate to the national defense.

The trial court instructed the jury that the government must prove either an intent or a reason to believe that the information was to be used either to the injury of the United States or to the advantage of the Soviet Union. The court also instructed the jury that they could consider the character of the information acquired, as to whether or not it was susceptible to use by the Soviet Union. The court also charged the jury that if there was no intent and no reason to believe that in so exchanging information that there would result an injury to the United States or advantage to the Soviet Union, then the defendants must be acquitted.

As to the fourth element of the first count, the trial court instructed the jury that it was not required that the documents or information alleged to have been taken necessarily injure the United States or benefit any foreign nation. The document need not in fact be vitally important or actually injurious. The document or information, however, had to be connected with or related to the national defense.

On appeal to the Ninth Circuit Court of Appeals, the defendants contended that the words "national defense" must be given a military and naval connotation. The appellate court found the contention untenable. The court maintained that the words used in the statute were to be read in a broad sense with a flexible meaning.

The defendants next argued that the statute was unconstitutional because it "would fix no immutable standard of guilt to govern conduct," but would instead be subject to interpretation by each court and jury. The defendants pointed out that on their face the naval intelligence reports did not relate to the national defense. The appellate court did not agree, concluding that it was unnecessary to determine what inferences were to be deducted from the reports.

However, as the court pointed out, one of the reports did name a number of Japanese "suspected" of being interested in intelligence work. The jury could properly infer that it was important for the Navy to know potential spy suspects, and that it was vital that foreign governments be ignorant of the Navy's knowledge. The court remarked that the jury could properly conclude from these inferences that the report "related" to the national defense.

The defendants contended that "intent" consists of two elements—will and knowledge—and that while there was evidence of will, there was no evidence that defendants *knew* these reports "related" to the national defense, or that their acts were unlawful. The appellate court maintained that the statute did not require unconditional intent, and that "reason to believe" was sufficient. Considering the source of the information divulged, and the desire of Gorin to obtain it, the jury could properly infer that the defendants had reason to believe that it would be used "to the injury of the United States, or to the advantage of" a foreign nation.

In its review of the case, the U.S. Supreme Court concluded:

The inquiry directed at the instructions is whether the jury is given sufficient guidance to enable it to determine whether the acts of the petitioners were within the prohibitions. These instructions set out the definition of national defense in a manner favorable and unobjectionable to petitioners. When they refer to facts connected with or related to defense, however, petitioners urge that the connection should be determined by the court. Instructions can, of course, go no farther than to say the connection must be reasonable, direct and natural. Further elaboration would not clarify.

The function of the court is to instruct as to the kind of information which is violative of the statute and of the jury to decide whether the information secured is of the defined kind. It is not the function of the court, where reasonable men may differ, to determine whether the acts do or do not come within the ambit of the statute. The question of the connection of the information with national defense is a question of fact to be determined by the jury as negligence upon undisputed facts is determined.

Viewing the instructions as a whole, the court found none of the defendants' objections were sufficient to justify reversal. And so Gorin and Salich would remain in prison to serve out their sentences.

OPINION EXCERPT

Mr. Justice Reed delivered the opinion of the Court.

Petitioners [Gorin and Salich] object to the convictions principally on the grounds (1) that the prohibitions of the act are limited to obtaining and delivering information concerning the specifically described places and things set out in [Section 1(a) of] the act, such as a vessel, aircraft, fort, signal station, code or signal book, and (2) that an interpretation which put within the statute the furnishing of any other information connected with or relating to the national defense than that concerning these specifically described places and things would make the act unconstitutional as violative of due process because of indefiniteness.

The philosophy behind the insistence that the prohibitions of Sections 1(b) ["anything connected with the national defense"] and 2(a) ["information relating to the national defense"], upon which the indictment is based, are limited to the places and things which are specifically set out in Section 1(a) ["any vessel, aircraft, work of defense, navy yard . . . "] relies upon the traditional freedom of discussion of matters connected with national defense which is permitted in this country. It would require, urge petitioners, the clearest sort of declaration by the Congress to bring under the statute the obtaining and delivering to a foreign government for its advantage of reports generally published and available which deal with food production, the advances of civil aeronautics, reserves of raw materials, or other similar matters not directly connected with, and yet of the greatest importance to, national defense. The possibility of such an interpretation of the terms "connected with" or "relating to" national defense is to be avoided by construing "to make it a crime only to obtain information as to places and things specifically listed in Section 1 as connected with or related to the national defense."

Petitioners argue that the statute should not be construed so as to leave to a jury to determine whether an innocuous report on a crop yield is "connected" with the national defense.

Petitioners rely upon the legislative history to support this position. The passage of the Espionage Act during the World War year of 1917 attracted the close scrutiny of Congress, and resulted in different bills in the two Houses which were reconciled only after a second conference report. Nothing more definite appears in this history as to the Congressional intention in regard to limiting the act's prohibitions upon which this indictment depends to the places and things in Section 1(a) than that a House definition of "national defense" which gave it a broad meaning was stricken out, and the conference report stated as to the final form of the present act: "Section 1 sets out the places connected with the national defense to which the prohibitions of the section apply." Neither change seems significant on this inquiry. The House bill had not specified the places under surveillance. The Conference change made them definite. The fact that the clause "or other place connected with the national defense" is also included in Section 1(a) is not an unusual manner of protecting enactments against inadvertent omissions. With this specific designation of prohibited places, the broad definition of Section 1202 of the House was stricken as no longer apt, and, as stated in Conference Report No. 69, Section 6 of the act was therefore adopted. Obviously the purpose was to give flexibility to the designated places. We see nothing in this legislative history to affect our conclusion, which is drawn from the meaning of the entire act.

An examination of the words of the statute satisfies us that the meaning of national defense in Sections 1(b) and 2(a) cannot be limited to the places and things specified in Section 1(a). Certainly there is no such express limitation in the later sections. Section 1(a) lays down the test of purpose and intent, and then defines the crime as going upon or otherwise obtaining information as to named things and places connected with the national defense. Section 1(b) adopts the same purpose and intent of 1(a), and then defines the crime as copying, taking or picturing certain articles such as models, appliances, documents, and so forth of anything connected with the national defense. None of the articles specified in 1(b) is the same as the things specified in 1(a). Apparently the draftsmen of the act first set out the places to be protected, and included in that connotation ships and planes, and then, in 1(b), covered much of the contents of such places in the nature of plans and documents. Section 2(a), it will be observed, covers in much the same way the delivery of these movable articles or information to a foreign nation or its agent. If a government model of a new weapon were obtained or delivered, there seems to be little logic in making its transfer a crime only when it is connected in some undefined way with the places catalogued under 1(a). It is our view that it is a crime to obtain or deliver, in violation of the intent and purposes specified, the things described in Sections 1(b) and 2(a) without regard to their connection with the places and things of 1(a).

2

SECRETS OF THE
ATOM BOMB

On the afternoon of January 31, 1951, a grand jury suddenly emerged from the depths of its walnut-paneled conference room and announced to the astonished world that it had just indicted three Americans of Russian ancestry—Julius and Ethel Rosenberg and Morton Sobell—for conspiring between 1944 and 1950 to communicate to leaders of the Union of Soviet Socialist Republics certain documents relating to the national defense of the United States, with the intent and the reason to believe that this information would be used to the advantage of the Soviet Union and to the detriment to the United States.

The indictment of these seemingly unassuming individuals for the crime of espionage sent considerable shock waves throughout the vast underground world of Soviet spies; and the ensuing trial of the Rosenbergs, who were parents of young boys—carrying with it the distinct possibility of capital punishment—captivated the world's attention.

These three defendants (among several others who were indicted alongside them) were, it turned out, clearly Soviet spies, and not insignificant ones at that. Not only did they pass along atomic bomb secrets from the heavily guarded vaults of the Manhattan Project in Tennessee and the clandestine corridors of Los Alamos national experimental laboratory in New Mexico, but they succeeded in handing over critical military research on sonar and radar that was undoubtedly used by the Russians to later shoot down planes in the Korean and Vietnam wars. During their lengthy trials and appeals, it became abundantly clear to the jurors and judges involved—and most of those who closely followed the trial—that Americans most certainly died as a result of their actions.

Before he graduated from high school in the lower east side of Manhattan in 1934, Julius Rosenberg had become a devoted Communist, having joined the Young Communist League when he was only 14 years old. The fervor with which the young Julius, whose parents were Russian, embraced the movement was unusual even by the enthusiastic socialistic impulses of the day. During his junior year of high school, this intense adolescent began to date Ethel Greenglass, whose father was Russian, against her parents' strong desires—Ethel was almost three years older than Julius. In time she too became a devoted party member.

They soon came to see the work of the party as the very purpose for their existence, and the movement's seemingly optimistic appeal for humanity occupied their every waking moment. The Rosenbergs happily devoured the party's inspiring propaganda by the shelfful, including copies of the remarkably strident *Daily Worker*. The cause of Communism would literally consume these young disciples.

After graduating from high school at the age of 16, the thin and somber Julius received a bachelor's degree in electrical engineering at City College of New York, and five years later, he and the even dourer Ethel were married; he was 21, she was 24. Julius went to work for the War Department, and Ethel was employed by the federal census bureau. In 1944, the U.S. government discovered that Julius was an active member of the party, and Julius was instantly fired from his job. This same investigation revealed that Ethel was a member of the party, and her position was also terminated, leaving the couple, now with small children, jobless, but nevertheless enthusiastic about Communism, which had clearly become their idol.

The Rosenbergs were anxious to spread their religious zeal to anyone who would listen. David Greenglass, Ethel's younger brother, was 12 years old when his 19-year-old sister was being courted by Julius. David, who was affectionately called "Doovey" by his older sister, initially rebuffed the couple's persistent efforts to have him join the organization, but after Julius brought the young man a chemistry set, the two became fast friends as a result of the gift. By the age of 14, Greenglass too had joined the Young Communist League, but his enthusiasm soon waned when he discovered that Yugoslavia's Marshal Tito was expelled from the Communist network for defying Soviet supremacy, which convinced Greenglass that the Soviet Union was perhaps more interested in world dominion than a blissful utopia.

Shortly after David and Ruth married, he enlisted in the U.S. Army in April of 1943, and he vigorously preached his political ideas to his fellow soldiers, sometimes to their annoyance. Greenglass often ended his letters to Ruth with "Your comrade," and referred to their common "Marxist outlook." In the work arena,

Greenglass proved highly skilled as a machinist. and he was assigned to the Manhattan Project in Oak Ridge, Tennessee, to assist the Allied forces in developing the first nuclear weapons. Greenglass knew nothing about the project at the time of his departure, but was warned that its activities were strictly confidential. He was soon transferred to the atomic experimental station at Los Alamos, New Mexico, where he was to help develop the implosion-type atomic bomb, while Ruth remained in New York. At the time, Los Alamos employed thousands of employees, including many Nobel Prize scientists, and its location in the remote mountains of New Mexico largely remained a secret to the outside world.

Ever attentive to the socialistic cause, the Rosenbergs immediately saw in Greenglass's new position an opportunity to advance Communism and the cause of the Soviet Union. In November 1944, Ruth traveled from New York to Albuquerque to visit David, and she mentioned that his sister Ethel and her husband Julius wanted David to give them information which they could turn over to the Soviet Union, even though they knew the disclosure constituted espionage and would prove detrimental to the country they called home. The Russians learned that the Americans and the Britons were working to develop the atomic weapon, and Julius believed that as an ally Russia deserved to have that technology. This was the argument Rosenberg gave to Greenglass, who fell for its appeal. Soon thereafter Greenglass was gladly assisting the Rosenbergs with the information they requested. Over the course of the next year, David gave the location and security measures of the atomic experimental station and the names of scientists working there. He also prepared detailed handwritten notes and sketches relating to a high-explosive lens mold being developed at Los Alamos. Greenglass's notes were either passed directly to Rosenberg while Greenglass was on furlough in New York, or to a Soviet courier named Harry Gold, who was sent to New Mexico to collect the information.

Julius and Ethel were undoubtedly aware of the grave risks of serving as Soviet spies, including the fact that they might be imprisoned—or even executed—for their activities, leaving behind as orphans their sons, Michael and Robert, who at the time were seven and three years old. Greenglass also seemed brazen about the range of federal espionage laws that he was violating as he handed over the materials to the Rosenbergs and other Soviet operatives. Such was the fervor of these young Communists as they toiled away to advance their agenda at the detriment of the United States.

In January of 1945, Greenglass arrived in New York City on vacation, and he promptly passed along to Rosenberg all the data he had been able to collect, along with a list of the scientists at Los Alamos and the names of possible recruits working there who might be sympathetic to the cause. Greenglass also turned over his hastily scribbled notes, and it was later alleged at trial that Rosenberg volunteered his wife Ethel to transcribe the notes on her portable typewriter, a fact that became incriminating when she was later tried for espionage and claimed to know nothing about the matter.

A few nights later Rosenberg mentioned that he would like Greenglass to meet a Russian colleague in Manhattan. In a scene reminiscent of a John le Carré novel, Rosenberg and Greenglass drove to First Avenue near 59th Street and parked the car by a bar in a dark street, where Rosenberg got out, walked down the street, and came back with an individual who got into Greenglass's car. Rosenberg stood alone while Greenglass drove away with the stranger. The man, Greenglass later testified, interrogated him about scientific information relating to the atomic bomb, and after driving around for a while, Greenglass returned and let the man out. Greenglass watched as he and Rosenberg walked away. The identity of the guest remains a mystery to this day.

The Russians' race to learn more about the bomb began to accelerate in earnest. A man by the name of Harry Gold soon entered what was becoming an increasingly complicated—and indeed peculiar—cast of characters assembled by the Rosenbergs. Gold was a chubby laboratory chemist who had been a courier for a number of Soviet spy rings during the Manhattan Project. He was born in Philadelphia to poor Russian Jewish immigrants, and as a young man he became interested in socialism, which eventually led to his involvement in the Communist movement. His superior was Anatoli Yakovlev, a former Soviet vice-consul in New York City whose diplomatic role was nothing but a thin veneer for his wide-ranging work in the Soviet spy network.

In the summer of 1944, Gold— who was known to drink heavily and to conduct himself in an undisciplined manner in his professional affairs— held a series of meetings in Queens, Brooklyn, and Central Park with the renowned physicist Dr. Karl Fuchs, a bespectacled Briton who grew up in Germany and who was currently working at Los Alamos in the theoretical physics division, where he was regarded as a superb scientist and a brilliant researcher with great intensity for his work. No one suspected that Fuchs had been transferring detailed notes about the project to a Soviet courier named "Raymond," who turned out to be Harry Gold. The work carried on at Los Alamos culminated in the creation of several bombs, the first of which was tested near Alamogordo, New Mexico, on July 16, 1945, while the other bombs—"Little Boy" and "Fat Man"—were used in attacks on Hiroshima and Nagasaki.

Fuchs was nothing if not prolific. He was responsible for a number of significant calculations relating to early models of the hydrogen bomb. His chief area of expertise was implosion, which was critical for the development of the plutonium bomb, and his data was critical to the Russians' understanding of the application of nuclear fission to the production of military weapons. In January of 1945, Gold again met Fuchs in Cambridge, Massachusetts, and received a stack of papers which he later turned over to Yakovlev. Gold would next meet with Fuchs in Santa Fe in June of 1945.

While Gold was in Santa Fe, Yakovlev asked him to take on an additional mission to meet with an individual named David Greenglass. Gold bitterly protested, but Yakovlev insisted that the assignment was of vital importance. Little did the two know that the brief contact between Gold and Greenglass would eventually lead to the exposure of the Rosenbergs, who were quickly getting in over their heads. Nonetheless, Yakovlev handed Gold a piece of onionskin paper on which was typed the name "Greenglass," an address on High Street in Albuquerque, and the recognition signal, "I am from Julius." Yakovlev also gave Gold a piece of cardboard cut from a "Jello" box and said Greenglass would have the matching piece. Yakovlev instructed Gold to take a circuitous route to Albuquerque in order to reduce the chance of surveillance.

Gold left Santa Fe and arrived in Albuquerque that evening. He went directly to the High Street address, found that Greenglass was not in, and then checked into a hotel for the evening. The next day he went back, and Greenglass opened the door. Gold asked, "Mr. Greenglass?" When Greenglass answered yes, Gold then replied, "I am from Julius," and showed Greenglass the piece of the "Jello" box Yakovlev had given him. Greenglass invited Gold to come in, took the piece of the "Jello" label from his wife's handbag and compared it to Gold's—the pieces matched perfectly.

Greenglass told Gold that it would take several hours to prepare the material he requested. Greenglass started to tell Gold about possible recruits at Los Alamos, but Gold cut him short, admonishing him that these matters were extremely sensitive and that he should be very circumspect in his behavior toward others. Gold quickly left the apartment, promising to return in a few hours. Greenglass immediately went to work on a report, drew sketches of experiments, composed descriptive material about them, and provided a list of possible recruits. Later that day, Gold returned and Greenglass handed him the documents. In exchange, Gold gave Greenglass an envelope with $500 in cash.

Gold returned to New York City by train and gave Yakovlev the envelopes from both Fuchs and Greenglass.

About two weeks later Gold arranged a meeting with Yakovlev in Flushing, New York. Yakovlev conveyed to Gold that the materials had been "extremely valuable" and had been sent immediately to the Soviet Union. Yakovlev also remarked that tremendous progress had been made on the development of the bomb.

For these Soviet spies, matters soon began to deteriorate. In September of 1945, Gold met Yakovlev in New York and turned over a package he had received from Fuchs, who remarked that there was no longer the open and free cooperation between the Americans and the British and that many departments were now closed to Fuchs. Fuchs said he would have to return to England, and that he was worried because the British had arrived at Kiel, Germany, ahead of the Russians and might discover the Gestapo dossier about Fuchs, revealing his strong Communist ties. Dr. Fuchs was right—the world would eventually close in around him.

Greenglass then returned to New York City from New Mexico. Rosenberg immediately came to his apartment, and Greenglass informed him that he now had obtained a remarkably good description of the bomb. Greenglass drew up a cross-section sketch of the bomb and prepared a fairly detailed ten-page analysis of it. He described to Rosenberg how the bomb was set off by a barometric pressure device. Rosenberg remarked that the information was very helpful and that his wife Ethel should transcribe it. As Ethel was typing, Rosenberg burned the handwritten notes in a frying pan, flushed them down a drain, and gave Greenglass two hundred dollars.

Gold met with Yakovlev again, this time in a small New York seafood restaurant. In typical fashion, Yakovlev told Gold it was imperative to get another Soviet agent involved. Yakovlev instructed Gold to take a letterhead from his pocket, tear off the top portion, and write on the back "Directions to Paul Street." Yakovlev then tore the paper in half in an irregular fashion. He kept one half and Gold kept the other. Yakovlev told Gold that he would soon receive two tickets in the mail, and that exactly five days after the date on the tickets Gold should go to the roadway stop of the Astoria Line for a meeting in the bar. Gold's new Soviet contact would be standing at the bar and approach him, asking to be directed to Paul Street. They would then compare the torn pieces of paper.

Early in December 1946, Gold received, in the mail, two tickets to a boxing match in New York City. Unfortunately, the tickets were incorrectly addressed, and they had arrived too late for Gold to keep the appointment. At 5:00 p.m. on December 26, he received a telephone call at work, and the voice simply said, "This is John." Gold arranged a meeting in a certain movie theater that night, and the man identified himself by handing Gold the torn letterhead. This man told Gold to proceed to 42nd Street and 3rd Avenue to meet Yakovlev.

When Gold arrived, Yakovlev was there, and he promptly asked Gold if he had received anything further from Fuchs. Yakovlev told Gold he should begin to plan for a trip to Paris in March, and he gave Gold directions for the meeting. During the conversation, Gold mentioned the name of his current employer, which sent Yakovlev into a rage. Yakovlev told Gold that he had almost ruined eleven years of work by working for this individual, who had been previously investigated by the U.S. government. Yakovlev dashed away, telling Gold he would never see him again.

In using Gold to contact Greenglass, the Soviet intelligence had made a serious breach in security that led to the uncovering of the Rosenberg spy ring, a network independent of the one that Gold was involved in. The Soviets typically never allowed a member of one network to know about another, under the presumption that in case one network was detected, the other would not be compromised. Gold's protest about contacting Greenglass in Albuquerque went unheeded, and the Soviets later regretted this serious breach of protocol.

In the meantime, Julius Rosenberg was undeterred, and he was working other angles, this time to advance the Soviet cause on the military front. He and a former college classmate, Morton Sobell, who regularly delivered materials for transmittal to the Soviet Union, solicited Max Elitcher, a U.S. Navy Department engineer, to obtain anti-aircraft and other military secrets for Russia. Rosenberg and Sobell also asked Elitcher for the names of young engineers who might help supply military secrets to the Russians.

It is a small world, and Elitcher had known Sobell and Rosenberg while attending City College of New York, where the three studied engineering. Elitcher saw Sobell almost daily while in school, but Rosenberg less frequently. Elitcher and Sobell lived together for a time in Washington, and at Sobell's urging Elitcher joined the newly formed branch of the Communist Party. Elitcher left government service to work elsewhere, and he and his wife moved to Queens. It turned out to be an even smaller world—the Elitchers' backyard neighbors were none other than the Sobells, and Sobell continued to recruit Elitcher to spy for the Soviets.

Sobell eventually moved away, and in June 1944, Elitcher received a telephone call from Rosenberg, suggesting they meet. Rosenberg told Elitcher what the Soviets were doing in the war effort and that they were being denied information from the United States. Rosenberg urged Elitcher to supply him with plans and reports regarding new military equipment which might be of value to the Soviet Union, but Elitcher refused.

Sometime later, Elitcher visited Sobell who mentioned that he had some information for Rosenberg that was too valuable to destroy. Sobell said he needed to get it to Rosenberg that very night, so Elitcher went with Sobell who placed a 35-millimeter film container in the glove compartment of his car, drove to a building on Catherine Street, took the film out of the glove compartment, and immediately left. Elitcher stayed in the car. He later recalled that Sobell had a sophisticated camera and an enlarger, and that the material Sobell worked on in his various places of employment was highly classified.

Rosenberg continued to contact Elitcher to get information that might be of interest to the Soviets, but Elitcher kept putting him off. In 1948, feeling that he was being followed by the FBI, Elitcher bluntly told Rosenberg to leave him alone.

After the war was over, Rosenberg and Greenglass went into business together for a number of years, and during this time Rosenberg confessed to Greenglass that he was still using spies in upstate New York and Ohio to provide him with information for the Soviets.

Unfortunately for the Rosenbergs and other Soviet spies, certain top-secret communications from Russia called the Venona cables were deciphered by late 1948. One of these cables contained a report on the progress of the atomic bomb research prepared by Fuchs, providing positive proof to U.S. authorities that the Soviets had penetrated the secrets of the Manhattan Project. By January of 1949 Fuchs had confessed to the FBI; and a few days after the news of the arrest of Dr. Fuchs was published, Rosenberg went to Greenglass's home and suggested they go for a walk. Rosenberg reminded Greenglass that the man he saw in Albuquerque—Harry Gold—was a contact of Fuchs. Rosenberg told Greenglass that he had no other choice but to immediately leave the United States. When Greenglass replied that he needed cash, Rosenberg said he would "get the money from the Russians."

Rosenberg persisted, and in April of 1950, he again urged Greenglass to immediately leave the country. He gave Greenglass $1,000 in cash, and said he would return with $6,000 more to help him leave the country. Rosenberg told Greenglass he would have to get a Mexican tourist card, and he handed him a form letter and precise instructions to memorize before he left for Mexico City. When Greenglass arrived in Mexico City he was to send the letter to the Soviet Embassy and sign it "I. Jackson." Three days later, Greenglass—making sure to carrying in his hand a guide to the city with his middle finger between the pages of the guide—was then to go to the Plaza De La Colon at 5:00 p.m. and look at the statue of Columbus there. He was to wait until a man came up to him, when Greenglass would say, "That is a magnificent statue," and mention that he was from Oklahoma. His contact would then answer, "Oh, there are much more beautiful statues in Paris," and he would give Greenglass a passport and additional money.

Greenglass was then to travel to Vera Cruz and eventually on to Sweden or Switzerland. If he went to Sweden, he was to send the same type of letter to the Soviet Ambassador or his secretary and sign the letter "I. Jackson." Three days later, Greenglass was to go to the Statue of Linnaeus in Stockholm at exactly 5:00 p.m. where a man would approach him. Greenglass would mention that the statue was beautiful and the man would answer, "There are much more beautiful ones in Paris." The man would then give Greenglass the means of transportation to Czechoslovakia, where upon arrival he was to write to the Soviet Ambassador advising him of his presence.

Shortly after this meeting with Rosenberg, Greenglass and his family went to a photography shop and had six sets of passport photos taken. On Memorial Day, Greenglass gave Rosenberg five sets of these photos, presumably for fake passports and visas. Later Rosenberg visited Greenglass and gave him $4,000 in $10 and $20 bills wrapped in brown paper, asking Greenglass to repeat to him the memorized instructions. After all was said and done, Greenglass never left the states, and he eventually used the cash to pay a lawyer to represent him.

On May 22, 1950, Harry Gold confessed to the FBI that he had been working with Greenglass, who then fingered Rosenberg as a spy. Less than two months later, Rosenberg was arrested while in his bathroom, shaving.

Sobell, on the other hand, had a different idea. On June 22, he fled to Mexico City with his wife Helen, infant son Mark, and Helen's daughter Sydney. Sobell tried to find passage for the four of them from Mexico to Europe, but without proper passports it was impossible to do so. On August 16, Sobell and his family were abducted by armed men, taken to the United States border, and

Sobell turned over to the FBI, who arrested him for conspiring to violate U.S. espionage laws.

All four individuals—Julius and Ethel Rosenberg, David Greenglass, and Morton Sobell—were prosecuted by the federal government. Greenglass pled guilty to the charges (in exchange for leniency in his sentencing), and the Rosenbergs and Sobell were tried for espionage and treason. The Rosenbergs took the stand and flatly denied any involvement with the Soviets. Sobell pled not guilty, but did not testify. Harry Gold and Ruth Greenglass were named in the indictment as conspirators but not as defendants, and a severance for trial purposes was granted as to Greenglass, who pleaded guilty, and as to Anatoli Yakovlev, who was excluded from the indictment due to diplomatic immunity. (Yakovlev, who was highly decorated in the Soviet Union for espionage activities, bragged in an interview forty years later that the FBI uncovered "less than half" of the information about his spy network.)

The indictment was extensive. It listed ten overt acts committed in furtherance of the conspiracy, including the sketches of experiments conducted at Los Alamos Project that Greenglass gave Rosenberg. On March 6, 1951, the trial of the Rosenbergs and of Sobell was held in the United States District Court for the Southern District of New York, with Judge Irving Kaufman presiding. Kaufman had recently been appointed to the bench by President Truman, and he was known to be a bright and hard-working jurist. (In 1961, President Kennedy promoted him to an appellate position on the federal court of appeals for the Second Circuit.)

At the time, Irving Saypol was the United States Attorney for the Southern District of New York, and he was the chief prosecutor. Saypol was extremely experienced prosecutor, having convicted Alger Hiss, along with other notorious Communists, and his was a sincere belief that he was punishing evil in doing so. (Saypol's success in the Rosenberg trial accelerated his career, and he was appointed to the New York Supreme Court just months later.) Saypol's prosecution team included Roy Cohn, who later became famous for his association with Senator Joseph McCarthy and the pursuit of Communist infiltration of the government.

The Rosenbergs and Sobell were defended by the father-and-son team of Emanuel "Manny" Bloch and his father Alexander. The two were well-known defenders of leftish sympathizers. During the course of the trial and its many subsequent appeals, Manny Bloch cast aside his other cases to focus completely on the Rosenbergs, and along the way he became very close to the family.

Bloch's frenetic efforts in the final days to spare the Rosenbergs from the electric chair were nothing short of heroic. After the couple's execution, a dispirited Bloch delivered the eulogy at their funeral and served as guardian for their children. In early 1954, he died of a heart attack in his apartment at the age of 52, and his father remarked that he too was a victim of the Rosenberg prosecution.

The trial began on March 6, 1951, and it lasted 14 days. The prosecutor's primary witnesses were David Greenglass, Ruth Greenglass, Harry Gold, and Max Elitcher. It is presumed that David chose to serve as a prosecution witness against his sister and brother-in-law in exchange for immunity for his wife Ruth, so that she might remain with their two children. David testified that Ethel had typed up his notes for Julius, and that it was Ethel who urged Ruth to convince David to become involved is espionage. Greenglass received a 15-year sentence for his role in the passing of information concerning the atomic bomb. Was he telling the truth? When asked forty years later if he would have done anything differently, David allegedly replied "Never." Another account holds that he admitted lying under oath to save his wife. Greenglass died in 2014 at the age of 92, having spent the last few years of his life under an assumed name in a nursing home.

Harry Gold's testimony was also influential in the conviction of the Rosenbergs. Gold was given several days warning that the FBI was going to search his home, but he didn't begin to remove incriminating evidence until hours earlier and there was simply too much to destroy. Gold eventually confessed to the FBI, and he was sentenced to 30 years in prison. He was paroled in May 1965, having served just half of his sentence.

Because of his close friendship with Sobell and Rosenberg, the testimony of Elitcher was the most damaging of all. Elitcher maintained that Rosenberg had attempted to recruit him as a spy from 1944 to 1948. Elitcher shared many political beliefs with Rosenberg and Sobell, but he refused to pass secret information to either.

Julius and Ethel were called to the stand to testify. They denied all allegations against them, and in doing so, they lied through their teeth. They vehemently denied that they had ever solicited Greenglass for information related to the bomb, or that they had participated in any kind of espionage work for Russia. Julius claimed that he did not even know Harry Gold. He admitted that he and David went into business together after the war, but noted that they did not enjoy good business relations. He said Ruth had told him that David had stolen things while in the Army, and Julius assumed David was in trouble for this reason. He said David asked him for a few thousand dollars in cash and when he refused David threatened he would be sorry. Julius denied that he gave David any money to leave the country. He admitted he knew Sobell and Elitcher, but claimed he never discussed anything pertaining to national security with them. On cross-examination, the Rosenbergs were asked about their Communist affiliations, but they refused to answer on the grounds of self-incrimination.

Sobell also pleaded not guilty, but unlike the Rosenbergs he refused to take the stand by asserting his Fifth Amendment rights. At the end of the trial, the jury found the three defendants guilty as charged. The judge sentenced the Rosenbergs to death, and Sobell to 30 years' imprisonment.

Judge Kaufman made the following terse statement when sentencing the Rosenbergs:

> I consider your crime worse than murder. Plain deliberate contemplated murder is dwarfed in magnitude by comparison with the crime you have committed. In committing the act of murder, the criminal kills only his victim. The immediate family is brought to grief and when justice is meted out the chapter is closed. But in your case, I believe your conduct in putting into the hands of the Russians the A-bomb years before our best scientists predicted Russia would perfect the bomb has already caused, in my opinion, the Communist aggression in Korea, with the resultant casualties exceeding 50,000 and who knows but that millions more of innocent people may pay the price of your treason. Indeed, by your betrayal you undoubtedly have altered the course of history to the disadvantage of our country.
>
> No one can say that we do not live in a constant state of tension. We have evidence of your treachery all around us every day—for the civilian defense activities throughout the nation are aimed at preparing us for an atom bomb attack. Nor can it be said in mitigation of the offense that the power which set the conspiracy in motion and profited from it was not openly hostile to the United States at the time of the conspiracy. If this was your excuse the error of your ways in setting yourselves above our properly constituted authorities and the decision of those authorities not to share the information with Russia must now be obvious.
>
> In the light of this, I can only conclude that the defendants entered into this most serious conspiracy against their country with full realization of its implications. The statute of which the defendants at the bar stand convicted is clear. I have previously stated my view that the verdict of guilty was amply justified by the evidence. In the light of the circumstances, I feel that I must pass such sentence upon the principals in this diabolical conspiracy to destroy a God-fearing nation, which will demonstrate with finality that this nation's security must remain inviolate; that traffic in military secrets, whether promoted by slavish devotion to a foreign ideology or by a desire for monetary gains must cease.
>
> The evidence indicated quite clearly that Julius Rosenberg was the prime mover in this conspiracy. However, let no mistake be made about the role which his wife Ethel Rosenberg played in this conspiracy. Instead of deterring him from

pursuing his ignoble cause, she encouraged and assisted the cause. She was a mature woman—almost three years older than her husband and almost seven years older than her younger brother. She was a full-fledged partner in this crime.

Indeed the defendants Julius and Ethel Rosenberg placed their devotion to their cause above their own personal safety and were conscious that they were sacrificing their own children, should their misdeeds be detected—all of which did not deter them from pursuing their course. Love for their cause dominated their lives—it was even greater than their love for their children.

When he refused to extend executive clemency to the Rosenbergs, President Eisenhower likewise issued a terse statement: "I can only say that, by immeasurably increasing the chances of atomic war, the Rosenbergs may have condemned to death tens of millions of innocent people all over the world. The execution of two humans is a grave matter. But even graver is the thought of the millions of dead whose deaths may be directly attributable to what these spies have done."

Two weeks before the date scheduled for their deaths, the Rosenbergs were visited by the director of the Federal Bureau of Prisons. After the meeting, the defiant Rosenbergs issued a public statement:

> Yesterday, we were offered a deal by the Attorney General of the United States. We were told that if we cooperated with the Government, our lives would be spared. By asking us to repudiate the truth of our innocence, the Government admits its own doubts concerning our guilt. We will not help to purify the foul record of a fraudulent conviction and a barbaric sentence. We solemnly declare, now and forever more, that we will not be coerced, even under pain of death, to bear false witness and to yield up to tyranny our rights as free Americans. Our respect for truth, conscience and human dignity is not for sale. Justice is not some bauble to be sold to the highest bidder. If we are executed it will be the murder of innocent people and the shame will be upon the Government of the United States.

Was it all just a bluff? Most observers find it surprising that Bloch did not encourage Julius to make the confession naming David Greenglass and Harry Gold, who had already made full confessions. Some have speculated that the Communist Party felt that Ethel's execution would provide propaganda against the "inhumanity of capitalism."

On June 19, 1952, at eight o'clock in the evening, after two years on death row at the New York state prison in Sing Sing, the Rosenbergs were sent to the electric chair together.

In the minds of most, time has confirmed the facts that lay behind the conviction of the Rosenbergs. Practically all of the grand jury transcripts have now been released, lending further credibility to the results of the trial. But the controversy still continues.

The Rosenberg boys Michael and Robert, who were then ten and seven years old, were looked after by the Blochs. The identity of their parents was kept from all but a few of their closest friends. The boys were eventually adopted by Abel and Ann Meerpool. Michael and Robert Meerpool for years adamantly protested the innocence of their parents, and in 1975 they wrote *We Are Your Sons*. When Sobell finally admitted in 2008 that he was a spy who worked with the Rosenbergs, they had to admit that their parents were part of the Soviet conspiracy to spy on the United States. Sobell, however, disparaged Greenglass's contributions as "junk" that was of no value to the Soviets.

For his role in the conspiracy, Greenglass went to prison for almost a decade, then changed his name and lived quietly until a journalist tracked him down. Nearly a half century later, he apparently admitted to a *New York Times* reporter that he had lied on the witness stand to save his wife from prosecution, providing testimony that he was never sure about but that nevertheless sent his sister and her husband to the electric chair. Greenglass confessed that to spare his wife from prosecution he testified that his sister typed his notes. In fact, he said, he could not recall who had done it. He was clear that he had no regrets, admitting that his wife and the mother of his children was more important to him than his sister. Greenglass's wife Ruth, who had played a minor role in the conspiracy and who also gave testimony that incriminated the Rosenbergs, died in 2008.

Over 50 years later, a number of detractors still claim that the death penalty was too harsh for the Rosenbergs, who seemingly never gathered information that was very valuable. However, many would say that the discovery and decryption of the Verona cables—which intercepted the messages of Soviet spies—strongly refuted that notion. It appears likely that spirited discussions about the greatest cold war trial in history will continue for the next 50 years.

OPINION EXCERPT

Mr. Justice Douglas, dissenting.

When the motion for a stay was before me, I was deeply troubled by the legal question tendered. After twelve hours of research and study I concluded, as my opinion indicated, that the question was a substantial one, never presented to this Court and never decided by any court. So I issued the stay order.

Now I have had the benefit of an additional argument and additional study and reflection. Now I know that I am right on the law.

The Solicitor General says in oral argument that the Government would have been laughed out of court if the indictment in this case had been laid under the Atomic Energy Act of 1946. I agree. For a part of the crime alleged and proved antedated that Act. And obviously no criminal statute can have retroactive application. But the Solicitor General misses the legal point on which my stay order was based. It is this—whether or not the death penalty can be imposed *without the recommendation of the jury* for a crime involving the disclosure of atomic secrets where a part of that crime takes place after the effective date of the Atomic Energy Act.

The crime of the Rosenbergs was a conspiracy that started prior to the Atomic Energy Act and continued almost four years after the effective date of that Act. The overt acts *alleged* were acts which took place prior to the effective date of the new Act. But that is irrelevant for two reasons. *First,* acts in pursuance of the conspiracy were proved which took place *after* the new Act became the law. *Second,* under *Singer* v. *United States,* no overt acts were necessary; the crime was complete when the conspiracy was proved. And that conspiracy, as defined in the indictment itself, endured almost four years after the Atomic Energy Act became effective.

The crime therefore took place in substantial part *after* the new Act became effective, *after* Congress had written new penalties for conspiracies to disclose atomic secrets. One of the new requirements is that the death penalty for that kind of espionage can be imposed *only* if the jury recommends it. And here there was no such recommendation. To be sure, this espionage included more than atomic secrets. But there can be no doubt that the death penalty was imposed because of the Rosenbergs' disclosure of atomic secrets. The trial judge, in sentencing the Rosenbergs to death, emphasized that the heinous character of their crime was trafficking in atomic secrets. He said:

"I believe your conduct in putting into the hands of the Russians the A-bomb years before our best scientists predicted Russia would perfect the bomb has already caused, in my opinion, the Communist aggression in Korea, with the resultant casualties exceeding 50,000 and who knows but that millions more of innocent people may pay the price of your treason. Indeed, by your betrayal you undoubtedly have altered the course of history to the disadvantage of our country."

But the Congress in 1946 adopted new criminal sanctions for such crimes. Whether Congress was wise or unwise in doing so is no question for us. The cold truth is that the death sentence may not be imposed for what the Rosenbergs did unless the jury so recommends.

Some say, however, that since *a part* of the Rosenbergs' crime was committed under the old law, the penalties of the old law apply. But it is law too elemental for citation of authority that where two penal statutes may apply—one carrying death, the other imprisonment—the court has no choice but to impose the less harsh sentence.

A suggestion is made that the question comes too late, that since the Rosenbergs did not raise this question on appeal, they are barred from raising it now. But the question of an unlawful sentence is never barred. No man or woman should go to death under an unlawful sentence merely because his lawyer failed to raise the point. It is that function among others that the Great Writ serves. I adhere to the views stated by Mr. Chief Justice Hughes for a unanimous Court in *Bowen v. Johnston*:

"It must never be forgotten that the writ of *habeas corpus* is the precious safeguard of personal liberty and there is no higher duty than to maintain it unimpaired. The rule requiring resort to appellate procedure when the trial court has determined its own jurisdiction of an offense is not a rule denying the power to issue a writ of *habeas corpus* when it appears that nevertheless the trial court was without jurisdiction. The rule is not one defining power but one which relates to the appropriate exercise of power."

Here the trial court was without jurisdiction to impose the death penalty, since the jury had not recommended it.

Before the present argument I knew only that the question was serious and substantial. Now I am sure of the answer. I know deep in my heart that I am right on the law. Knowing that, my duty is clear.

OPINION EXCERPT

Mr. Justice Clark, with whom The Chief Justice, Mr. Justice Reed, Mr. Justice Jackson, Mr. Justice Burton, and Mr. Justice Minton join.

Seven times now have the defendants been before this Court. In addition, the Chief Justice, as well as individual Justices, has considered applications by the defendants. The Court of Appeals and the District Court have likewise given careful consideration to even more numerous applications than has this Court.

The defendants were sentenced to death on April 5, 1951. Beginning with our refusal to review the conviction and sentence in October 1952, each of the Justices has given the most painstaking consideration to the case. In fact, all during the past Term of this Court one or another facet of this litigation occupied the attention of the Court. At a Special Term on June 15, 1953, we denied for the sixth time the defendants' plea. The next day an application was presented to Mr. Justice Douglas, contending that the penalty provisions of the Atomic Energy Act governed this prosecution; and that, since the jury did not find that the defendants committed the charged acts with intent to injure the United States nor recommend the imposition of the death penalty, the court had no power to impose the sentence of death. After a hearing Mr. Justice Douglas, finding that the contention had merit, granted a stay of execution. The Court convened in Special Term to review that determination.

Human lives are at stake; we need not turn this decision on fine points of procedure or a party's technical standing to claim relief. Nor did Mr. Justice Douglas lack the power and, in view of his firm belief that the legal issues tendered him were substantial, he even had the duty to grant a temporary stay. But for me the short answer to the contention that the Atomic Energy Act of 1946 may invalidate defendants' death sentence is that the Atomic Energy Act cannot here apply. It is true that Section 10 (b) (2) and (3) of that Act authorizes capital punishment only upon recommendation of a jury and a finding that the offense was committed with intent to injure the United States. (Notably, by that statute the death penalty may be imposed for *peacetime* offenses as well, thus exceeding in harshness the penalties provided by the Espionage Act.) This prosecution, however, charged a wartime violation of the Espionage Act of 1917 under which these elements are not prerequisite to a sentence of death. Where Congress by more than one statute proscribes a private course of conduct, the Government may choose to invoke either applicable law: "At least where different proof is required for each offense, a single act or transaction may violate more than one criminal statute." Nor does the partial overlap of two statutes necessarily work a *pro tanto* repealer of the earlier Act. "It is a cardinal principle of construction that repeals by implication are not favored. When there are two acts upon the same subject, the rule is to give effect to both if possible. The intention of the legislature to repeal "must be clear and manifest." It is not sufficient "to establish that subsequent laws cover some or even all of the cases provided for by the prior act; for they may be merely affirmative, or cumulative, or auxiliary." There must be "a positive repugnancy between the provisions of the new law, and those of the old." Otherwise the Government when charging a conspiracy to transmit both atomic and non-atomic secrets would have to split its prosecution into two alleged crimes. Section 10 (b) (6) of the Atomic Energy Act itself, moreover, expressly provides that Section 10 "shall not exclude the applicable provisions of any other laws . . . ," an unmistakable reference to the 1917 Espionage Act. Therefore this section of the Atomic Energy Act, instead of repealing the penalty provisions of the Espionage Act, in fact preserves them in undiminished force. Thus there is no warrant for superimposing the penalty provisions of the later Act upon the earlier law.

In any event, the Government could not have invoked the Atomic Energy Act against these defendants. The crux of the charge alleged overt acts committed in 1944 and 1945, years before that Act went into effect. While some overt acts did in fact take place as late as 1950, they related principally to defendants' efforts to avoid detection and prosecution of earlier deeds. Grave doubts of unconstitutional *ex post facto* criminality would have attended any prosecution under that statute for transmitting atomic secrets before 1946. Since the Atomic Energy Act thus cannot cover the offenses charged, the alleged inconsistency of its penalty provisions with those of the Espionage Act cannot be sustained.

Our liberty is maintained only so long as justice is secure. To permit our judicial processes to be used to obstruct the course of justice destroys our freedom. Over two years ago the Rosenbergs were found guilty by a jury of a grave offense in time of war. Unlike other litigants they have had the attention of this Court seven times; each time their pleas have been denied. Though the penalty is great and our responsibility heavy, our duty is clear.

While [Section] 10 (b) (6) additionally contains an exception, providing that "no Government agency shall take any action under such other laws inconsistent with the provisions of this section," that exception is not applicable here. As disclosed by the legislative history of the Act (which must be read to refer to [Section] 10 (b) (6)), it "prohibits any agency from placing information in a restricted category under the authority of this or any other law once such information has been released from the category by official action of the Atomic Energy Commission." And see 92 Cong. Rec. 6096 (1946): "Section 10 also establishes the Commission as the top authority in the Government with reference to what will or will not remain as restricted data."

3

BACK IN THE USSR

Sometimes Russian agents defect to the United States. One such event occurred in the early days of May 1957, when a Soviet lieutenant colonel
named Reino Hayhanen walked into the American embassy in Paris and announced to the diplomats assembled there that for the past five years he had
been a Soviet spy working in the United States.

Hayhanen was told to have a seat, and for the next several hours he was
extensively interrogated about his activities on behalf of the Soviet Union. After
the embassy personnel had gathered an impressive dossier, they arranged for
Hayhanen to fly to Washington, DC, to be further interrogated by the FBI.

Hayhanen had grown tired of the Soviet way of life, and he was ready to
move to the states, where he knew life would be easier. Hayhanen was a gold-
mine of details about the current Soviet spy ring in the states, and it was largely
through his testimony that American authorities learned of the activities of one
Rudolph Ivanovich Abel.

Abel was an influential colonel in the KGB, who a decade earlier had entered
the United States illegally through Canada. To disguise his identity as a Soviet
spy, he adopted two creative aliases: Emil Robert Goldfus—an infant who
had died in New York City in 1903—and Martin Collins—a fictitious person
purportedly born in New York City. The KGB assigned Abel the code name
"Mark" for use in communicating with other Soviet agents.

Hayhanen was given the code name "Vik" to conduct his espionage activities. Hayhanen lived in Finland and began to establish his identity as the Amer-
ican-born Eugene Maki. The real Eugene Nicolai Maki was born in Enaville,
Idaho, on May 30, 1919; his mother was a Native American, but his father

had immigrated to the United States from Finland in 1905. In the mid-1920s, Eugene Maki's parents heard about the "new" Russia, and they sold all of their belongings and left the Idaho farm to book passage on a ship to Europe.

After leaving the United States, the Maki family settled in Estonia. As the years passed, even the older residents of Enaville forgot about the Maki family. In Moscow, plans were made for a recreated Eugene Maki—one thoroughly grounded in Soviet intelligence techniques—to enter the scene. Hayhanen was given instruction in the finer aspects of photography, with particular emphasis on "microdots" (photographic reduction of a document can be enlarged so that it is readable) and "soft film" (ordinary film chemically treated to remove its backing to make it pliable and capable of being folded to a small size). Hayhanen was taught how to carefully secrete messages in tiny, hollowed-out objects such as coins, bolts, screws, and matchbooks. He was also given training in cryptography for transmitting exceptionally sensitive information.

On July 3, 1951, Hayhanen traveled to the American embassy in Finland and presented a birth certificate from the state of Idaho showing he was born in Enaville on May 30, 1919. There he executed an affidavit in which he explained that when he was ten years old his family had left the United States for Estonia, that he accompanied his mother until her death and that he then left Estonia for Finland. A year later, the U.S. government issued to Hayhanen a passport in Helsinki; and several months later, he sailed aboard the *Queen Mary* and arrived at New York City on October 21, 1952, ready to serve the Soviet Union.

Hayhanen was told that a Soviet agent, whose code name was "Mikhail," would serve as his superior in this country. In order to establish contact with this agent, Hayhanen was instructed that after arriving in New York he should go to the Tavern on the Green in Central Park. There, he was told, he would find a signpost marked "Horse Carts," and he was instructed to place a small red thumbtack in the signpost to show he had arrived safely. If he suspected he was under surveillance, he was to place a white thumbtack on the board.

From the fall of 1952 until early in 1954, "Mikhail" served as Hayhanen's superior in New York. They met only when necessary, at Prospect Park subway station. To exchange messages and intelligence data, they used "dead drops"—inconspicuous hiding places—in the New York area.

Hayhanen had been sent to the states to serve as an assistant to an individual whom he then knew only as "Mark." Hayhanen did not actually see Abel until the summer of 1954, when the two met in the men's smoking room at a theater in Flushing, New York. Thereafter, Hayhanen saw Abel frequently, received his salary from him, and carried out several discrete missions at his direction. Hayhanen watched Abel use the predesignated drops for messages to other agents, and Abel told Hayhanen that several agents were working for him. Abel said he received coded messages from the Soviet Union, and on one occasion Hayhanen observed him attempting to receive (unsuccessfully, it turned out) the signals of a shortwave radio station.

The activities of Abel on behalf of the Soviet government were no doubt extensive. Sometime between July and December 1954, Abel received instructions from Moscow to find a Soviet agent named Roy Rhodes, whose code name was *Quebec*. The communication from the Soviet Union informed Abel that Rhodes's wife owned several businesses in Red Bank, New Jersey, but Abel and Hayhanen were unable to find Rhodes there. They later learned that Rhodes's family had moved to Salida, Colorado, and Abel told Hayhanen to go there and find him. Hayhanen didn't, but he did learn from Rhodes's father and sister that Rhodes had moved to Tucson, Arizona, a lead he never had time to follow up on.

In April 1957, Hayhanen boarded the ocean liner *Liberté* and sailed from New York to Europe on vacation. Shortly after arriving in Paris, he notified Soviet agents that he was proceeding to West Berlin. Instead, he went straight to the American embassy, where he informed the officials of his espionage activities on behalf of the Soviet government.

Hayhanen was quite useful to the U.S. authorities, and he was able to help them solve several mysteries that had perplexed them for years. The FBI had years before found a hollowed-out bolt in one of the "dead drops" mentioned by Hayhanen—a hole in a set of cement steps in Prospect Park. The bolt was about two inches long and one-fourth inch in diameter. It contained the following typewritten message:

> Nobody came to meeting either 8 or 9th . . . as I was advised he should. Why? Should he be inside or outside? Is time wrong? Place seems right. Please check.

Hayhanen confirmed that containers such as this were often used. Among the items he had been supplied by the Soviets were hollow pens, pencils, screws, batteries, and coins. In the modest home of Hayhanen and his wife, FBI agents found such items as a 50 Markka coin from Finland. It had been hollowed out, and there was a small hole in the first "*a*" of the word "*Tasavalta*" on the coin. FBI lab experts examined the coin, and they immediately noted that it bore a great similarity to the Jefferson nickel that the Brooklyn newsboy had discovered in 1953.

On the evening of Monday, June 22, 1953, a delivery boy for the *Brooklyn Eagle* knocked on the door of one of his customers to collect money for the paper. One of the coins felt lighter, and when he dropped this coin to the floor, it fell apart. Inside was a tiny photograph which appeared to include a series of numbers. Two days later, a detective of the New York City Police Department told an FBI agent about the strange hollow nickel which, he had heard, was discovered by a Brooklyn youth. When the New York detective contacted the boy, he handed over the hollow nickel and the photograph it contained. In examining the nickel, agents of the FBI's New York Office noted that the microphotograph appeared to portray nothing more than ten columns of typewritten numbers. The agents immediately suspected that they had found a coded espionage message, but the effort to decipher the microphotograph met with failure.

During the FBI's extensive interviews with him, Hayhanen was carefully questioned regarding the codes and cryptosystems which he had used in the various Soviet intelligence agencies he had served. The information which he provided was applied by FBI Laboratory experts to the microphotograph from the Jefferson nickel.

With this data, the FBI Laboratory succeeded in breaking through the curtain of mystery which surrounded the coded message. The message apparently was intended for Hayhanen, and had been sent from the Soviet Union shortly after his arrival in the United States. It read:

1. We congratulate you on a safe arrival. We confirm the receipt of your letter.
2. We gave instructions to transmit to you three thousand in local currency. Consult with us prior to investing it in any kind of business, first advising us of the character of the business.
3. According to your request, we will transmit the formula for the preparation of soft film, along with your mother's letter.
4. It is too early to send you the gammas. Encipher short letter. All the data about yourself, place of work, address, etc. must not be transmitted in one cipher message.
5. The package was delivered to your wife personally. Everything is all right with the family. We wish you success. Greeting from the comrades.

Although Hayhanen assisted the FBI in solving the mystery of the hollow nickel, "Mikhail" was yet to be identified. Hayhanen had the impression that Mikhail was a Soviet diplomatic official and possibly attached to the embassy or the United Nations. He described Mikhail as between 40 and 50 years old; medium build; long thin nose; dark hair; and about five feet, nine inches tall. This description was matched against those of Soviet representatives who had been in the United States between 1952 and 1954. From the long list of possible suspects, the most logical "candidate" appeared to be Mikhail Nikolaevich Svirin.

From the latter part of August 1952 until April 1954, Svirin had served as the first secretary to the Soviet United Nations Delegation in New York. On May 16, 1957, FBI agents showed several photographs to Hayhanen. The moment his eyes fell on the photo of Mikhail Nikolaevich Svirin, he shouted, "That's the one. There is absolutely no doubt about it. That's Mikhail." Unfortunately, Svirin had returned to the Soviet Union in October 1956 and was beyond the long arm of American justice.

The FBI's next task was to identify "Mark." Hayhanen did not know where Mark was residing or the name he was using, but he was able to furnish many other details: Mark was a colonel in the KGB; had been engaged in espionage work since approximately 1927; and had come to the United States in 1948 or 1949, entering by illegally crossing the Canadian border. In keeping with instructions he received from Soviet officials, Hayhanen met Mark at a movie theater in Flushing, Long Island, during the late summer of 1954. As identification, Hayhanen wore a blue and red striped tie and he smoked a pipe.

After their introduction at this theater, Hayhanen and Mark held frequent meetings in Prospect Park, on crowded streets, and in other inconspicuous places throughout New York. They also made several short trips together to Atlantic City, Philadelphia, Albany, Greenwich, and other eastern cities. Unfortunately for Abel, he had shown Hayhanen the location of his art studio in Brooklyn.

Immediately after Hayhanen showed the FBI Abel's art studio in Brooklyn, FBI agents placed Abel under round-the-clock surveillance. Meanwhile, Hayhanen continued to cooperate fully with U.S. officials. Abel was apparently none the wiser as his former colleague provided a stream of evidence to help convict Abel for his espionage activities.

On June 13, 1957, the Immigration and Naturalization Service (INS) was informed that the FBI had information concerning an alien living illegally in this country. Sam Papich, the FBI liaison officer, contacted Mario Noto, the INS deputy assistant commissioner for special investigations. Papich also told Noto that there was substantial evidence that Abel was a Soviet spy. Interestingly enough, Noto never asked about Abel's espionage activities because he was focused on the immigration issue.

Furthermore, Papich never suggested that the INS treat the case in any particular way, and no special arrangements were made between the two agencies. Papich soon provided Noto with the information he requested—that Abel had entered the country by way of Canada, that he had used a false birth certificate, and that he had confided to several people that he was in this country illegally. Noto was also told that Abel was an officer in the KGB.

Noto again met with the FBI and told them he would promptly order the arrest of Abel for failing to notify the U.S. Attorney General as required by the Immigration and Nationality Act. INS officials agreed the evidence was sufficient to justify issuance of a show cause order as to Abel's deportability. It was decided that Abel should be arrested for a deportation hearing, rather than a criminal espionage offense. The show cause order and arrest warrant were drawn up in Washington, DC, and Noto instructed two INS agents to apprehend Abel in New York. The FBI asked to talk with Abel before his arrest in order to determine whether Abel would agree to "cooperate."

At 7:00 a.m. on June 21, FBI agents broke into Abel's hotel room while INS agents waited nearby. The FBI informed Abel that they were charged with investigating matters relating to the internal security of the United States. Abel was interrogated, and he refused to answer a number of questions. He was told that the FBI was aware he had engaged in espionage and that if he refused to cooperate he would be arrested before he left the room. After half an hour of questioning, the FBI agents decided to have the INS arrest Abel. The INS agents did so, and they searched the room for weapons and evidence of alienage. The FBI agents were present when the search was made, but they did not participate in it. The only articles seized during this search were: (1) a birth certificate in the name of "Martin Collins," (2) a birth certificate in the name of "Emil Goldfus," (3) an international certificate of vaccination issued in the name of "Martin Collins," and (4) a bank book issued by the East River Savings Bank in the name of "E. R. Goldfus."

While they were in Abel's room, the INS agents also seized three slips of paper. The agents told Abel that he could take with him anything he wanted. When he finished packing, he asked for permission to repack one of his bags. While he was doing that, one of the INS agents noticed Abel was trying to hide some papers in his sleeve, and these papers were quickly seized. One of the documents later introduced into evidence at Abel's trial was a strip of graph paper containing a coded message in grouped digits.

At approximately 8:30 a.m., the INS agents left the hotel with Abel and drove to the district office of the INS. As soon as they left, FBI agents inquired of the hotel manager whether Abel had checked out of the hotel. When told that he had, they received written consent to search the room. These agents seized the contents of a wastebasket which contained several articles that Abel had discarded while packing. Two of the items were admitted into evidence: a piece of wood wrapped in sandpaper and containing a cipher pad and a hollowed-out wooden pencil containing microfilm. These items were clearly incriminating— who but a spy would have them?

On August 7, 1957, a grand jury in the eastern district of New York charged Rudolf Ivanovich Abel (whose real name was Vilyam "Willie" Genrikhovich Fisher) with violation of a number of U.S. espionage laws, and specifically, communicating information about the national defense of the United States to the Soviet Union and acting as an agent of a foreign government without prior notification to the Secretary of State.

Prior to trial, Abel did everything he could to suppress the government's evidence on the grounds that it was obtained by unlawful search and seizure in violation of the Fourth Amendment. The trial judge rejected Abel's contention, holding that INS agents making an arrest pursuant to an administrative warrant may, as an incident of that arrest, conduct a search of the adjacent premises. The search of Abel's room, the court said, was made in good faith for the purpose of discovering weapons and evidence of alienage— *not* for uncovering evidence of Abel's espionage activities. Abel's evidentiary suppression motion was denied.

The Soviet agent Roy Rhodes was called as a witness by the government. He testified that in 1951 he was assigned to serve as motor sergeant at the American embassy in Moscow. When he first arrived, he was not accompanied by his family, who were awaiting their visas. In December he received word that his wife and child had been granted visas, and to celebrate the good news, Rhodes had several drinks with two Russian nationals who were employed at the embassy garage. Late that afternoon, the girlfriend of one of the Russians came to the garage, along with a female companion. The foursome spent the evening together, eating, drinking, dancing, and otherwise carousing. The following morning, Rhodes recounted, he "woke up in bed with this girl in what I had taken to be her room."

Rhodes did not see the woman again for several weeks, but he later met with a number of Soviet citizens, some of whom were members of the military. At these meetings, Rhodes was given cash (usually between $2,500 and $3,000) in exchange for information about his duties at the embassy and the personal habits of American military and State Department personnel.

Rhodes also testified that his father and his sister lived near Salida, Colorado, where they had spoken with Hayhanen. Counsel for Abel strenuously objected to this damaging testimony, contending it was irrelevant and highly prejudicial to his case. The government countered that the evidence simply corroborated Hayhanen's testimony concerning the diligent efforts that he and Abel had made to locate Rhodes. The judge admitted the evidence. The test for admission of the evidence, the appellate court concluded, was whether the jury would know more about the circumstances of the case with the evidence than without it.

Abel was tried by a jury and convicted on each of the counts listed in the indictment, and he was sentenced to thirty years in prison.

Abel appealed his conviction to the Second Circuit Court of Appeals, and the primary issue raised on his appeal was whether the prohibition of unreasonable searches and seizures was violated when government agents, without a search warrant, searched his hotel and seized certain articles they found there. The appellate court was also to determine (a) whether there was sufficient evidence to find that Abel conspired to transmit to the Soviet government information prohibited by the espionage laws, and (b) whether the trial judge erred by allowing testimony of a non-commissioned army officer who cooperated with the Soviet government while serving in the American embassy in Moscow.

The search-and-seizure issue raised several important legal questions. The appellate court found that government agents may, pursuant to a lawful arrest, conduct a search of the premises where the arrest is made. The attorneys for Abel pointed out that in every case where such a search has been upheld the arrest was made for the commission of a crime, and that the issuance of an *administrative* arrest warrant did not confer the same right to search the premises where the arrest was made.

Identical charges for which Abel was arrested could have been made the subject of either a criminal prosecution *or* a deportation hearing. Arrest and detention for deportation offenses are allowed by statute, and the court pointed out that there was no legitimate basis to distinguish between the right of government agents to conduct a search incident to arrest for the commission of a crime and the same search for deportation proceedings.

Abel next contended that the search conducted by the INS agents violated the Fourth Amendment because the *true* objective of the arresting officers was to uncover evidence of espionage rather than to discover weapons or evidence of alienage. This contention was soundly rejected by the court. It was true, of course, that the INS first learned of Abel's illegal presence in this country from the FBI, but that fact alone did not necessarily indicate that the INS search was made in bad faith.

The head of the INS testified that the agency's interest in Abel was limited to his illegal presence in the United States. This testimony was seemingly corroborated by the articles seized from Abel's room: (1) the Martin Collins birth certificate, (2) the Emil Goldfus birth certificate, (3) the international certificate of vaccination in the name of Martin Collins, (4) a bank book issued by the East River Savings Bank to E. R. Goldfus, and (5) several slips of paper which Abel tried to hide in his sleeve.

The seizure of the first four items was clearly consistent with a search intended to obtain evidence of alienage. The fact that the agents limited themselves to seizing these articles, the court said, was convincing evidence that their search was conducted in good faith. And the seizure of the slips of paper by the INS agents occurred only after Abel desperately tried to hide them.

Abel argued that even if the INS search was lawful, the seizures were unreasonable because they did not relate to the offense charged in the arrest warrant. The court held that with the exception of the papers, everything seized was related to the offense charged in the arrest warrant. The court concluded that the papers taken from Abel's person were subject to seizure because it was clear that they were the instrumentalities by which he might commit the crime of espionage.

The appellate court also found that the record contained more than ample evidence that Abel conspired with others to act on behalf of the Soviet government. Abel argued that the evidence did not support the government charges showing that the conspiracy's purpose was to gather and transmit to the USSR information relating to the national defense of the United States. Abel pointed out that there was no evidence showing that he ever *succeeded* in communicating any information other than the type which could lawfully be sent abroad. The court conceded there was not the slightest hint that these espionage agents met with any success. However, Abel was convicted of having *conspired* with others to gather and transmit secret information pertaining to the national defense of the United States, and the record was clear that Abel knew of the unlawful purpose of this conspiracy. In other words, a conspirator's lack of success does not mitigate the criminality of his activities.

Abel then complained that the Hayhanen testimony was not specific enough to warrant his conviction for conspiracy. Hayhanen specifically mentioned "military information" and "atomic secrets." But his failure to elaborate was readily explained in light of his response to a question by the prosecution:

Q: During this conversation or during the receipt of these oral instructions from Pavlov [the supervising agent], did he give you any directions as to the type of information [you should obtain]?

A: Yes, he did. He told that it depends what kind of illegal information agents will have, so it depends then what kind of information they can give, where they work or whom they have as friends and such and such things.

It was not surprising, then, that Hayhanen's testimony failed to reveal any *specific* plans for obtaining secret information. Hayhanen, however, did testify to a sequence of events that not only proved the purpose of the conspiracy but also the fact that Abel was fully aware of the conspiracy's purpose. The jury was therefore justified in inferring that Abel and his co-conspirators were interested in establishing contact with another Soviet agent named Roy Rhodes, who was said to be a valuable source of information about atomic bombs.

The jury was no doubt impressed by the elaborate precautions taken by the conspirators to keep their activities secret. The court pointed out that individuals intent upon gathering public information do not find it necessary to employ secret codes, microdots, hollowed-out coins, and drop-off points for cryptic messages. The use of such methods was sufficient to justify the jury's finding that the object of the conspiracy was to transmit to the USSR information relating to the national defense of the United States.

The court noted:

> Moreover, the jury cannot have failed to be impressed by the elaborate precautions taken by the conspirators to keep their activities secret. Men intent upon gathering and transmitting only such information as is available to the general public do not ordinarily find it necessary to employ secret codes; microdots; hollowed-out coins, pencils, or matchbooks; "drops"; and the variety of other devices which Abel and his colleagues used. To be sure, the defendant in *Heine* had employed devious methods to transmit information which this court later held might lawfully be transmitted but our reversal of his conviction does not establish that evidence of such devious methods has no probative value. In *Heine* the information which the defendant had gathered and transmitted was known to the court. No room was left for inference.
>
> The present case is quite the contrary. Abel and his co-conspirators—unlike Heine and his— did not, as far as we know, succeed with their plans. Hence, an inference as to their purpose is properly drawn from the methods which they employed. We do not intimate that proof of the methods alone would be sufficient to sustain a conviction. We merely hold that the justifiable inference from the use of such methods by the appellant and his associates, when considered together with the other evidence which we have discussed, was sufficient to justify the jury in finding that the object of the conspiracy in the present case was to gather and transmit to the USSR information concerning the national defense of the United

States which was not "lawfully accessible to anyone who was willing to take the pains to find, sift and collate it."

In light of the overwhelming evidence that Rudolph Ivanovich Abel was a Soviet spy, his conviction was affirmed by the Second Circuit Court of Appeals and then the U.S. Supreme Court. But in a strange twist of fate, four years later Abel was back in the USSR, having been exchanged for the famous U-2 aviator Francis Gary Powers, an American spy who had been caught and imprisoned by the Soviet government for his espionage activities on behalf of the United States.

Spying, it seems, is frequently a busy and vicious two-way street, and one that can be exceedingly dangerous to cross in certain traffic conditions.

OPINION EXCERPT

Mr. Justice Frankfurter delivered the opinion of the Court.

The underlying basis of petitioner's attack upon the admissibility of the challenged items of evidence concerns the motive of the Government in its use of the administrative arrest. We are asked to find that the Government resorted to a subterfuge, that the Immigration and Naturalization Service warrant here was a pretense and sham, was not what it purported to be. According to petitioner, it was not the Government's true purpose in arresting him under this warrant to take him into custody pending a determination of his deportability. The Government's real aims, the argument runs, were (1) to place petitioner in custody so that pressure might be brought to bear upon him to confess his espionage and cooperate with the FBI, and (2) to permit the Government to search through his belongings for evidence of his espionage to be used in a designed criminal prosecution against him. The claim is, in short, that the Government used this administrative warrant for entirely illegitimate purposes and that articles seized as a consequence of its use ought to have been suppressed.

Were this claim justified by the record, it would indeed reveal a serious misconduct by law-enforcing officers. The deliberate use by the Government of an administrative warrant for the purpose of gathering evidence in a criminal case must meet stern resistance by the courts. The preliminary stages of a criminal prosecution must be pursued in strict obedience to the safeguards and restrictions of the Constitution and laws of the United States. A finding of bad faith is, however, not open to us on this record. What the motive was of the INS officials who determined to arrest petitioner, and whether the INS in doing so was not exercising its powers in the lawful discharge of its own responsibilities but was serving as a tool for the FBI in building a criminal prosecution against petitioner, were issues fully canvassed in both courts below. The crucial facts were found against the petitioner.

On this phase of the case the district judge, having permitted full scope to the elucidation of petitioner's claim, having seen and heard witnesses, in addition to testimony by way of affidavits, and after extensive argument, made these findings:

"The evidence is persuasive that the action taken by the officials of the Immigration and Naturalization Service is found to have been in entire good faith. The testimony of Schoenenberger and Noto leaves no doubt that while the first information that came to them concerning the petitioner was furnished by the FBI—which cannot be an unusual happening—the proceedings taken by the Department differed in no respect from what would have been done in the case of an individual concerning whom no such information was known to exist." "The defendant argues that the testimony establishes that the arrest was made under the direction and supervision of the FBI, but the evidence is to the contrary, and it is so found." "No good reason has been suggested why these two branches of the Department of Justice should not cooperate, and that is the extent of the showing made on the part of the defendant."

The opinion of the Court of Appeals, after careful consideration of the matter, held that the answer "must clearly be in the affirmative" to the question "whether the evidence in the record supports the finding of good faith made by the court below."

Among the statements in evidence relied upon by the lower courts in making these findings was testimony by Noto that the interest of the INS in petitioner was confined to petitioner's illegal status in the United States; that in informing the INS about petitioner's presence in the United States the FBI did not indicate what action it wanted the INS to take; that Noto himself made the decision to arrest petitioner and to commence deportation proceedings against him; that the FBI made no request of him to search for evidence of espionage at the time of the arrest; and that it was "usual and mandatory" for the FBI and INS to work together in the manner they did. There was also the testimony of Schoenenberger, regarding the purpose of the search he made of petitioner's belongings, that the motive was to look for weapons and documentary evidence of alienage. To be sure, the record is not barren of evidence supporting an inference opposed to the conclusion to which the two lower courts were led by the record as a whole: for example, the facts that the INS held off its arrest of petitioner while the FBI solicited his cooperation, and that the FBI held itself ready to search petitioner's room as soon as it was vacated. These elements, however, did not, and were not required to, persuade the two courts below in the face of ample evidence of good faith to the contrary, especially the human evidence of those involved in the episode. We are not free to overturn the conclusion of the courts below when justified by such solid proof.

Petitioner's basic contention comes down to this: even without a showing of bad faith, the FBI and INS must be held to have cooperated to an impermissible extent in this case, the case being one where the alien arrested by the INS for deportation was also suspected by the FBI of crime. At the worst, it may be said that the circumstances of this case reveal an opportunity for abuse of the administrative arrest. But to hold illegitimate, in the absence of bad faith, the cooperation between INS and FBI would be to ignore the scope of rightful cooperation between two branches of a single Department of Justice concerned with enforcement of different areas of law under the common authority of the Attorney General.

The facts are that the FBI suspected petitioner both of espionage and illegal residence in the United States as an alien. That agency surely acted not only with propriety but in discharge of its duty in bringing petitioner's illegal status to the attention of the INS, particularly after it found itself unable to proceed with petitioner's prosecution for espionage. Only the INS is authorized to initiate deportation proceedings, and certainly the FBI is not to be required to remain mute regarding one they have reason to believe to be a deportable alien, merely because he is also suspected of one of the gravest of crimes and the FBI entertains the hope that criminal proceedings may eventually be brought against him. The INS, just as certainly, would not have performed its responsibilities had it been deterred from instituting deportation proceedings solely because it became aware of petitioner through the FBI, and had knowledge that the FBI suspected petitioner of espionage. The Government has available two ways of dealing with a criminally suspect deportable alien. It would make no sense to say that branches of the Department of Justice may not cooperate in pursuing one course of action or the other, once it is honestly decided what course is to be preferred. For the same reasons this cooperation may properly extend to the extent and in the manner in which the FBI and INS cooperated in effecting petitioner's administrative arrest. Nor does it taint the administrative arrest that the FBI solicited petitioner's cooperation before it took place, stood by while it did, and searched the vacated room after the arrest. The

FBI was not barred from continuing its investigation in the hope that it might result in a prosecution for espionage because the INS, in the discharge of its duties, had embarked upon an independent decision to initiate proceedings for deportation.

The Constitution does not require that honest law enforcement should be put to such an irrevocable choice between two recourses of the Government. For a contrast to the proper cooperation between two branches of a single Department of Justice as revealed in this case, see the story told in *Colyer v. Skeffington*. That case sets forth in detail the improper use of immigration authorities by the Bureau of Investigation of the Department of Justice when the immigration service was a branch of the Department of Labor and was acting not within its lawful authority but as the cat's paw of another, unrelated branch of the Government.

We emphasize again that our view of the matter would be totally different had the evidence established, or were the courts below not justified in not finding that the administrative warrant was here employed as an instrument of criminal law enforcement to circumvent the latter's legal restrictions, rather than as a bona fide preliminary step in a deportation proceeding. The test is whether the decision to proceed administratively toward deportation was influenced by, and was carried out for, a purpose of amassing evidence in the prosecution for crime. The record precludes such a finding by this Court.

OPINION EXCERPT

Mr. Justice Douglas, with whom Mr. Justice Black concurs, dissenting.

With due deference to the two lower courts, I think the record plainly shows that FBI agents were the moving force behind this arrest and search. For at least a month they investigated the espionage activities of petitioner. They were tipped off concerning this man and his role in May; the arrest and search were made on June 21. The FBI had plenty of time to get a search warrant, as much if not more time than they had in *Johnson v. United States*, and *Kremen v. United States*, where the Court held warrantless searches illegal. But the FBI did not go to a magistrate for a search warrant. They went instead to the INS and briefed the officials of that agency on what they had discovered. On the basis of this data a report was made to John Murff, Acting District Director of the INS, who issued the warrant of arrest.

No effort was made by the FBI to obtain a search warrant from any judicial officer, though, as I said, there was plenty of time for such an application. The administrative warrant of arrest was chosen with care and calculation as the vehicle through which the arrest and search were to be made. The FBI had an agreement with the officials of INS that this warrant of arrest would not be served at least until petitioner refused to "cooperate." The FBI agents went with agents of the INS to apprehend petitioner in his hotel room. Again, it was the FBI agents who were first. They were the ones who entered petitioner's room and who interrogated him to see if he would "cooperate"; and when they were unable to get him to "cooperate" by threatening him with arrest, they signaled agents of the INS who had waited outside to come in and make the arrest. The search was made both by the FBI agents and by officers of the INS. And when petitioner was flown 1,000 miles to a special detention camp and held for three weeks, the agents of the FBI as well as INS interrogated him.

Thus the FBI used an administrative warrant to make an arrest for criminal investigation both in violation of 242 (a) of the Immigration and Nationality Act and in violation of the Bill of Rights. The issue is not whether these FBI agents acted in bad faith. Of course they did not. The question is how far zeal may be permitted to carry officials bent on law enforcement. As Mr. Justice Brandeis once said, "Experience should teach us to be most on our guard to protect liberty when the Government's purposes are beneficent." The facts seem to me clearly to establish that the FBI agents wore the mask of INS to do what otherwise they could not have done. They did what they could do only if they had gone to a judicial officer pursuant to the requirements of the Fourth Amendment, disclosed their evidence, and obtained the necessary warrant for the searches which they made.

If the FBI agents had gone to a magistrate, any search warrant issued would by terms of the Fourth Amendment have to "particularly" describe "the place to be searched" and the "things to be seized." How much more convenient it is for the police to find a way around those specific requirements of the Fourth Amendment! What a hindrance it is to work laboriously through constitutional procedures! How much easier to go to another official in the same department! The administrative officer can give a warrant good for unlimited search. No more showing of probable cause to a magistrate! No more limitations on what may be searched and when!

In *Rea v. United States*, federal police officers, who obtained evidence in violation of federal law governing searches and seizures and so lost their case in the federal court, repaired to a state court and proposed to use it there in a state criminal prosecution. The Court held that the Federal District Court could properly enjoin the federal official from using the illegal search and seizure as basis for testifying in the state court. The federal rules governing searches and seizures, we held, are "designed as standards for federal agents" no more to be defeated by devious than by direct methods. The present case is even more palpably vulnerable. No state agency is involved. Federal police seek to do what immigration officials can do to deport a person but what our rules, statutes, and Constitution, forbid the police from doing to prosecute him for a crime.

The tragedy in our approval of these short cuts is that the protection afforded by the Fourth Amendment is removed from an important segment of our life. We today forget what the Court said in *Johnson v. United States*, that the Fourth Amendment provision for "probable cause" requires that those inferences "be drawn by a neutral and detached magistrate" not "by the officer engaged in the often competitive enterprise of ferreting out crime." This is a protection given not only to citizens but to aliens as well, as the opinion of the Court by implication holds. The right "of the people" covered by the Fourth Amendment certainly gives security to aliens in the same degree that "person" in the Fifth and "the accused" in the Sixth Amendments also protects them. Here the FBI works exclusively through an administrative agency—the INS —to accomplish what the Fourth Amendment says can be done only by a judicial officer. A procedure designed to serve administrative ends—deportation—is cleverly adapted to serve other ends—criminal prosecution. We have had like examples of this same trend in recent times. Lifting the requirements of the Fourth Amendment for the benefit of health inspectors was accomplished by *Frank v. Maryland*, as I have said. Allowing the Department of Justice rather than judicial officers to determine whether aliens will be entitled to release on bail pending deportation hearings is another.

4

OPERATION SCORPION

The Directorate of Intelligence—the primary intelligence agency in Cuba—maintained an active organization for espionage in South Florida known as *La Red Avispa* ("The Wasp Network"). Among other things, The Wasp Network reported information to the Cuban government about the operation of U.S. military facilities, U.S. political and law enforcement activities, and the work of U.S. organizations that supported a change of regime in Cuba.

Five secret agents working for The Wasp Network, who were later tried for espionage in the United States, were clearly industrious. For example, they constructed false identities in an attempt to penetrate the Miami facility of the Southern Command, which planned and oversaw operations of U.S. military forces in Cuba, Latin America, and the Caribbean. One of these agents even acted as a fraudulent informant to the FBI, monitored the activities of other Cuban-American organizations in Florida, and sought the assistance of a member of Congress to have his wife (also a Cuban agent) enter the United States.

Of particular interest to The Wasp Network was a Miami-based organization called "Brothers to the Rescue" (BTTR) that flew small aircraft over the Florida straits in order to help rescue those fleeing Cuba. BTTR was the brainchild of an individual named Jose Basulto, who was also one of the organization's pilots. The Cuban government was aware that BTTR pilots often violated its airspace, so the Cuban government launched a special mission code-named "Operation Scorpion" in order to stop the rescue missions of BTTR. Among other things, the Cuban intelligence officers transmitted encrypted radio messages that allowed the Cuban military to determine specific flight plans of BTTR.

BTTR was extremely active, and it had knowingly violated Cuban airspace thousands of times since its inception. In July of 1995, the organization notified both U.S. and Cuban officials of its plan to commit "civil disobedience" within Cuban territorial waters.

Cuba prepared itself: placing gun boats in the water and fighter jets in the air. The U.S. State Department issued a public announcement stating that pilots should under *no* circumstance violate Cuban airspace. Despite the warning, BTTR flew four planes there. As the plane approached Cuban territory, Havana Air Traffic Control told Jose Basulto to leave, but he refused to do so. Basulto flew his plane low over downtown Havana, dropping nearly 20,000 leaflets and religious medals. Miraculously, all of the BTTR pilots returned safely to Miami.

Following the incident, Cuba notified the FAA of the violations by BTTR. The letter from Cuba sternly warned that future actions would bring "grave consequences," and Cuba demanded that American officials adopt whatever measures were necessary to avoid "provocation" of Cuban sovereignty. The U.S. State Department then issued another statement advising American pilots to avoid penetrating Cuban boundaries, and that the State Department should take this situation seriously.

Despite the warnings from both Cuba and the United States, BTTR flew again on January 13, 1996, and it escalated its efforts further—dropping almost 500,000 leaflets over Havana and nearby communities. Two days later, the Cuban government contacted the FAA. The letter made clear that Cuba has "the necessary measures to guarantee integrity of its national territory" and that violators of Cuban airspace should "be prepared to face serious consequences."

On February 24, three BTTR planes flew in international airspace close to Cuban territorial waters. As the planes approached Cuba, they were warned that they were "in danger" and were flying into an area that was "activated." Basulto brazenly ignored these warnings and nosed his plane into Cuban territory. The other two planes on the mission were shot down five and ten miles away from Cuba, killing the pilots and passengers inside. When the shoot-down occurred, Basulto's plane was two miles into Cuban airspace, but somehow he managed to escape unharmed.

Three Cuban intelligence officers operating in America—Ruben Campa, Gerardo Hernandez, and Luis Medina—and two Cuban agents operating in America—Rene Gonzalez and Antonio Guerrero were apprehended for their part in the shoot-down incident and subsequently indicted. Following a trial in Miami that lasted more than six months, all five men were found guilty of espionage charges, and one of them was convicted of conspiracy to murder.

After the trial, intelligence officer Ruben Campa was convicted of five counts: acting as an agent of a foreign government, fraud and misuse of documents, and possession with intent to use fraudulent identification documents. He was sentenced to a total of 228 months in prison.

Intelligence officer Gerardo Hernandez—who was the kingpin of the operation—was convicted of thirteen counts: conspiracy to gather and transmit national defense information, acting as an agent of a foreign government without notifying the Attorney General, fraud and misuse of documents, possession with intent to use fraudulent identification documents, and conspiracy to murder. Hernandez was sentenced to concurrent terms of life imprisonment on the counts of conspiracy to murder and conspiracy to gather and transmit national defense information. On the other counts, he was sentenced to shorter terms of imprisonment which ran concurrently with one another and with his life sentences.

Intelligence officer Luis Medina was convicted of ten counts: acting as a foreign agent, fraud and misuse of documents, making a false statement in a passport application, and possession with intent to use fraudulent identification documents. Medina was sentenced to life imprisonment on the conspiracy charge. On the other charges he was sentenced to shorter terms of imprisonment that ran concurrently with his life sentence.

Agent Rene Gonzalez was convicted of two counts of acting as an agent of a foreign government. He was sentenced to five years of imprisonment on the conspiracy count and a consecutive term of ten years in prison on the substantive count.

Agent Antonio Guerrero was convicted of three counts of acting as a foreign agent and conspiring to gather and transmit national defense information. Guerrero was sentenced to life imprisonment for conspiracy to gather and transmit national defense information. For each of the other counts, Guerrero was sentenced to shorter terms of imprisonment, which ran concurrently with his life sentence.

The defendants raised a number of issues on appeal to the Eleventh Circuit Court of Appeals. They challenged the rulings on the following grounds: (1) the suppression of evidence from searches conducted under the Foreign Intelligence Surveillance Act, (2) sovereign immunity, (3) discovery of information under the Classified Information Procedures Act, (4) the exercise of peremptory challenges, (5) prosecutorial and witness misconduct, (6) jury instructions, (7)

the sufficiency of the evidence in support of their convictions, and (8) several sentencing issues.

The appellate court concluded that the arguments concerning suppression of evidence, sovereign immunity, discovery, jury selection, and the trial were meritless, and that sufficient evidence supported each conviction. In the end, the court affirmed the sentences of two of the defendants, but it remanded in part for resentencing of the other three.

Guererro, Hernandez, and Medina argued that the evidence introduced at trial was insufficient to convict them of acting as an agent of a foreign government without notifying the Attorney General. They next argued that their convictions for conspiracy to transmit national defense information were not supported by clear and sufficient evidence. The appellate court disagreed, holding that the government introduced sufficient evidence to support the convictions.

The indictment charged that Guerrero, Hernandez, and Medina conspired to "communicate, deliver, and transmit" to the Republic of Cuba information relating to the national defense of the United States, intending that it be used to the injury of the United States and to the advantage of Cuba. The defendants conceded that they conspired to transmit information to Cuba but argued that the information they transmitted was *not* information relating to national defense. Once again, the court took exception to their contentions.

An individual named Joseph Santos, who also worked as a spy for The Wasp Network, testified that he received instructions from Medina to penetrate the facility of the Southern Command in Miami to gather information. Santos testified that as part of his training for penetration work, he was instructed that it was especially important to gather information classified as restricted, classified, or secret.

Furthermore, the U.S. government introduced evidence that Guerrero was assigned to gather intelligence from the Naval Air Station at Key West. Guerrero discovered that a command post building there was being remodeled to accommodate "top secret activities." Correspondence from a Cuban military specialist instructed Guerrero to "obtain anything else that you can get related to the use of that building." The Chief of Naval Operations at the Pentagon testified that the storage of classified documents at this facility was unknown to the general public.

The U.S. government introduced correspondence from Medina to Guerrero that included a chart of both military and other "secret information." The government also introduced a report from Guerrero that described the aircraft frequency settings he observed while working on a repair job in the "greenhouse" (an alternate air control tower) at the Key West station. The Chief of Naval

Operations at the Pentagon testified that Guerrero's report included frequencies that were not published.

In the view of the Eleventh Circuit Court of Appeals, a reasonable jury could have found that Guerrero, Hernandez, and Medina conspired to transmit to Cuba information relating to the national defense. As a result, the court concluded that the government presented ample evidence that the purpose of the conspiracy was to transmit secret information relating to national defense. The fact that the conspirators were often prevented from achieving their goal was immaterial.

Campa presented two arguments that the evidence introduced at trial was insufficient to convict him. Campa first argued that the evidence did not prove he knew of the requirement to register as a foreign agent with the U.S. government. Campa next argued that the government failed to offer sufficient evidence to support his remaining convictions for fraud and misuse of documents and for possession with intent to use fraudulent identification documents. These convictions were based on an allegation that Campa possessed a fraudulent passport. Campa argued that there was insufficient evidence that he possessed this passport.

The government introduced a document that appeared to be a standard U.S. passport. The document bore Campa's photograph and the name and signature of "Osvaldo Reina," and a government expert testified that it was a counterfeit passport. An agent of the FBI, who was present when the passport was seized, testified that the passport was found along with a social security card, a Florida driver's license, business cards for an agent of a Spanish book publishing company, and a membership card for a Florida club, all bearing the name (and sometimes the photograph) of Reina. These items were found hidden inside a notebook in Hernandez's apartment.

The appellate court explained: "The government need not prove actual possession in order to establish knowing possession; it need only show constructive possession through direct or circumstantial evidence. Constructive possession exists when the defendant exercises ownership, dominion, or control over the item or has the power and intent to exercise dominion or control."

The U.S. government also introduced an encrypted report found in Campa's residence of "work directives." The primary legend was in the name of Ruben Campa and contained biographical data associated with that name. The reserve legend was in the name of Osvaldo Reina and included the biographical data that appeared on the counterfeit passport. The government also introduced an "escape plan" found at Campa's residence, and it instructed Campa to "change identity and assume the one in your reserve documentation" in the event of a situation that "might demand an emergency exit from the country."

From this evidence, the court said, a reasonable jury could have found that Campa had control over the counterfeit passport. A reasonable jury could have inferred from the appearance of Campa's photograph on the passport and accompanying documents that Campa was aware of the documents and intended to use them if necessary.

Gonzalez conceded that evidence presented at trial established that he and his co-defendants acted as emissaries of the Cuban government, but he argued that the evidence never revealed that he was *aware* of the reporting requirements. The court pointed out that the statute described a "general intent" crime, so the government was only required to prove the intent to do the prohibited acts. The government was *not* required to prove that Gonzalez knew of the registration requirement.

Gonzalez's argument that the evidence introduced at trial was insufficient to prove a conviction for conspiracy also failed. To sustain a conviction for conspiracy, the government had to prove (a) an agreement to achieve an unlawful objective, (b) the defendant's knowing and voluntary participation in the conspiracy, and (c) the commission of an overt act in furtherance of it. The government did *not* need to prove that the defendants accomplished the purpose of the conspiracy. In the view of the court, the government presented sufficient evidence to establish that Gonzalez furthered the conspiracy.

The indictment also charged that Gonzalez solicited from a U.S. congressman the admission of Gonzalez's wife into the states. Gonzalez argued that the evidence did not prove that his efforts were tantamount to interference with any governmental function. A report that Gonzalez sent to Hernandez described his efforts to secure his wife's entry into the United States and explained that his efforts were "designed more to give an appearance, rather than to seek action to have my family leave." The court stated that a reasonable jury could have found that this report furthered the conspiracy by keeping other members of the conspiracy informed about his actions. Whether this report actually interfered with any governmental function was irrelevant.

Another allegation in the indictment stated that Gonzalez met with the FBI in the guise of cooperating with them. The government introduced communications from Cuba which directed Gonzalez to meet with FBI agents, as well as reports from Gonzalez to Hernandez describing these meetings with the FBI.

The government also introduced a report in which Gonzalez wrote to Hernandez, "As you told me to do, I have been flying in the vicinity of Homestead Air Base in order to be able to observe any strange movement," and it described

Gonzalez's observations of aircraft, their movement, and their positioning. The report supported the allegation in the indictment that this overt act furthered the conspiracy.

The government pointed to a number of intercepted communications between the Cuban government and Hernandez to prove the conspiracy to commit murder. Hernandez argued that his conviction should be reversed because the government failed to prove that (a) he intended the murder to occur within the jurisdiction of the United States, (b) he knew of the object of the conspiracy, and (c) he acted with malice aforethought. Hernandez urged that because the government did not prove that there was a plan to "confront" BTTR in international (as opposed to Cuban) airspace, his conviction for conspiracy to murder should be reversed. The court ultimately held that "intent" showing the murder occurred within the jurisdiction of the United States was not an element of the statute.

Second, Hernandez argued that the government did not introduce sufficient evidence to establish that he knew the *object* of the conspiracy. But additional intercepted messages to Hernandez stated that it was important for Cuban officials to know when its agents would be on board BTTR flights. A January 30 message instructed Hernandez that if other intelligence officers were asked to fly at the last minute, they should find an excuse not to do so. If they could not avoid flying, they should transmit code words to alert the Cuban military. A message transmitted on February 18 instructed Hernandez that "under no circumstances" should Cuban agents fly with BTTR "on days 24, 25, 26, and 27 in order to avoid any incident of provocation that they may carry out and our response to it." The message continued: "Immediately confirm when you instruct both of them." Hernandez met with these agents on February 22 and 23, and the shoot-down occurred the next day.

The U.S. government offered proof that Hernandez and the Cuban regime considered the operation a success. Correspondence from Hernandez sent after the shoot-down stated: "It's a great satisfaction and source of pride to us that the operation to which we contributed a grain of salt ended successfully." The government also introduced an order from the chief of the Cuban directorate of intelligence that granted Hernandez "recognition for the outstanding results achieved on the job, during the provocations carried out by the government of the United States this past 24th of February of 1996."

The government introduced evidence that the encrypted messages were transmitted to Hernandez's call sign. The messages were decrypted with materials found at Hernandez's apartment. From this evidence—Hernandez's instructions to Gonzalez, the scheduling of Hernandez's meetings with other agents, and the timing of the shoot-down—a reasonable jury could have found that Hernandez received the messages.

In the court's mind, there were at least two reasons to conclude that a shoot-down was contemplated. First, the instructions that Hernandez received from the Cuban directorate of intelligence and relayed to the agents who had infiltrated BTTR supported an inference that a shoot-down was planned. Second, the correspondence from Hernandez after the shoot-down stating that the operation "ended successfully," established Hernandez's guilt.

In the end, the convictions of the five Cuban spies were affirmed by the appellate court, and Campa, Guerrero, and Medina were resentenced in light of the irregularities that occurred at trial. Because Hernandez was sentenced to life imprisonment for his murder and conspiracy conviction, any error in the calculation of his concurrent sentence for conspiracy to gather and transmit national defense information was irrelevant to the time he would serve in prison.

At long last, The Wasp Network and Operation Scorpion had lost its sting.

OPINION EXCERPT

Kravitch, Circuit Judge, concurring in part and dissenting in part.

A country cannot lawfully shoot down aircraft in international airspace, in contrast to a country shooting down foreign aircraft within its own territory when the pilots of those aircraft are repeatedly warned to respect territorial boundaries, have dropped objects over the territory, and when the objective of the flights is to destabilize the country's political system. Thus, the question of whether the Government provided sufficient evidence to support Hernandez's conviction turns on whether it presented sufficient evidence to prove that he entered into an agreement to shoot down the planes in international, as opposed to Cuban, airspace.

The majority opinion discusses the airspace issue, but it does so in the context of a different analytical framework: whether the *mens rea* requirement in subsection (a) of Section 1111 carries over to subsection (b). The opinion fails to address, however, whether the Government produced sufficient evidence to prove beyond a reasonable doubt that Hernandez agreed to commit an unlawful act. Such a discussion is necessary because our conspiracy law requires that those entering into a conspiracy have an agreement to commit an unlawful act and the substantive murder offense requires that the killing be unlawful. A shoot down in Cuban airspace would not have been unlawful; thus, Hernandez could not have been convicted of conspiracy to murder unless the Government proved beyond a reasonable doubt that he agreed for the shoot down to occur in international, as opposed to Cuban, airspace.

Here, the Government failed to provide sufficient evidence that Hernandez entered into an agreement to shoot down the planes at all. None of the intercepted communications the Government provided at trial show an agreement to shoot down the planes. At best, the evidence shows an agreement to "confront" BTTR planes.

But a "confrontation" does not necessarily mean a shoot down. BTTR's videotape on January 9th clearly shows that BTTR members seriously contemplated that MiGs would "confront" them by forcing them to land. Richard Nuccio—an advisor to President Clinton on Cuban affairs—also thought BTTR's repeated violations of Cuban airspace would result in a forced landing. He testified (and documents show) that conversations within the State Department suggested the same. And Basulto testified that on the day of the shoot down he thought MiGs would fire warning shots. This evidence demonstrates the obvious: there are many ways a country could "confront" foreign aircraft. Forced landings, warning shots, and forced escorted journeys out of a country's territorial airspace are among them—as are shoot downs. But the Government presented no evidence that when Hernandez agreed to help "confront" BTTR that the agreed confrontation would be a shoot down. To conclude that the evidence does show this goes beyond mere inferences to the realm of speculation.

Moreover, even assuming that Hernandez agreed to help Cuba shoot down the BTTR planes, the Government presented no evidence that Hernandez agreed to a shoot down in international airspace. It is not enough for the Government to show that a shoot down merely occurred in international airspace: the Government must prove beyond a reasonable doubt that Hernandez agreed to a shoot down in international airspace. Although such an agreement may be proven with circumstantial evidence, here, the Government failed to provide either direct or circumstantial evidence that Hernandez agreed to a shoot down in international airspace. Instead, the evidence points toward a confrontation in Cuban airspace, thus negating the requirement that he agreed to commit an unlawful act.

Basulto testified that in his nearly 2000 BTTR flights, MiGs never confronted him in international airspace. Further, every communication between Cuba and the FAA discussed the consequences for invading

Cuba's sovereign territory, including the letter Cuba sent on January 15th—only a month before the tragic events of February 24th. The evidence also shows that American officials at the White House and in the State Department never contemplated a confrontation in international airspace. And the intercepted communications between Cuba and Hernandez speak of a confrontation only if BTTR "provokes" Cuba. Further, the fact that the intercepted communications after the shoot down show that Hernandez was congratulated for his role and that he acknowledged participation and called it a "success" does not clearly establish an agreement to a shoot down in international airspace. The Government cannot point to *any evidence* that indicates Hernandez agreed to a shoot down in international, as opposed to Cuban, airspace.

OPINION EXCERPT

Pryor, Circuit Judge.

[The defendant] Hernandez argues that his conviction for conspiracy to murder, 18 U.S.C. §§ 1111, 1117, is not supported by sufficient evidence. Hernandez argues that his conviction should be reversed because the government failed to prove that he intended the murder to occur within the jurisdiction of the United States, failed to prove that he knew of the object of the conspiracy, and failed to prove that he acted with malice aforethought. Each of these arguments fails. We address each argument in turn.

First, Hernandez argues that the government was required to prove that he intended the murder to occur within the special maritime and territorial jurisdiction of the United States. Hernandez contends that, because the government did not prove that there was a plan to "confront" Brothers in international, as opposed to Cuban, airspace, his conviction for conspiracy to murder should be reversed. We disagree.

Whether Sections 1111 and 1117 require proof that Hernandez intended the murder to occur within the special maritime and territorial jurisdiction of the United States "is a question of statutory construction." The language of the statute, the starting place of our inquiry provides, "Murder is the unlawful killing of human being with malice aforethought. Every murder perpetrated by poison, lying in wait, or any other kind of willful, deliberate, malicious, and premeditated killing . . . is murder in the first degree." 18 U.S.C. § 1111(a). Section 1111(b) provides, "Within the special maritime and territorial jurisdiction of the United States, whoever is guilty of murder in the first degree shall be punished by death or by imprisonment for life." Section 1117 provides a penalty of "imprisonment for any term of years or for life" for a conspiracy to violate Section 1111.

Although the statute explicitly describes the *mens rea* required for murder, the statute is silent about *mens rea* that the murder occur in the special jurisdiction of the United States. Ordinarily, we interpret statutes that are silent as to *mens rea* to require proof of general intent. This rule is subject to an exception when the nature of the statute is such that "congressional silence concerning the mental element of the offense should be interpreted as dispensing with conventional *mens rea* requirements." An exception applies to Section 1111.

When a criminal statute is otherwise silent, no proof of *mens rea* is necessary for elements that are "jurisdictional only." As the Supreme Court has explained, "the existence of the fact that confers federal jurisdiction need not be one in the mind of the actor at the time he perpetrates the act made criminal by the federal statute." "Knowledge of jurisdictional facts is not required in determining guilt." In *Feola*, the Court held that a statute that prohibits assault of a federal officer does not require knowledge that the victim is a federal officer because the victim's status as a federal officer is a fact that is jurisdictional only. The *Feola* Court explained that its holding "poses no risk of unfairness to defendants" because "the situation is not one where legitimate conduct becomes unlawful solely because of the identity of the individual or agency affected."

Hernandez argues that the requirement that the murder occur in the special jurisdiction of the United States is more than a jurisdictional requirement. Hernandez argues that, because the government did not introduce evidence that Cuban law prohibits murder, the jurisdictional language in Section 1111(a) distinguishes between potentially legitimate conduct (murder in Cuba under Hernandez's theory) and conduct that is unlawful (murder in the special jurisdiction of the United States).We disagree.

5

A VIETNAMESE CAPER

Truong Dinh Hung—more commonly known to his friends and acquaintances as David Truong—was a Vietnamese citizen and the son of a prominent Vietnamese politician who had come to the United States in 1965 to study at Stanford. Truong pursued a scholarly interest in Vietnam and the complicated relationship between North Vietnam and the United States, and he soon became an activist in the anti-war movement.

In 1976, Truong met a woman named Dung Krall, a Vietnamese-American and the wife of an American naval officer, who apparently had extensive contacts among the Vietnamese community in Paris.

Truong eventually persuaded Ms. Krall to transport packages to certain Vietnamese operatives in Paris. The recipients were representatives of the Socialist Republic of Vietnam at the time of the 1977 Paris negotiations between Vietnam and the United States. The packages contained copies of diplomatic cables and other classified documents of the U.S. government. Truong, it was later revealed, procured these papers from Ronald Humphrey, an employee of the U.S. Information Agency, who surreptitiously gathered the documents, copied them, and removed their classification markings. In a statement given after his arrest, Humphrey said that his motive was to "improve" relations between the North Vietnamese government and the United States so that he could be reunited with a woman he loved, who was a prisoner of the North Vietnamese government.

Unbeknownst to Truong (and unfortunately for him), Ms. Krall was an undercover informant for the CIA and the FBI. Krall kept these two agencies fully informed of Truong's activities and presented the documents Truong had given her for their inspection, copying, and approval before Krall delivered them to Paris. The FBI supervised this operation from approximately September 1976 until January 1978.

When the U.S. intelligence agencies first learned that Truong was transmitting classified documents to Paris, they were naturally interested in locating his source. Top Carter administration officials approved an extensive electronic surveillance, and Truong's phone was tapped and his apartment bugged from May 1977 to January 1978. The telephone interception continued for 268 days, and virtually every conversation was monitored and taped. The eavesdropping device ran continuously for 255 days. No court authorization was ever sought for the telephone tap or the bug. As a result of these diligent efforts, the government learned that Humphrey was providing Truong with this top-secret information.

After a protracted trial in Alexandria, Virginia, that brought into focus national security concerns as they conflicted with civil liberties in an early era of electronic surveillance by the government, Truong and Humphrey were convicted of espionage and conspiracy to commit espionage. They were also convicted of:

- conspiring to convert classified government documents,
- acting as agents of a foreign government without prior notification to the Secretary of State,
- delivering material related to the national defense to unauthorized persons, and
- conspiring to violate the statute penalizing government employees who transmit, and foreign agents who thereby receive classified information.

On appeal to the Fourth Circuit Court of Appeals, Truong and Humphrey challenged their convictions on the grounds that the FBI surveillance violated the Fourth Amendment, and that the resulting evidence should have been suppressed. The government had not sought a warrant for the eavesdropping or the bugging, but instead relied on the "foreign intelligence" exception to the Fourth Amendment's warrant requirement. The government contended that the President can authorize surveillance without seeking a warrant because of his delegated duties in the area of foreign affairs. On that basis, the FBI received approval for the surveillance from the President's delegate, the Attorney General. This approval alone, according to the government, was constitutionally sufficient to authorize the surveillance.

The district court accepted the government's argument but observed that the executive branch could proceed without a warrant only as long as the investigation was primarily a *foreign intelligence* investigation. The court decided that the FBI investigation had become primarily a *criminal* investigation by July 20, 1977, and it excluded all evidence obtained *after* that date.

In reviewing the matter, the appellate court agreed with the district court that the executive branch need not always obtain a warrant for foreign intelligence surveillance. If the legitimate need of government to safeguard domestic security requires the use of electronic surveillance, the question is whether the needs of citizens for privacy and free expression may not be better protected by requiring a warrant before such surveillance is undertaken.

The appellate court also considered whether a warrant would unduly frustrate the efforts of government to protect itself from acts of subversion against it. Balancing individual privacy and government needs, the Supreme Court in previous cases had held that the executive must seek a warrant before it undertakes *domestic* security surveillance.

But in the area of *foreign* intelligence, the Supreme Court pointed out, the needs of the executive are so compelling that a uniform warrant requirement would "unduly frustrate" the president in carrying out his responsibilities. Attempts to counter foreign threats to the national security require "the utmost stealth, speed, and secrecy." A warrant requirement would hamper the flexibility of executive foreign intelligence efforts and increase the chance of disclosure concerning sensitive operations.

However, because individual privacy interests are compromised, any time the government conducts surveillance without prior judicial approval, the foreign intelligence exception must be carefully examined. The government is relieved of seeking a warrant *only* when the object of the surveillance concerns a foreign power, its agent, or collaborators.

The appellate court ruled that surveillance in the present case clearly satisfied this limitation. Ms. Krall, the CIA agent, received a letter of introduction to Truong through the president of the Vietnamese Association in Paris. Truong transmitted to Krall documents which were eventually handed to representatives of the Vietnamese government. The Vietnamese ambassador to the United Nations told Krall that Truong had *volunteered* to obtain documents for the Vietnamese government. Obviously, there was sufficient evidence that tended to show collaboration with Vietnam on the part of Truong.

As the district court ruled, the executive should be excused from securing a warrant only when the surveillance is conducted "primarily" for foreign intelligence reasons. The appellate court felt that the district court adopted the proper test, because once surveillance becomes a criminal investigation, the courts are competent to make the probable cause determination. Individual privacy interests come to the fore—and foreign policy concerns recede—when the government moves forward with a criminal prosecution. The appellate court thus rejected the government's assertion that if surveillance is to any degree directed at gathering foreign intelligence, the executive may ignore the warrant requirement of the Fourth Amendment.

The defendants urged that the "primarily" test does not go far enough to protect privacy interests. They argued that the government should be able to avoid the warrant requirement *only* when the surveillance is conducted "solely" for foreign policy reasons. But the court found that position unacceptable, because almost all foreign intelligence investigations are in part criminal investigations.

Although espionage prosecutions are rare, there is always the possibility that the targets of the investigation will be prosecuted for criminal violations. If the defendants' test was adopted, the executive would be required to obtain a warrant every time it undertook foreign intelligence surveillance.

In the present case, the district court concluded that July 20, 1977, was the operative date. It was then that the investigation of Truong had become primarily a *criminal* investigation. Although the Justice Department had been aware of the investigation from its inception, until then the criminal division had not taken a central role. On July 19 and July 20, several memoranda circulated between the Justice Department and the various intelligence and national security agencies, and they indicated that the government had begun to assemble a criminal prosecution.

The Fourth Circuit Court of Appeals noted that even if a warrant is not required, the Fourth Amendment requires that the surveillance be "reasonable" under the circumstances of the particular case.

For seventy days prior to July 20, FBI agents intercepted all of Truong's phone calls, and the agents listened to Truong's conversations with visitors in his apartment. As the court observed, this intrusive surveillance was reasonable in order to determine Truong's source of government documents. It was necessary to intercept all of Truong's calls, because the government agents could never be sure whether a particular caller would reveal that he was a source of the documents. Furthermore, investigators often find it critical to review all calls in order to determine code language or oblique references to the illegal scheme.

The FBI and the CIA also searched one of the packages that Truong sent to Paris by way of Ms. Krall without the authorization of the Attorney General or a search warrant. Because the government agents did not receive executive authorization, the foreign intelligence exception to the warrant requirement did not render this search legitimate. Nevertheless, because Truong did not have a reasonable expectation of privacy, the district court did not err in admitting the package's contents into evidence.

The documents at issue were stored inside an unsealed manila envelope, and inside that envelope was a transparent book bag, loosely tied with twine. Although the documents were partially shielded from view, parts of the documents could be seen through the book bag. Truong had not made a diligent effort to conceal the documents from view. Moreover, Truong knew that this flimsily wrapped package would cross at least two national boundaries on its way to Paris. This risk of inspection, when Ms. Krall left the states and entered France, mitigated against any reasonable expectation of privacy by Truong that the contents of the package would remain entirely undisclosed. Therefore, neither a search warrant nor executive authorization was necessary for this search.

The jury found that the defendants had violated three espionage provisions: 18 U.S.C. § 794(a), § 794(c), and § 793(e):

A common prerequisite for a conviction under each of the statutes is that the defendant transmits information "relating to the national defense." The defendants argued that this phrase limited the statutory reach to military matters, and they maintained that none of the materials transmitted by Truong and Humphrey fit that category.

Contrary to the defendants' argument, the legislative history of the espionage statutes demonstrated that Congress intended "national defense" to encompass a broad range of information and that Congress rejected attempts to narrow the reach of the statutory language. The appellate court agreed that the words "national defense" in the Espionage Act carry that meaning. Thus, the defendants' attempt to narrow the scope of national defense to strictly military matters was summarily rejected by the court.

Under either the narrow definition urged by the defendants or the broad definition endorsed by the Supreme Court, the appellate court held that the defendants transmitted information relating to the national defense. The materials sent to Paris related directly to the U.S. military, including data concerning Vietnamese designs on Thailand, American POWs in Indochina, and American military matériel which had fallen into the hands of the Vietnamese government. Additionally, the packages contained names of U.S. intelligence sources. There could be no doubt that the transmitted information related to "national defense."

Truong and Humphrey based their second principal objection on their claim that a constitutional conviction under the espionage statutes must include a finding of evil intent (i. e., intent to injure the United States or to aid a foreign nation). They contended that their convictions were invalid because the trial judge failed to instruct the jury that a finding of evil intent was essential, and because the statute did not contain evil intent as a necessary element.

Under the espionage statute the prosecution had to prove that the defendant acted "with intent or reason to believe" that transmission of the information would injure the United States or aid a foreign nation. This *scienter* require-ment was critically important to rebut a claim that the espionage statutes were unconstitutionally overbroad. The defendants insisted that the district judge's instructions in this case diluted this critical requirement by suggesting that the defendant could be convicted for mere negligence.

The district judge had instructed the jury that it must find that the defen-dants acted "willfully and with an intent or reason to believe" that the informa-tion would be used to injure the United States or to aid a foreign power. The jury was also told that "reason to believe" meant that a defendant knew facts from which he concluded, or reasonably should have concluded, that the in-formation could be used for the prohibited purposes. The latter standard did not mean, however, that the jury could convict merely upon a finding that a defendant acted "negligently." Rather, the jury was instructed that a defendant must act "willfully" (i.e., "voluntarily and intentionally and with a specific intent to do something the law forbids").

In addition to their convictions under the espionage statutes, Truong and Humphrey were found guilty of violating criminal statutes relating to foreign agents and classified information.

The jury found that Truong and Humphrey had acted as unregistered agents of the Socialist Republic of Vietnam. The defendants argued that the statute violated their privilege against self-incrimination because they would have been forced to confess participation in illegal espionage if they had registered. The appellate court held that a registration provision violates the Fifth Amendment only if it is directed at a *class* of persons who are inherently suspect of illegal activities. A neutral registration requirement, such as the instant one, did not offend the Fifth Amendment.

Truong and Humphrey were convicted of conspiracy to commit espionage. The statute makes it unlawful for a U.S. government employee knowingly to *transmit* classified information to an agent of a foreign government. Conversely, the statute makes it illegal for an agent of a foreign government knowingly to *receive* classified information from a U.S. government employee.

Truong argued that he could not be bound by the classification system because he himself was not a government employee. But the appellate court reasoned that Truong could not hide behind his civilian status when he encouraged a U.S. government employee to copy classified documents. Second, the fact that the president did not personally classify the documents did not place them outside the scope of the act.

Both defendants were convicted and sentenced to fifteen years in prison. Three years later, the appellate court affirmed the convictions of David Truong and Ronald Humphrey.

According to *The Washington Post*, Truong maintained his innocence and told reporters, "I'm nobody's agent, and nobody's spy." Truong died of cancer at the age of 68 on June 26, 2014, at a hospital in Penang, Malaysia.

OPINION EXCERPT

Winter, Circuit Judge.

The defendants [David Truong and Ronald Humphrey] raise a substantial challenge to their convictions by urging that the surveillance conducted by the FBI violated the Fourth Amendment and that all the evidence uncovered through that surveillance must consequently be suppressed. As has been stated, the government did not seek a warrant for the eavesdropping on Truong's phone conversations or the bugging of his apartment. Instead, it relied upon a "foreign intelligence" exception to the Fourth Amendment's warrant requirement. In the area of foreign intelligence, the government contends, the President may authorize surveillance without seeking a judicial warrant because of his constitutional prerogatives in the area of foreign affairs. On this basis, the FBI sought and received approval for the surveillance from the President's delegate, the Attorney General. This approval alone, according to the government, is constitutionally sufficient to authorize foreign intelligence surveillance such as the surveillance of Truong.

The district court accepted the government's argument that there exists a foreign intelligence exception to the warrant requirement. The district court, however, also decided that the executive could proceed without a warrant only so long as the investigation was "primarily" a foreign intelligence investigation. The district court decided that the FBI investigation had become primarily a criminal investigation by

July 20, 1977, and excluded all evidence secured through warrantless surveillance after that date. Conversely, all evidence secured before July 20 was not suppressed by the district court, because it determined that during that period the investigation primarily concerned foreign intelligence.

We agree with the district court that the Executive Branch need not always obtain a warrant for foreign intelligence surveillance. Although the Supreme Court has never decided the issue which is presented to us, it formulated the analytical approach which we employ here in an analogous case, *United States v. United States District Court (Keith)*. In *Keith*, the executive had conducted warrantless domestic security surveillance. The Court posited two inquiries to guide the Fourth Amendment determination of whether a warrant is required:

If the legitimate need of Government to safeguard domestic security requires the use of electronic surveillance, the question is whether the needs of citizens for privacy and free expression may not be better protected by requiring a warrant before such surveillance is undertaken. We must also ask whether a warrant would unduly frustrate the efforts of Government to protect itself from acts of subversion and overthrow directed against it.

Balancing individual privacy and government needs, the Supreme Court concluded that the executive must seek a warrant before it undertakes domestic security surveillance.

For several reasons, the needs of the executive are so compelling in the area of foreign intelligence, unlike the area of domestic security, that a uniform warrant requirement would, following *Keith*, "unduly frustrate" the President in carrying out his foreign affairs responsibilities. First of all, attempts to counter foreign threats to the national security require the utmost stealth, speed, and secrecy. A warrant requirement would add a procedural hurdle that would reduce the flexibility of executive foreign intelligence initiatives, in some cases delay executive response to foreign intelligence threats, and increase the chance of leaks regarding sensitive executive operations.

More importantly, the executive possesses unparalleled expertise to make the decision whether to conduct foreign intelligence surveillance, whereas the judiciary is largely inexperienced in making the delicate and complex decisions that lie behind foreign intelligence surveillance. The executive branch, containing the State Department, the intelligence agencies, and the military, is constantly aware of the nation's security needs and the magnitude of external threats posed by a panoply of foreign nations and organizations. On the other hand, while the courts possess expertise in making the probable cause determination involved in surveillance of suspected criminals, the courts are unschooled in diplomacy and military affairs, a mastery of which would be essential to passing upon an executive branch request that a foreign intelligence wiretap be authorized. Few, if any, district courts would be truly competent to judge the importance of particular information to the security of the United States or the "probable cause" to demonstrate that the government in fact needs to recover that information from one particular source.

Perhaps most crucially, the executive branch not only has superior expertise in the area of foreign intelligence, it is also constitutionally designated as the pre-eminent authority in foreign affairs. The President and his deputies are charged by the constitution with the conduct of the foreign policy of the United States in times of war and peace. Just as the separation of powers in Keith forced the executive to recognize a judicial role when the President conducts domestic security surveillance, so the separation of powers requires us to acknowledge the principal responsibility of the President for foreign affairs and concomitantly for foreign intelligence surveillance.

In sum, because of the need of the executive branch for flexibility, its practical experience, and its constitutional competence, the courts should not require the executive to secure a warrant each time it conducts foreign intelligence surveillance.

6

SUITCASE SCANDAL

Franklin Duran was a resident of Caracas, Venezuela. He was convicted in a U.S. federal court for serving as an agent of a foreign government (in this case Venezuela) when he attempted to cover up the so-called "Suitcase Scandal." Duran's business partner and two other co-conspirators pled guilty to the charges, and they turned state's evidence and testified against Duran at trial.

Duran was a co-owner of Venoco, the largest private petro-chemical company in Venezuela. Venoco's corporate survival depended on the operations of Petroleos de Venezuela, S.A. (PDVSA), an energy monopoly owned and operated by the Venezuelan government. Several of Duran's other ventures were also heavily dependent on the favor of the Venezuelan government.

Duran's main business partner was Carlos Kauffmann, the other owner of Venoco. Also prominent among Duran's business partners was Guido Alejandro Antonini Wilson, a dual citizen of Venezuela and the United States, who engaged in commercial dealings with the Venezuelan government and other ventures involving Venezuelan investors. Duran, Kauffmann, and Antonini were also personal friends.

The "Suitcase Scandal" between Venezuela and Argentina unfurled on August 4, 2007, when Argentine customs agents searched a suitcase that Antonini was carrying when he arrived in Buenos Aires, Argentina, on a private plane chartered by the oil company PDVSA. A customs agent discovered about $800,000 in U.S. currency in the suitcase. Coincidentally, it was a criminal violation in Argentina to import more than $10,000 into the country without declaring it.

Antonini, traveling on his Venezuelan passport, had completed a customs statement in which he listed as his residence Duran's apartment in Caracas, and this disclosure turned out to be extremely problematic for Duran.

Shortly after his arrival in Buenos Aires, Antonini attended a reception for Venezuelan President Hugo Chavez, and he then flew to Miami. Antonini left Argentina without resolving the currency declaration issue, so the Argentine authorities instituted extradition proceedings against him. Not surprisingly, communications between Duran, Kauffmann, and Antonini commenced shortly thereafter.

The incident received much attention in the press, and the media speculated that the cash was evidence that Venezuela and Argentina had been secretly channeling large sums of money from the oil company PDVSA to Argentine presidential candidate Cristina Fernandez de Kirchner, who was favored by Hugo Chavez and the Venezuelan regime.

After being implicated in the "Suitcase Scandal," Duran contacted the Director of the Venezuelan intelligence agency, Dirección de los Servicios de Inteligencia y Prevención (DISIP). The agency reassured Duran not to worry—they would handle the matter.

On August 10, 2007, Duran and his brother, a DISIP agent, traveled to Miami to persuade Antonini to set forth a full written account of the suitcase incident. Antonini gave the Durans an oral rendition of the facts, but declined to provide the written narrative. Antonini then hired an attorney and entered into a cooperation agreement with the FBI.

In Venezuela, the intelligence agency DISIP formulated a strategy to defuse the "Suitcase Scandal" in hopes of concealing the fact that the $800,000 was a campaign contribution from the Venezuelan government to the Argentine presidential candidate. The DISIP proposed that a forged, back-dated document attesting to Antonini's removal of $800,000 of his "own" money from Venezuela be placed in the files of the Venezuelan customs authority. The DISIP would then retain an Argentine lawyer to represent Antonini for failing to declare the money when he arrived in Argentina. If Antonini were to claim the money as his own, it was assumed that the matter would be quickly resolved.

In order to secure Antonini's cooperation, the DISIP retained a Venezuelan attorney to counsel with Antonini and to prepare a power of attorney. The DISIP also enlisted the assistance of Duran and Kauffmann because of their personal relationship with Antonini.

Duran, Kauffmann, and the Venezuelan attorney met with Antonini several times in Miami to discuss the DISIP's strategy and to convince Antonini to cooperate. Unbeknownst to them, Antonini wore a recording device provided by the FBI. These three men assured Antonini that the Venezuelan and Argentine governments would come to an agreement, and that Argentina would drop the charges once Antonini executed the power of attorney. Antonini raised some concerns and remained noncommittal.

In September 2007, Duran again met with Antonini and encouraged him to sign the power of attorney, but Antonini refused. Duran was frustrated and did not meet with Antonini again until December 2007. In early October 2007, Antonini sent a written offer to President Hugo Chavez, requesting $2 million in compensation for his assistance with the DISIP in forging sufficient documentation about his ownership of the $800,000 seized by Argentine officials.

On October 28, Antonini met with a DISIP agent in a conference secretly recorded by the FBI, and Antonini reiterated the demands he had made to Chavez. The DISIP agent accepted the offer on behalf of Chavez. At a meeting in Miami on December 11, 2007, Duran supplied Antonini with the falsified documents, and they discussed the power of attorney and the payment of the $2 million.

As soon as Duran and the DISIP agent left the meeting, the FBI arrested them.

Before trial, the U.S. government sought to preclude evidence regarding the foreign policy—or lack thereof—between the United States and Venezuela. The government was concerned that Duran would introduce such evidence to show that Duran was the subject of a political prosecution designed to embarrass the Venezuelan government for contributing to an Argentine presidential candidate. The government argued that relations between the United States and Venezuela had nothing to do with Duran's criminal conduct. Additionally, the government contended that permitting Duran to raise the defense of political prosecution would be an invitation for jury disqualification.

Duran responded that the evidence of foreign policy relations between the United States and Venezuela was directly relevant to the motives of the government witnesses, and that the motive of the prosecution was to embarrass the Chavez government by using Duran as a scapegoat. Duran, however, agreed at the status conference that he would not defend the case on the basis that it was a political prosecution. The district court granted the government's motion to suppress the evidence.

Second, the government sought to preclude Duran from introducing evidence about Duran's assertion that he did not know that as a foreign agent he had the duty to notify the Attorney General. The government contended that such an argument was irrelevant and confusing to the jury. Duran responded that knowledge of the notification requirement was clearly relevant to the jury's determination of whether Duran acted with knowledge that his conduct was unlawful. The district court granted the government's motion on the ground that the statute was a general intent crime which did not require proof that the defendant knew of the notification requirement.

The government also sought to introduce evidence of Duran's and Kauffmann's numerous schemes of giving kickbacks to officials of various agencies of the Venezuelan government, as well as to officials of various states of Venezuela. The government urged that such evidence was admissible because it was relevant to issues other than Duran's character, including (a) whether Duran knowingly conspired with Kauffmann and others to act as agents of the Venezuelan government, (b) whether Duran knowingly acted as an agent of the Venezuelan government, and (c) whether there was a preexisting relationship between Duran and the Venezuelan government.

In response, Duran argued that the alleged kickback schemes were irrelevant because none of them involved the DISIP. The district court initially denied the government's request to introduce such evidence, and it only permitted Kauffmann to testify generally about the kickbacks that he and Duran gave to Venezuelan government officials.

However, in the middle of the trial, the district court permitted Duran to raise the defense of entrapment. Duran initially advanced the theory that he acted wholly independently of the Venezuelan government based upon concern for his own affairs. Duran later revised this defense to argue that he became entrapped into acting as Venezuela's agent by Antonini's insistence that the aid he sought be provided by the Venezuelan government. After a request by the government, the district court permitted the introduction of Duran's kickbacks through Kauffmann's rebuttal testimony because the evidence was directly relevant to show Duran's predisposition to act as an agent of the Venezuelan government, and was thus admissible to negate Duran's entrapment defense.

At trial, the prosecution presented its case through the testimonies of Antonini, Maionica, and Kauffmann, as bolstered by the FBI's recorded conversations. A jury convicted Duran, and the district court sentenced him to 48 months in prison, followed by three years of supervised release.

Duran's primary issue on appeal to the Eleventh Circuit Court of Appeals was whether the foreign agent notification statute is unconstitutionally vague.

The foreign agent registration statute at issue provided that "whoever, other than a diplomatic or consular officer or attaché, acts in the United States as an agent of a foreign government without prior notification to the Attorney General" is guilty of a crime. Duran argued to the appellate court that the foreign agent notification statute was unconstitutionally vague, and that he did not have notice, and could not have had notice of his obligation to notify the attorney general of his conduct in the United States on behalf of the Venezuelan government because he was *not* an employee of or spy for the Venezuelan government. However, the jury found to the contrary—that Duran was *in fact* an agent of a foreign government.

In analyzing a vagueness claim, the first step taken by a court is the language of the statute itself. Where the act sets forth plainly delineated boundaries no further inquiry is necessary. To violate the statute a person must act, and the action must be taken at the direction of, or under the control of, a foreign government. The appellate court held that the statute at bar *plainly* identified the prohibited conduct, and the statute's language was clear and unambiguous.

Duran argued that the statute was unconstitutionally vague because it did not require an element of *specific* intent: that a defendant knew of the duty to notify the attorney general. Specifically, Duran argued that he could *not* have had notice of the notification requirement without that *specific* intent.

However, the appellate court remarked that it routinely validated general intent statutes against vagueness challenges. The plain language of the act made it clear that it was a general intent crime, since there was no *mens rea*. The silence of the statute was dispositive of the fact that Congress intended it to be one of general intent.

Despite the plain language of the statute, Duran argued that it must be read to require *actual* knowledge of the notification requirement by affirmatively engaging in espionage or other subversive activities. Duran argued that in order to have sufficient notice of the requirement, his conduct must also have necessarily involved an intent to engage in espionage. He contended that his innocent conduct could not have provided him with knowledge of the registration requirement. Duran also relied on the legislative history of the statute arguing that all of the previous cases involving criminal prosecution under the statute related to some form of subversive activity or espionage-related component.

The appellate court, however, found that there was no such suggestion in the plain language of the statute, its legislative history, or previous convictions under the statute. To the contrary, the activities that fell within the statute's purview had never been limited to those bearing upon national security.

The government, the court conceded, is vested with sound discretion in determining those it chooses to prosecute. In this case the government chose to pursue Duran for violating a statute which permitted prosecution so long as Duran acted on behalf of a foreign government and failed to notify the attorney general. The court acknowledged that the government has a legitimate interest in knowing the identity of those acting on behalf of a foreign government, whether the action is legal or not. By its plain text the statute placed Mr. Duran on notice that his conduct was prohibited. His conviction was therefore affirmed.

According to the *Miami Herald*, after his conviction Duran maintained his innocence when he said:

> I am a man of principles and convictions, which were put to the test when they tried to force me to accept a set-up against the institutions of Venezuela. Despite all the weight of the empire's media, and having spent more than nine months in solitary confinement, I never gave up my values.

The FBI's recorded conversations between Duran and others, however, painted a much different story.

OPINION EXCERPT

Wilson, Circuit Judge.

Relying on legislative history, Duran asserts that his failure to have anticipated the statute's registration requirement stemmed from the fact that his conduct did not involve espionage or traditional spying on the United States government, what he categorizes as the primary focus of Section 951.When the text of a statute is plain, however, we need not concern ourselves with contrary intent or purpose revealed by the legislative history. Duran contends that for over ninety years, the only application of Section 951 has been to prosecute cases dealing with espionage or subversive activities against the United States. However, the plain language of Section 951 does not exclude from its scope cases that do not involve such subversive activities. Congress is free to pass laws with language covering areas well beyond the particular crisis *du jour* that initially prompted legislative action.

Although Congress' original intent in 1917 was national security, defense, and targeting espionage and subversive acts, over time, the original 1917 Act broke off into three directions to form three separate registration or notification statutes dealing with agents of foreign governments. Congress enacted legislation targeted specifically at such subversive acts through the Foreign Agents Registration Act of 1938 ("FARA"). The limited legislative history persuasively suggests that Congress chose to separate Section 951 and treat it as a catch-all statute that would cover all conduct taken on behalf of a foreign government.

https://casetext.com/-idm301511008-fn7. Thus, Duran's argument that he could not have had notice of the registration requirement under Section 951 is meritless because registration is not only required of spies or foreign agents engaged in subversive acts under FARA or Section 851, but it also reaches beyond such classifications to *any* affirmative conduct undertaken as an agent of a foreign government.

The earliest form of Section 951 was enacted on June 15, 1917, shortly after the United States entered World War I. Legislative history suggests that the 1917 Act was a war-time act to protect the United States from subversive elements that could threaten America's war effort. This is because, in its Congressional Reports, Congress labeled the act, "To Punish Espionage and Enforce the Criminal Laws of the United States" and "Espionage Bill."

The Foreign Agents Registration Act is primarily aimed at foreign political propagandists and political activists that the United States has an interest in keeping track of, and it requires agents of foreign principals to identify themselves and their foreign principals, disclose their activities, and file and label political propaganda. FARA's registration provision states in pertinent part, "No person shall act as an agent of a foreign principal unless he has filed with the Attorney General a true and complete registration statement unless he is exempt from registration." Thus, this is one example of a statutory registration requirement enacted after the 1917 Act that specifically covers "agents of foreign principals" as defined under 22 U.S.C. § 611(c).

Thus, Section 851 is an espionage registration statute, while Section 951 is a broader, catch-all notification statute aimed at all foreign relations in general. Thus, it became a completely separate notification statute from FARA, and it continues to cover any action of conduct by an agent of a foreign government.

The Government is vested with sound discretion in determining who to prosecute and under what laws to prosecute. Here, the Government exercised its prosecutorial discretion to convict Duran for violating Section 951, which permits prosecution so long as Duran acted on behalf of a foreign government and failed to notify the Attorney General of such action, regardless of the nature of such action.

7

DOCUMENT DROP

Richard Miller, a former FBI agent assigned to the Soviet Foreign Counter-Intelligence Unit in Los Angeles, was convicted of several espionage crimes:

- bribery
- conspiracy to commit espionage
- copying national defense information and delivering it to a foreign government
- communicating confidential information to a foreign government with the intent to harm the United States

At trial, the government charged Miller with various offenses relating to the delivery of documents to representatives of the Soviet Union. In his defense, Miller vehemently denied that he ever intended to harm the United States, and he urged that, to the contrary, his actions were actually taken to *benefit* the FBI.

Miller had met the co-defendant—Svetlana Ogorodnikova—in 1984. Svetlana had emigrated from the Soviet Union in 1973 with her husband Nikolay, another co-defendant. She entertained Soviet officials in Los Angeles and performed various errands for them. Among other things, Svetlana rented Soviet "cultural" (which were really propaganda) films to the Russian-American community. Svetlana and Nikolay apparently performed these tasks to earn a "right to return" to the Soviet Union.

In 1982, the FBI tried to recruit Svetlana as an informant. Her recruiter, an agent named John Hunt, testified that he and Svetlana were building rapport during an "evaluation period" which spanned some 55 meetings. Hunt said that Svetlana provided some intelligence information and was used in an FBI operation but that the FBI eventually decided not to use her as an operative.

Svetlana confessed that she and Hunt were lovers. Hunt claimed that in 1982 he attempted a double-agent scheme by approaching the Soviets through Svetlana. He claimed that the Soviets were aware of his meetings with Svetlana and he was testing whether the Soviets would attempt to recruit him.

Svetlana contacted the FBI in May of 1984, claiming to have valuable information. Agent Richard Miller was given the necessary authority to meet with her. After that meeting, he continued to see her, sometimes without reporting the meetings to his supervisors. They too became lovers.

Svetlana then asked Miller to provide information to help her locate three defectors, and Miller asked an FBI superior if the CIA could provide the information. Svetlana soon left to visit the Soviet Union. When she returned to Los Angeles, she and Miller resumed their meetings. She gave gifts to Miller and offered him money on numerous occasions. In early August, Svetlana asked Miller to work for the Soviet Union and provide her with classified documents.

Miller requested $15,000 in cash and $50,000 in gold, but later contended that he solicited the money only to "play along." He claimed that he wanted to convince the Soviets that he intended to provide classified information but that he never really intended to do so. Miller had something of a checkered career with the FBI, and he told Svetlana he wanted to leave in "a blaze of glory." Svetlana said Miller had told her that he would promise the Soviets everything but would do nothing without the approval of his boss.

Svetlana and Miller traveled to San Francisco in late August 1984. She entered the Soviet consulate while Miller waited a few blocks away. Svetlana delivered to the Soviets Miller's FBI credentials and a classified document—the Positive Intelligence Reporting Guide (PIRG)—which was an annual document that set forth the intelligence needs of the United States worldwide.

In late September, Svetlana and Miller made arrangements for a trip to Vienna to meet with Soviet officials. Miller prepared for the trip by updating his passport and shopping with Svetlana, but he said he never really planned to go and was surprised to learn she had reserved airline tickets for the two of them. Miller insisted that when the plans with the Soviets were sufficiently advanced, he would then inform the FBI.

The FBI, however, had already begun surveillance of Miller and Svetlana. They placed wiretaps in Miller's home, car, and office, as well as in the home and cars of Svetlana and Nikolay. The FBI also employed physical surveillance. Miller soon became aware of the surveillance, and he approached his supervisor with a "cover" story about a double agent scheme.

Miller then underwent five days of interrogation. He talked to the FBI voluntarily and waived his *Miranda* rights in writing, but at trial he contested the reliability of his admissions during this period. Miller eventually admitted giving the PIRG to Svetlana. He consented to searches of his two houses and his office, which yielded numerous FBI documents, some of which were classified.

The Ogorodnikovas' trial was severed from that of Miller. After a six-week trial, Svetlana and Nikolay pleaded guilty to conspiracy to commit espionage. Miller's first trial lasted three months and resulted in a mistrial when the jury, after three weeks of deliberations, became deadlocked. After a new trial lasting four months, a jury convicted Miller on six counts, and he was sentenced to two concurrent life terms plus an additional concurrent term of 50 years. He was also fined $60,000.

Miller insisted that he had acted only to benefit the FBI. He agreed to take several polygraph tests, but an FBI polygraph examiner, James Murphy, told Miller that he had failed the tests. Miller said he did not trust Murphy, and he asked for a new examiner. The FBI's chief polygrapher Paul Minor met with Miller the next day to conduct preliminary interviews, and surprisingly enough, Miller confessed that Svetlana had taken his FBI credentials into the Soviet Consulate in San Francisco. Miller then admitted that he had given Svetlana the PIRG, a classified document.

Before trial, Miller moved to have the polygraph results excluded because their prejudicial effect outweighed its probative value. The government argued that if the defendant contested the voluntariness of his admissions, then the polygraph evidence should be admitted to explain the sequence of events that led to his admissions. Miller said that he would not challenge the voluntariness of his admissions, but would attack its reliability. The trial court ruled that it was only fair then to permit the government to "set the scene" precipitating the admissions.

On appeal to the Ninth Circuit Court of Appeals, Miller challenged the admission of this testimony. The appellate court noted that it generally disfavored the admission of polygraph evidence unless the parties stipulated to its admission and the court determined that the polygraph was administered in a reliable manner, given the procedure's overall "questionable reliability" and its "misleading appearance of accuracy."

The court did note, however:

> A number of cases in other circuits have addressed the issue of the extent to
> which polygraph evidence may be used for limited purposes. In the leading case

of *Tyler v. United States*, the defendant confessed to murder after being told by a polygrapher that his reactions during a lie detector test indicated that he was not telling the truth. When the polygrapher subsequently testified to this fact at trial, the defendant objected. The trial court overruled the objection, holding that the testimony was admissible "as revealing circumstances leading to the confession," although the trial court agreed that the testimony was not admissible for the purpose of showing that the defendant lied.

The court gave the jury a limiting instruction to this effect, admonishing them that the polygrapher's testimony was only admitted for the purpose of deciding whether the confession was voluntary. The D.C. Circuit affirmed, holding that the limiting instruction obviated any prejudicial effect.

In the present case, the court concluded that the admission of polygraph evidence was *not* narrowly tailored to limit its prejudicial effect. The jury was fully exposed to the prejudicial impact of Miller's polygraph examinations—a result that clearly outweighed the probative value of the admitted testimony—even in light of the limited purpose for which it was introduced.

The court reasoned:

> By contrast, in the trial below, the prosecution questioned each of two witnesses concerning the specific questions Miller was asked and the answers he gave. The prosecution thus effectively introduced a thorough account of Miller's polygraph examinations. Unlike the earlier cases, the admission of polygraph evidence in this case was not narrowly tailored to limit the prejudicial effect of such evidence. The jury here was exposed to the full prejudicial impact of Miller's polygraph examinations, an impact that clearly outweighed the probative value of the admitted testimony, even considering the limited purpose for which it was introduced.
>
> The operative fact the government sought to establish through the polygraph evidence was that Miller's admissions were reliable because he decided to make them only after being told that he had failed the polygraph. As in *Tyler*, this fact could have been established without revealing the specific questions and answers given during the examinations.
>
> Compared to the overwhelming potential prejudice, the marginal probative value of this additional detailed testimony was slight indeed. We hold that the district court abused its discretion in admitting this testimony.

Since the admission of this evidence was erroneous, the appellate court considered whether it resulted in substantial prejudice to Miller's rights and affected the verdict. The probable impact of the polygraph evidence, the court said, was to convince the jury that Miller's answers were false and that his admissions were true. Since Miller's admissions were at the heart of the prosecution's case, the court held that it was more likely than not that the jury's verdict *was* affected by the polygraph evidence.

Additionally, the district court had improperly allowed evidence to prove the defendant's motive and character traits. Given these significant errors, Miller's conviction was reversed and the case was remanded for a new trial.

At long last, Miller would have a new day in court, but there would still be the damaging testimony of Svetlana to contend with.

OPINION EXCERPT

Nelson, Circuit Judge.

Before trial, [the defendant] Miller moved to have any evidence concerning his polygraph examinations excluded on the ground that its prejudicial effect outweighed its probative value. The government argued that, if the defendant intended to contest the voluntariness of his admissions before the jury, then the polygraph evidence should be admitted solely for the purpose of explaining the sequence of events that led to Miller's admissions. Miller responded that he would not challenge the voluntariness of his admissions at trial, but that he would attack their reliability. The trial court ruled that if Miller chose to challenge the admissions at trial, then it was only fair to permit the government, in response, to "set the scene" which it believed precipitated the admissions. At trial, the defendant did challenge the reliability of his admissions, through both cross-examination and other evidence. Accordingly, the trial court permitted the government to introduce evidence concerning Miller's polygraph examinations. An FBI interrogator (Torrence), as well as Murphy, testified that Miller had been told that he had failed the exams. Indeed, the government went further and questioned each of these witnesses about the specific questions Miller was asked and the responses he gave.

On appeal, Miller challenges the trial court's admission of this testimony, arguing that the court was incorrect in its determination that the prejudicial effect did not outweigh the probative value. We review such a ruling only for abuse of discretion.

We begin by noting that this circuit generally disfavors the admission of polygraph evidence. In *Brown v. Darcy*, we held it erroneous to admit polygraph evidence to establish the truth or falsity of a party's statements unless the parties stipulate to the admission of the evidence and the court determines that the polygraph was administered in a reliable manner. We concluded that such a holding was consistent with our uniformly "inhospitable view" towards the admission of unstipulated polygraph evidence. Polygraph evidence has an "overwhelming potential for prejudice," given its questionable reliability and its "misleading appearance of accuracy." Thus, polygraph evidence is generally excluded because of the danger that the jury will misuse it, giving it substantially more weight than it deserves.

However, we also noted in *Brown* that polygraph evidence might be admissible if it is introduced for a limited purpose that is unrelated to the substantive correctness of the results of the polygraph examination. Nonetheless, we cautioned in *Brown* that polygraph evidence should not be admitted, even for limited purposes, unless the trial court has determined that "the probative value of the polygraph evidence outweighs the potential prejudice and time consumption involved in presenting such evidence."

By contrast, in the trial below, the prosecution questioned each of two witnesses concerning the specific questions Miller was asked and the answers he gave. The prosecution thus effectively introduced a thorough account of Miller's polygraph examinations. Unlike the earlier cases, the admission of polygraph evidence in this case was not narrowly tailored to limit the prejudicial effect of such evidence. The jury here was exposed to the full prejudicial impact of Miller's polygraph examinations, an impact that clearly outweighed the probative value of the admitted testimony, even considering the limited purpose for which it was introduced. The operative fact the government sought to establish through the polygraph evidence was that Miller's admissions were reliable because he decided to make them only after being told that he had failed the polygraph. As in *Tyler*, this fact could have been established without revealing the specific questions and answers given during the examinations. Compared to the overwhelming potential prejudice, the marginal probative value of this additional detailed testimony was slight indeed. We hold that the district court abused its discretion in admitting this testimony.

Given that the admission of this evidence was erroneous, we must consider whether it resulted in substantial prejudice to Miller's rights. Nonconstitutional errors do not require reversal unless, viewing the evidence as a whole, it was more probable than not that the errors affected the verdict. We must therefore evaluate the potential prejudicial impact of the admitted testimony on the evidence that was presented to the jury. The prejudicial impact of the polygraph evidence would be to convince the jury unduly that Miller's answers during the polygraph examinations were false, and *a fortiori* that his admissions were true. Since Miller's admissions were at the heart of the prosecution's case, we conclude that it is more likely than not that the jury's verdict was affected by the introduction of the polygraph evidence. Accordingly, Miller's conviction must be reversed.

8

ECONOMIC ESPIONAGE

An individual named Dongfan "Greg" Chung was a Boeing engineer who handed over to the Chinese government extremely sensitive technical information and trade secrets developed by the company. As a result, Chung was convicted of:

- six counts of violating the Economic Espionage Act (EEA)
- one count of conspiring to violate the EEA
- one count of acting as an unregistered foreign agent
- one count of making a false statement to federal agents

Before sentencing, U.S. District Judge Cormac J. Carney said that he was not sure exactly what information had been transmitted to China, but "What I do know is what he did, and what he did pass hurt our national security and Boeing."

Chung begged the judge for mercy, "Your honor, I am not a spy. I am only an ordinary man." He continued, "Your honor, I beg your pardon, and let me live with family peacefully." Chung conveniently forgot to mention that in the process of selling the stolen information he had amassed a wealth of more than three million dollars.

Chung was more or less caught red-handed. According to an article in *The New Yorker*, the FBI had conducted a lengthy surveillance of Chung's home:

> The following week, shortly after sunrise, Chung wheeled out a large recycling bin and placed it next to two trash cans, which he had put out the night before. He then stopped behind the bushes in front of his front yard and waited for a

minute, watching the street, before he returned to the house. When the investigators retrieved the contents of the recycling bin, they found more than six hundred pages from Boeing, full of graphs and line drawings. The words "proprietary" or "trade secret" appeared on several of the pages.

Chung's primary argument on appeal was that his convictions were not supported by "sufficient evidence." In the course of his trial, it was revealed that Chung worked for Boeing, Rockwell, and McDonnell Douglas for 38 years (from 1964 to 2002), primarily as a stress analyst on the forward fuselage section of the space shuttle. After retiring, Chung returned to Boeing as a contractor in 2003 to help evaluate the crash of the space shuttle *Columbia*.

Federal agents first suspected that Chung was spying for China after their investigation of an individual named Chi Mak, an engineer who worked for a naval defense contractor. In October of 2005, FBI agents searched Mak's residence and saw Chung's contact information in several of Mak's address books.

During a second search of Mak's home in June 2006, federal agents found a letter addressed to Chung from Gu Weihao, a senior official with the China Aviation Industry Corporation. Weihao requested that Chung provide data about various aircraft and the space shuttle, and he thanked Chung for providing previous information.

Following those discoveries, agents conducted surveillance of Chung's home. There they discovered that Chung was disposing of Boeing technical documents by hiding them inside Chinese newspapers and throwing them into the trash.

On September 11, 2006, agents interviewed Chung and searched his home. They discovered underneath his house a massive trove of Boeing and Rockwell documents, many of which related to the space shuttle, Delta IV Rocket, F-15 Fighter, B-52 Bomber, and Chinook Helicopter. They also uncovered a number of business cards, letters, briefings, travel documents, and technical information related to aerospace or the space shuttle program.

On appeal the Ninth Circuit Court of Appeals described the documents this way:

> Most significantly, as discovered by federal agents on September 11, 2006, Defendant possessed approximately 300,000 pages of Boeing documents, including: (1) more than 700 SDS [Shuttle Drawing System] documents, one of which bears Chi Mak's name and telephone numbers; (2) documents related to the X-37 space vehicle; (3) documents related to the thermal protection system on the International Space Station; (4) documents related to the F-15 Fighter; (5) documents related to the CH-46 and CH-47 Chinook Helicopter; and (6)

documents related to the B-52 Bomber. Defendant told federal agents that he had taken the documents home because he planned to write a book. He also claimed that, although Boeing policy generally prohibited taking home work documents, his supervisor, William Novak, had given him permission to keep the documents.

The government identified six documents in Defendant's possession that allegedly contained trade secrets: four documents about a phased array antenna for the space shuttle and two documents about the Delta IV Rocket.

As noted, the government presented evidence that, between August 4, 2006, and September 1, 2006, federal agents discovered more than 1,000 pages of Boeing documents hidden between the pages of Chinese newspapers that Defendant had placed in the trash. Defendant's journals also record that, between November 12, 2004, and August 5, 2006, he "got rid of old newspaper," on 27 separate occasions. Defendant told agents that he had disposed of the documents in that fashion because he did not want NASA documents flying around the trash disposal area.

A grand jury indicted Chung on February 6, 2008. After a bench trial without a jury, he was convicted, and the district court sentenced him to prison for fifteen years and eight months and then to three years of supervised release. Chung appealed the decision.

During the trial, the government presented many of the documents retrieved from Chung's home. Included in the record was a series of letters between Chung and Chen Qinan, the project manager of the China National Aero Technology Import/Export Corporation. Those letters largely concerned the information Chung would supply while visiting China on a "technical exchange."

Qinan sought information relating to the fatigue life and structural design of aircraft and armed helicopters. Chung offered to provide information about the space shuttle as well, even though he acknowledged that the space shuttle was "classified as secret." In another letter, Chung expressed an interest in visiting several Chinese aircraft manufacturers, noting his desire to "contribute his expertise."

The government also presented a "tasking list" from the Nanchang Aircraft Company—a production factory of the Chinese Ministry of Aviation—which Chung received during his visit to the Nanchang plant. The list requested information concerning methods for determining the fatigue life of aircraft and helicopters, including information regarding U.S. military specifications.

There was also an undated letter from Chung to Chief Engineer Feng of the Nanchang Aircraft Company. In that letter, Chung stated that he had "attached the answers for the questions that were not answered when I was in Nanchang." In another letter, Chung referred to 27 manuals that he had previously sent them, and he attached a list cataloguing 24 structure manuals developed by Rockwell's B-1 Division.

The government presented several letters between Chung and his purported "handler," Gu Weihao. In the first letter, Weihao stated that he was engaged in research on damage tolerance and expressed his hope that Chung could "provide his advice in this area." In the second letter, Weihao requested Chung's assistance on some "difficult technical issues" concerning the design for the space shuttle, particularly quality control information. Weihao suggested a meeting in Guangzhou to discuss these matters "in a small setting, which is very safe."

Chung's journals further documented that in April 2001 he traveled to China and gave presentations on the space shuttle. Immediately before his visit to China in 2002, Chung downloaded more than 500 space shuttle specifications from the Shuttle Drawing System (SDS), a restricted Boeing database. In early 2003, Chung recorded in his journal that he organized "spec material" on 21 separate occasions.

By way of background, the Economic Espionage Act (EEA) provides in pertinent part:

> Whoever, intending or knowing that the offense will benefit any foreign government, foreign instrumentality, or foreign agent, knowingly—
> [. . .]
> (3) receives, buys, or possesses a trade secret, knowing the same to have been stolen or appropriated, obtained, or converted without authorization;
> [. . .]
> shall be fined not more than $500,000 or imprisoned not more than 15 years, or both.

The EEA defines "trade secret" as information that "the owner thereof has taken reasonable measures to keep secret," and that "derives independent economic value, actual or potential, from not being generally known to, and not being readily ascertainable through proper means by, the public."

NASA had contemplated replacing the space shuttle's dish antenna with a phased array antenna in the 1990s. Boeing competed with other companies to supply the antenna, but Boeing was the sole-source contractor at the time for integrating technologies (including the new antenna) into the shuttle. The proposed communications upgrade required Boeing's engineers to determine the feasibility of installing the new antenna at the existing antenna on the shuttle's forward fuselage by enlarging or adding an opening. Those potential structural changes required conducting stress analyses, and the engineers had to figure out how to dissipate the heat generated by the new antenna.

Chung possessed four documents related to the phased array antenna project. Two documents listed the tasks and hours necessary to complete the integration project. The other two documents were slide presentations about the communications upgrade. Among the data contained in the slides was a list of the antenna's specifications, including the proposed number of elements in the antenna.

The government pointed out that the tasks-and-hours lists were never made public. With regard to the slide presentations, the documents contained information similar to that presented by Boeing engineers at a NASA-sponsored conference, but the portions of those documents relating to the number of elements in the phased array antenna were *not* disclosed at the conference. As a result, there was sufficient evidence that all four phased array antenna documents contained secret information.

None of the documents was kept under lock and key, but Boeing implemented general physical security measures for its entire plant. Security guards required employees to show identification before entering the building, and Boeing reserved the right to search all employees' belongings and cars. Boeing also held training sessions instructing employees not to share documents with outside parties, and it required employees, including Chung, to sign confidentiality agreements. Furthermore, two of the four phased array documents were marked as proprietary. There was sufficient evidence to support the conclusion that Boeing took reasonable measures to keep all four phased array antenna documents secret.

Finally, Boeing derived some economic value from keeping the phased antenna array documents secret. The estimates of hours, tied to the list of tasks, would tip off competitors to more than just the costs associated with this specific project. A competing company, for example, might bid against Boeing for integration work when the sole-source contract ran out. Moreover, the documents would reveal to a competitor how Boeing operates in general. The documents would give a competitor the advantage of knowing how Boeing worked and would reveal Boeing's relative costs for performing each type of work.

The antenna documents contained information regarding the number of elements in the antenna. This was significant because it established that Boeing could install antenna modules on the space shuttle without a system for active cooling, and it was economically valuable because it would give competitors insight into the efficiency that Boeing had obtained and how the number of elements affected the cost of developing the antenna. Boeing thus derived economic value from keeping secret the information regarding the number of elements in its proposed antenna.

The government also had to prove that Chung acted with the intent to benefit a "foreign government, foreign instrumentality, or foreign agent." The court concluded that the government presented ample evidence that Chung intended to benefit China by providing technical information responsive to requests from Chinese officials and by delivering presentations to Chinese engineers.

The Ninth Circuit Court of Appeals remarked that given Chung's history of passing technical documents to China, a rational trier of fact could reasonably infer his intent to benefit China extended to his possession of trade secrets. There was therefore sufficient evidence to conclude, beyond a reasonable doubt, that Chung possessed the trade secret documents with the intent to benefit China.

There was the issue of the value of the documents Chung handed to the Chinese, as described by the appellate court:

> Defendant argues that there is insufficient evidence to prove that his intent to benefit China extended to the possession of trade secrets, as opposed to technical documents in general. Given Defendant's history of passing technical documents to China, however, a rational trier of fact reasonably could infer from Defendant's more recent possession of similar documents that his intent to benefit China persisted well into the limitations period and extended to his possession of the trade secrets.
>
> Moreover, given Defendant's history of delivering information to China, and the absence of any evidence (other than his own exculpatory testimony) regarding his scholarly or literary intentions, a rational fact-finder could reasonably discount Defendant's explanation that he possessed the documents because he intended to write a book. Thus, viewing the evidence in the light most favorable to the prosecution, there was sufficient evidence to conclude, beyond a reasonable doubt, that Defendant possessed the trade secret documents with the intent to benefit China. We therefore affirm Defendant's convictions for violating the EEA.

The court concluded that rational trier of fact could conclude beyond a reasonable doubt that Chung was acting at the direction or control of Chinese officials when he: (1) downloaded, input, and organized SDS specification materials, (2) traveled to China in 2003, (3) wrote a letter to Gu Weihao in 2003, (4) possessed a huge library of Boeing's and Rockwell's proprietary information, and (5) disposed of Boeing technical documents by hiding them between the pages of newspapers, which he deposited in the trash.

Chung was also convicted of acting as an unregistered foreign agent pursuant to the statute which provides criminal liability for anyone "other than a diplomatic or consular officer or attaché, who acts in the United States as an agent of a foreign government without prior notification to the Attorney General." The statute defines "agent of a foreign government" as "an individual who agrees to operate within the United States subject to the direction or control of a foreign government or official."

The appellate court therefore had no trouble affirming the conviction of Dongfan "Greg" Chung as an active Chinese spy. And it would be a long time before Chung would be making trips to the trash cans in front of his house.

OPINION EXCERPT

Graber, Circuit Judge.

In the 1990s, NASA contemplated replacing the space shuttle's dish antenna with a phased array antenna. Boeing competed with other companies to supply the antenna. But Boeing was the sole-source contractor at the time for integrating technologies, including the new antenna, into the shuttle. The proposed communications upgrade required Boeing's engineers to determine the feasibility of installing the new antenna at the existing antenna locations on the shuttle's forward fuselage by enlarging or adding an opening. Those potential structural changes required conducting the appropriate stress analyses. Additionally, engineers had to figure out how to dissipate the heat generated by the new antenna—either by reducing the number of "elements" used in the antenna or by installing an active cooling system—so that the shuttle could reenter the atmosphere safely. Ultimately, however, NASA opted not to place a phased array antenna on the shuttle.

Defendant [Dongfan "Greg" Chung] possessed four documents related to the phased array antenna project. Two documents listed the tasks and hours necessary to complete the integration project. Those documents underlie counts 2 and 4 of the indictment. The other two documents, which underlie counts 3 and 5, were slide presentations about the communications upgrade. Among the data contained in the slides was a list of the antenna's specifications, including the proposed number of elements in the antenna.

First, we look to whether the phased array antenna documents were secret and not readily ascertainable. The government points out, and Defendant does not contest, that the tasks-and-hours lists underlying counts 2 and 4 were never made public. With regard to the slide presentations underlying counts 3 and 5, Defendant correctly argues that the documents contain information similar to that presented by

Boeing engineers at a NASA-sponsored conference that was attended by Boeing's competitors. But the portions of those documents relating to the number of elements in the phased array antenna were not disclosed at the conference. Therefore, sufficient evidence supports the conclusion that all four phased array antenna documents contained secret information. Moreover, as we previously noted, Defendant does not contend that the secret information in those four documents was readily ascertainable.

Next, we consider whether Boeing took reasonable measures to maintain the four documents' secrecy. Although none of the documents was kept under lock and key, Boeing implemented general physical security measures for its entire plant. Security guards required employees to show identification before entering the building, and Boeing reserved the right to search all employees' belongings and cars. Boeing also held training sessions instructing employees not to share documents with outside parties, and it required employees, including Defendant, to sign confidentiality agreements. Further, two of the four phased array documents (underlying counts 3 and 5) were marked as proprietary. Thus, there was sufficient evidence to support the conclusion that Boeing took reasonable measures to keep all four phased array antenna documents secret.

Finally, Boeing derived some economic value from keeping the phased antenna array documents secret. The documents underlying counts 2 and 4 listed the tasks and hours necessary for the antenna's integration into the space shuttle. Boeing engineer Emad Farag testified that the estimates of hours, tied to the list of tasks, would tip off competitors to more than just the costs associated with this specific project. Although Boeing had no competitors for the integration project itself, Farag suggested that a competing company might bid against Boeing for integration work when the sole-source contract ran out. Moreover, the documents would show a competitor how Boeing operates, "not just related to the integration, but it has implication for everything else we're working on." The documents, he testified, would give a competitor who studies them the advantage of knowing how Boeing accomplishes its work, including engineering and processing, and would reveal Boeing's relative costs for performing each type of work. A reasonable inference is that the information could assist a competitor in understanding how Boeing approaches problem-solving and in figuring out how best to bid on a similar project in the future, for example, by underbidding Boeing on tasks at which Boeing appears least efficient.

The antenna documents underlying counts 3 and 5 contained information regarding the number of elements in the antenna. Farag testified that such information was significant because it established that Boeing could install antenna modules on the space shuttle without a system for active cooling. The information was economically significant, according to Farag, because it would give competitors insight into the efficiency that Boeing had obtained and because the number of elements affected the cost of developing the antenna. Importantly, Farag also testified that, unlike the integration project, the development of the antenna itself was not pursuant to a sole-source contract. That project was open to competition from other companies, and Farag specifically identified a potential competitor. Consequently, Boeing derived economic value from keeping secret the information regarding the number of elements in its proposed antenna.

Viewing the evidence in the light most favorable to the prosecution, we therefore conclude that there was sufficient evidence to support the district court's finding that the documents underlying counts 2 through 5 contained trade secrets.

Defendant also possessed two documents related to the Delta IV Rocket, a booster rocket that is designed to launch manned space vehicles. His possession of those documents underlies counts 6 and 7 of the indictment. Defendant does not contest the district court's finding that the Delta IV documents contained trade secrets.

To convict under Section 1831 of the EEA, the government must prove that Defendant acted with the intent to benefit a "foreign government, foreign instrumentality, or foreign agent." Unlike the foreign agent count, which required evidence of a foreign government's direction or control, criminal liability under the EEA may be established on the basis of Defendant's intent alone.

We hold that there was sufficient evidence to support the district court's finding that Defendant possessed the relevant trade secret documents during the limitations period with the intent to benefit China. The government presented ample evidence that, during the 1980s, Defendant intended to benefit China by providing technical information responsive to requests from Chinese officials and by delivering presentations to Chinese engineers. Defendant also delivered a presentation on the space shuttle to Chinese engineers in 2001. Five years later, federal agents discovered that Defendant possessed thousands of Boeing's technical documents, some of which he had downloaded and catalogued in 2003, and some of which contained trade secrets.

Defendant argues that there is insufficient evidence to prove that his intent to benefit China extended to the possession of trade secrets, as opposed to technical documents in general. Given Defendant's history of passing technical documents to China, however, a rational trier of fact reasonably could infer from Defendant's more recent possession of similar documents that his intent to benefit China persisted well into the limitations period and extended to his possession of the trade secrets. Moreover, given Defendant's history of delivering information to China, and the absence of any evidence (other than his own exculpatory testimony) regarding his scholarly or literary intentions, a rational fact-finder could reasonably discount Defendant's explanation that he possessed the documents because he intended to write a book. Thus, viewing the evidence in the light most favorable to the prosecution, there was sufficient evidence to conclude, beyond a reasonable doubt, that Defendant possessed the trade secret documents with the intent to benefit China. We therefore affirm Defendant's convictions for violating the EEA.

Defendant argues that there is not sufficient evidence to prove beyond a reasonable doubt that, during the limitations period, he conspired with others to violate the EEA. We disagree.

To prove a criminal conspiracy, the government must show: "(1) an agreement to engage in criminal activity, (2) one or more overt acts taken to implement the agreement, and (3) the requisite intent to commit the substantive crime."

Again, the record amply demonstrates that Defendant agreed to collect and transmit technical information to China in the 1980s. In May 1987, Gu Weihao wrote to Defendant to request assistance on technical issues concerning aircraft and the space shuttle. He suggested that Defendant pass any information through Chi Mak because that "channel was much safer than others." In 1988, Gu Weihao wrote that he hoped Defendant would "provide information on advanced technologies" and that "there was no need to limit the scope that we proposed while we were in the United States." Again, Gu Weihao suggested that Defendant should forward all information through Chi Mak because it would be "safer and faster." Thus, the record demonstrates that Defendant, Gu Weihao, and Chi Mak agreed that Defendant would pass information on advanced technologies to China. Although there is no direct evidence that Defendant specifically agreed to pass *trade secrets* to China, a rational trier of fact could reasonably infer from Gu Weihao's letters and from Defendant's possession of the trade secret documents that Defendant did not intend to accept such documents from the scope of the agreement.

The difficult issue presented by this case is whether the agreement between Defendant, Gu Weihao, and Chi Mak continued into the limitations period. Viewing the evidence in the light most favorable to the prosecution, we conclude that there is insufficient evidence to support the finding that Defendant conspired with Gu Weihao during the limitations period. The bare fact that Defendant wrote to Gu Weihao in 2003 is insufficient to prove a continuing conspiracy, given that Gu Weihao last requested information in 1988 and purportedly retired in 1992. All subsequent correspondence between Defendant and Gu Weihao that appears in the record discusses only personal issues and makes no mention of technical information.

By contrast, the record does support the district court's finding that Defendant conspired with Chi Mak to pass trade secrets to China during the limitations period. As recounted above, the record shows that Defendant agreed with Chi Mak in the 1980s to deliver information on advanced technologies to China. The government also presented evidence that Defendant downloaded shuttle design documents from a restricted Boeing database in 2002, approximately four months before the limitations period began. Chi Mak's name and telephone numbers were written in Chinese on one of those documents. During the limitations period, Defendant downloaded, indexed, and modified shuttle design specifications. Although the government does not allege that the shuttle design documents contained trade secrets, a rational trier of fact could reasonably infer from Defendant's unauthorized collection of such data that Defendant continued to work with Chi Mak to pass technological information to China. It is equally reasonable to infer that Defendant's possession of the trade secret documents was part of that same effort. Thus, viewing the evidence in the light most favorable to the prosecution, we conclude that a rational trier of fact could have found, beyond a reasonable doubt, that Defendant conspired with Chi Mak to violate the EEA after February 6, 2003.

9

MONITORING FOREIGN INTELLIGENCE

Americans first learned of their government's extensive telephone metadata program on June 5, 2013, when the British newspaper *The Guardian* published a Foreign Intelligence Surveillance Court (FISC) order leaked by a former CIA agent and government contractor named Edward Snowden, whose visage quickly flooded the public media before he managed to escape to safer ground in Russia.

Snowden had leaked to journalists highly classified information that he had stolen from the National Security Agency (NSA), and in the process, he revealed numerous global surveillance programs, many of which were run by the NSA with the cooperation of telecommunication companies and European governments.

Two weeks later, the U.S. Department of Justice filed charges against Snowden for violating the Espionage Act of 1917 and for the theft of government property, and the Department of State revoked his passport. Several days later, Snowden landed in Moscow, where Soviet authorities noted that his passport had been cancelled. He was confined to the airport terminal for over a month, but Russia eventually gave him a visa for a year. Repeated extensions have allowed him to stay there.

The FISC order that Snowden revealed to the public directed Verizon Communications to produce to the National Security Agency (NSA) "on an ongoing daily basis" all call detail records created by Verizon for communications within the United States and between the United States and abroad. The order thus required Verizon to produce the call detail records of all telephone calls where one or both ends of the call were located in the United States. The NSA would then aggregate this metadata into a repository that could later be examined for evidence related to terrorist activities.

As a result of this revelation, the American Civil Liberties Union (ACLU) filed suit against the government, challenging the telephone metadata program on statutory and constitutional grounds. The complaint asked the court to strike down the program as exceeding its statutory authority, as well as violating the First and Fourth Amendments to the U.S. Constitution. The district court granted the government's motion to dismiss the ACLU's petition, remarking:

> There is no evidence that the Government used any of the bulk telephony metadata it collected for any purpose other than investigation and disrupting terrorist attacks. While there have been unintentional violations of guidelines, those appear to stem from human error and the incredibly complex computer programs that support this vital tool. And once detected, those violations were self-reported and stopped. The bulk telephony metadata collection program is subject to executive and congressional oversight, as well as continual monitoring by a dedicated group of judges who serve on the Foreign Intelligence Surveillance Court.
>
> No doubt, the bulk telephone metadata collection program vacuums up information about virtually every telephone call to, from, or within the United States. That is by design, as it allows the NSA to detect relationships so attenuated and ephemeral they would otherwise escape notice. As the September 11 attacks demonstrate, the cost of missing such a threat can be horrific. Technology allowed al-Qaeda to operate decentralized and plot international terrorist attacks remotely. The bulk telephony metadata collection programs represents the Government's counter-punch: connecting fragmented and fleeting communications to re-construct and eliminate al-Qaeda's terror network.

On appeal, the Second Circuit Court of Appeals held that the telephone metadata program *exceeded* the scope of what Congress had authorized, and therefore the court found it unnecessary to decide the constitutional arguments propounded by the ACLU.

The appellate court acknowledged that the nation faces serious threats to national security, including the threat of foreign-generated acts of terrorism, and that Congress has the difficult responsibility of balancing the safety of our nation with the privacy interests of its citizens in a world where surveillance capabilities are vast and it is difficult to avoid exposing personal information. As a result of the terrorist attacks of September 11, 2001, Congress amended the Foreign Intelligence Survey Act (FISA) in what is known as the Patriot Act.

The court described the challenge it faced in this way:

We must confront the question whether a surveillance program that the government has put in place to protect national security is lawful. That program involves the bulk collection by the government of telephone metadata created by telephone companies in the normal course of their business but now explicitly required by the government to be turned over in bulk on an ongoing basis. As in the 1970s, the revelation of this program has generated considerable public attention and concern about the intrusion of government into private matters. As in that era, as well, the nation faces serious threats to national security, including the threat of foreign-generated acts of terrorism against the United States. Now, as then, Congress is tasked in the first instance with achieving the right balance between these often-competing concerns. To do so, Congress has amended FISA, most significantly, after the terrorist attacks of September 11, 2001, in the PATRIOT Act.

In the present case, the government argued that Section 215 of the Act authorized the telephone metadata program, which included the collection of information about Verizon telephone calls, such as the phone number called, the phone number from which the call was made, and the length of the call. The metadata could also reveal the user or device making or receiving a call through unique "identity numbers" associated with the equipment, and thus it could provide information about the routing of a call through the telephone network. This information could sometimes convey information about a caller's general location.

The government acknowledged that the FISC order was part of a broader program of bulk collection of telephone metadata from other telecommunications providers carried out pursuant to Section 215. It was revealed that the government had been collecting such telephone metadata information since at least May 2006, when the FISC first authorized it to collect "all call-detail records or telephony metadata, including comprehensive communications routing information, including but not limited to session identifying information (e.g., originating and terminating telephone numbers, communications device identifiers, etc.), trunk identifier, and time and duration of call."

The FISC order specified (1) that the items were to be produced to the NSA; (2) that there were reasonable grounds to believe the tangible things sought were relevant to authorized investigations to protect against international terrorism; and (3) that the items sought could be obtained with a subpoena *duces tecum* issued by a court of the United States in aid of a grand jury investigation or with any other order issued by a court of the United States directing the production of records or tangible things.

The order required the recipient (in this case, Verizon), after receiving the appropriate secondary order, to continue production on an ongoing daily basis for the duration of the order, and contemplated the creation of a data archive that would only be accessed when the NSA identified a known telephone number for which there were facts giving rise to a reasonable, articulable suspicion that the telephone number was associated with what was presumably terrorist activity or a specific terrorist organization. The order also stated that the NSA would "exclusively operate" the network on which the metadata were stored and processed.

At trial, the government disclosed additional FISC orders reauthorizing the program. It was revealed that FISC orders had to be renewed every 90 days; and at that point the program had been renewed 41 times since May 2006. The government disputed the plaintiff's characterization of the program as one requiring the collection of "virtually all telephony metadata" associated with calls made or received in the United States, but the government declined to elaborate on the scope of the program or specify how the program fell short of such a description.

The court remarked that "on its face" the Verizon order required the production of "all call detail records or 'telephony metadata'" relating to Verizon communications within the United States or between the United States and abroad. The government did not assert that Verizon was the *only* telephone service provider subject to such an order, and it did not seriously dispute the plaintiffs' contention that *all* significant service providers in the United States were subject to similar orders.

The government explained that it used the bulk metadata collected to make "queries" using metadata "identifiers," or particular phone numbers that it believed, based upon "reasonable articulable suspicion," to be associated with a foreign terrorist organization. The identifier was used as a "seed" to search across the government's database. The search yielded phone numbers (and the metadata associated with them) that had been in contact with the seed. That step was referred to as the "first hop."

Then the NSA could also search for the numbers (and associated metadata) that have been in contact with the numbers resulting from the first search, which was referred to as the "second hop." The program also allowed for another iteration of the process, such that a "third hop" could then be conducted, pulling in results that included, essentially, the metadata of the contacts of the contacts of the contacts of the original "seed." The government, however, strongly contended that it did not conduct any "general browsing" of the data it collected.

In challenging the government's practices, the ACLU claimed that even though telephone metadata did not directly reveal the content of telephone calls, it did raise privacy concerns: pointing to the startling amount of detailed information uncovered—information it claimed could traditionally only be obtained by examining the contents of communications and was therefore "often a proxy for content." According to the ACLU, such metadata could possibly reveal sensitive civil, political, or religious affiliations, among other personal information.

The Court of Appeals agreed, explaining:

> That telephone metadata do not directly reveal the content of telephone calls, however, does not vitiate the privacy concerns arising out of the government's bulk collection of such data. Appellants [the ACLU] and *amici* take pains to emphasize the startling amount of detailed information metadata can reveal— "information that could traditionally only be obtained by examining the contents of communications" and that is therefore "often a proxy for content." For example, a call to a single-purpose telephone number such as a "hotline" might reveal that an individual is: a victim of domestic violence or rape; a veteran; suffering from an addiction of one type or another; contemplating suicide; or reporting a crime. Metadata can reveal civil, political, or religious affiliations; they can also reveal an individual's social status, or whether and when he or she is involved in intimate relationships.

The court explained that the original version of Section 215, which predated the Patriot Act, allowed the Director of the FBI or his designee to obtain orders from the FISC authorizing common carriers to provide to the government certain business records for the purpose of foreign intelligence and international terrorism investigations where there existed "specific and articulable facts giving reason to believe that the person to whom the records pertain was a foreign power or an agent of a foreign power." The Patriot Act substantially revised Section 215 to provide for the production not only of "business records," but also of "any tangible things," and to *eliminate* the restrictions on the types of businesses such orders could reach.

As amended by successor bills to the Patriot Act, the current version of Section 215 allows the Director of the FBI or his designee to make an application for an order requiring the production of any tangible things (including books, records, papers, documents, and other items) for an investigation to obtain foreign intelligence information not concerning a United States person or to protect against international terrorism or clandestine intelligence activities.

In its current form, the law requires such an application to include a statement of facts showing that there are reasonable grounds to believe that the tangible things sought are relevant to an authorized investigation (other than a threat assessment) conducted to obtain foreign intelligence information not concerning a United States person or to protect against international terrorism or clandestine intelligence activities. Such an order "may only require the production of a tangible thing if such thing can be obtained with a subpoena duces tecum issued by a court of the United States in aid of a grand jury investigation or with any other order issued by a court of the United States directing the production of records or tangible things."

Finally, the statute requires the Attorney General to "adopt specific minimization procedures governing the retention and dissemination by the FBI of any tangible things, or information therein, received by the FBI in response to an order under this subchapter."

The order in the present case specified that the items were to be produced to the NSA and that there were reasonable grounds to believe the tangible things sought were relevant to authorized investigations to protect against international terrorism. The order required Verizon to continue production on an ongoing daily basis for the duration of the order, and it contemplated creation of a data archive that would only be accessed when NSA had identified a known telephone number for which there were facts giving rise to a reasonable, articulable suspicion that the telephone number was associated with terrorist activity or a specific terrorist organization. The order also stated that only the NSA would operate the network on which the metadata was stored and processed.

Section 215 requires the Attorney General to adopt specific minimization procedures governing the retention and dissemination by the government of information received. The procedures include (1) the requirement that the NSA store the metadata within secure networks, (2) that the metadata not be accessed for any purpose other than what is allowed under the FISC order, (3) that the results of queries not be disseminated outside the NSA except in accordance with the minimization and dissemination requirements of NSA procedures, and (4) that the relevant personnel receive comprehensive training on the minimization procedures and technical controls. And—as the government pointed out—the program is subject to oversight by the Department of Justice, the FISC, and Congress.

The ACLU contended that the program was *not* authorized by the legislation on which the government relied for the issuance of FISC orders to telephone service providers to collect and turn over the metadata like that at issue.

In its analysis of the case, the appellate court remarked that it was clear that Section 215 is broad enough to provide the government with essential tools to investigate and forestall acts of terrorism. The government may apply for an order requiring the "production of any tangible things for an investigation to protect against international terrorism or clandestine intelligence activities." A Section 215 order may require the production of anything that "can be obtained with a subpoena duces tecum issued by a court of the United States in aid of a grand jury investigation" or any other court order.

While the types of "tangible things" subject to such an order would appear to be virtually unlimited, such "things" may only be produced upon a specified factual showing by the government. To obtain a Section 215 order, the government must provide the FISC with "a statement of facts showing that there are reasonable grounds to believe that the tangible things sought are relevant to an authorized investigation (other than a threat assessment) conducted under guidelines approved by the Attorney General." The basic requirements for metadata collection under Section 215, then, are simply that the records be relevant to an authorized investigation (other than a threat assessment).

In spite of the complexity of the statutory framework, the parties' positions were relatively straightforward. The government emphasized that "relevance" is an extremely broad standard, particularly in the context of the grand jury investigations to which the statute analogizes orders under Section 215.

The ACLU, on the other hand, contended that relevance is *not* an unlimited concept, and that the government's own use (or non-use) of the records obtained demonstrated that most of the records sought were *not* relevant to any particular investigation. According to the ACLU, the government did not seek the records—as was usual in a grand jury investigation—in order to review them in search of evidence bearing on a particular subject. In this case the government sought the records to create a vast data bank to be kept in reserve, and the government then determined if and when some particular set of records might be relevant to a particular investigation.

The government responded that in the case of grand jury subpoenas, courts have authorized discovery of large volumes of information where the requester sought to identify within that volume smaller amounts of information that could directly bear on the matter. The ACLU, however, disputed that metadata from every phone call with a party in the United States, over a period of many years, could be considered "relevant" to an authorized investigation, regardless of the definition of that term.

The parties did not discuss whether the records required by the orders in question were relevant to any particular inquiry. The records sought by the government were all-inclusive, and the government did not suggest that all of the records sought—or indeed any of them—were relevant to any specific defined inquiry. Rather, the parties asked the court to decide whether Section 215 au-

thorized the creation of a historical repository of information that bulk aggrega-
tion of the metadata allows, because bulk collection to create such a repository
is necessary to the application of certain analytic techniques.

The government took the position that the metadata collected was relevant
because it might allow the NSA, at some unknown time in the future, to utilize
its ability to sift through the trove of data it had collected in order to identify
information that is relevant.

In the end, the court agreed with the ACLU that such an expansive concept
of "relevance" was unprecedented and unwarranted. The court remarked:

> We should be cautious in inferring legislative action from legislative inaction, or
> inferring a Congressional command from Congressional silence. At most, the
> evidence cited by the government suggests that Congress assumed, in light of the
> expectation of secrecy, that persons whose information was targeted by a § 215
> order would rarely even know of such orders, and therefore that judicial review
> at the behest of such persons was a non-issue. But such an assumption is a far cry
> from an unexpressed intention to withdraw rights granted in a generally appli-
> cable, explicit statute such as the APA [Administrative Procedures Act].

The litigation at hand, the court said, suggested that the matter was not as
routine as the government suggested. Normally, the question of whether records
demanded by a subpoena or other court order are "relevant" to a proceeding is
raised in the context of a motion to quash a subpoena. The grand jury undertakes
to investigate a particular subject matter to determine whether there is probable
cause to believe crimes have been committed, and seeks by subpoena records
that might contain evidence that will help in making that determination. Given
the wide investigative scope of a grand jury, the standard is easy to meet, but
the determination of relevance is constrained by the subject of the investigation.

The government argued that the metadata collected— a vast amount of
which did not contain directly "relevant" information, as the government conceded—was relevant because it may allow the NSA, at some unknown time in
the future, utilizing its ability to sift through the trove of irrelevant data it has
collected up to that point, to identify information that is relevant.

The court agreed with the plaintiffs that such an expansive concept of "relevance" was unprecedented and unwarranted, and that the statutes to which
the government referred had never been interpreted to authorize anything approaching the breadth of the sweeping surveillance at issue here. In the court's
view, by limiting the use of Section 215 to "investigations" rather than "threat
assessments," Congress clearly meant to prevent Section 215 orders from being
issued where the FBI—without any particular, defined information that would

permit the initiation of even a preliminary investigation— sought to conduct an inquiry in order to identify a potential threat in advance.

The telephone metadata program and the orders that the government sought, the court said, were even more remote from a concrete investigation than the threat assessments that Congress found not to warrant the use of Section 215 orders. When conducting a threat assessment, FBI agents must have both a reason to conduct the inquiry and an articulable connection between the particular inquiry being made and the information being sought. The telephone metadata program, by contrast, sought to compile data in advance of the need to conduct any inquiry and was based on no evidence of any current connection between the data being sought and any existing inquiry.

The court concluded that the government's rationale for the relevance of the bulk collection of telephone metadata undermined the prohibition on using Section 215 orders for threat assessments, reasoning that the interpretation urged by the government would require a drastic expansion of the term "relevance," not only with respect to Section 215, but a number of national security-related statutes, and extend further than those statutes were ever intended.

The court reasoned that to allow the government to collect phone records only because they may become relevant to a possible authorized investigation in the future failed even the permissive "relevance" test. The text of Section 215, the court pointed out, could not bear the weight the government requested, and therefore does not authorize the telephone metadata program.

The court also explained:

> The government has pointed to no affirmative evidence, whether "clear and convincing" or "fairly discernible," that suggests that Congress intended to preclude judicial review. Indeed, the government's argument from secrecy suggests that Congress did not contemplate a situation in which targets of Section 215 orders would become aware of those orders on anything resembling the scale that they now have. That revelation, of course, came to pass only because of an unprecedented leak of classified information. That Congress may not have anticipated that individuals like appellants, whose communications were targeted by Section 215 orders, would become aware of the orders, and thus be in a position to seek judicial review, is not evidence that Congress affirmatively decided to revoke the right to judicial review otherwise provided by the APA in the event the orders were publicly revealed.

If Congress chooses to authorize a far-reaching program such as the government advocated, the court said, it is certainly capable of doing so. But until then, the court refused to deviate from well-established legal standards.

OPINION EXCERPT

Gerard E. Lynch, Circuit Judge.

This appeal concerns the legality of the bulk telephone metadata collection program (the "telephone metadata program"), under which the National Security Agency ("NSA") collects in bulk "on an ongoing daily basis" the metadata associated with telephone calls made by and to Americans, and aggregates those metadata into a repository or data bank that can later be queried. Appellants [the ACLU] challenge the program on statutory and constitutional grounds. Because we find that the program exceeds the scope of what Congress has authorized, we vacate the decision below dismissing the complaint without reaching appellants' constitutional arguments. We affirm the district court's denial of appellants' request for a preliminary injunction.

In the early 1970s, in a climate not altogether unlike today's, the intelligence-gathering and surveillance activities of the NSA, the FBI, and the CIA came under public scrutiny. The Supreme Court struck down certain warrantless surveillance procedures that the government had argued were lawful as an exercise of the President's power to protect national security, remarking on "the inherent vagueness of the domestic security concept [and] the necessarily broad and continuing nature of intelligence gathering." In response to that decision and to allegations that those agencies were abusing their power in order to spy on Americans, the Senate established the Select Committee to Study Governmental Operations with Respect to Intelligence Activities (the "Church Committee") to investigate whether the intelligence agencies had engaged in unlawful behavior and whether legislation was necessary to govern their activities. The Church Committee expressed concerns that the privacy rights of U.S. citizens had been violated by activities that had been conducted under the rubric of foreign intelligence collection.

The findings of the Church Committee, along with the Supreme Court's decision in *Keith* and the allegations of abuse by the intelligence agencies, prompted Congress in 1978 to enact comprehensive legislation aimed at curtailing abuses and delineating the procedures to be employed in conducting surveillance in foreign intelligence investigations. That legislation, the Foreign Intelligence Surveillance Act of 1978 ("FISA"), established a special court, the Foreign Intelligence Surveillance Court ("FISC"), to review the government's applications for orders permitting electronic surveillance. Unlike ordinary Article III courts, the FISC conducts its usually ex parte proceedings in secret; its decisions are not, in the ordinary course, disseminated publicly.

We are faced today with a controversy similar to that which led to the *Keith* decision and the enactment of FISA. We must confront the question whether a surveillance program that the government has put in place to protect national security is lawful. That program involves the bulk collection by the government of telephone metadata created by telephone companies in the normal course of their business but now explicitly required by the government to be turned over in bulk on an ongoing basis. As in the 1970s, the revelation of this program has generated considerable public attention and concern about the intrusion of government into private matters. As in that era, as well, the nation faces serious threats to national security, including the threat of foreign-generated acts of terrorism against the United States. Now, as then, Congress is tasked in the first instance with achieving the right balance between these often-competing concerns. To do so, Congress has amended FISA, most significantly, after the terrorist attacks of September 11, 2001, in the Patriot Act. The government argues that Section 215 of that Act authorizes the telephone metadata program.

Before proceeding to explore the details of Section 215 of the PATRIOT Act, we pause to define "telephone metadata," in order to clarify the type of information that the government argues Section 215 authorizes it to collect in bulk. Unlike what is gleaned from the more traditional investigative practice of wiretapping, telephone metadata do not include the voice content of telephone conversations. Rather, they include details about telephone calls, including, for example, the length of a call, the phone number from which the call was made, and the phone number called. Metadata can also reveal the user or device making or receiving a call through unique "identity numbers" associated with the equipment (although the government maintains that the information collected does not include information about the identities or names of individuals), and provide information about the routing of a call through the telephone network, which can sometimes (although not always) convey information about a caller's general location. According to the government, the metadata it collects do not include cell site locational information, which provides a more precise indication of a caller's location than call-routing information does.

That telephone metadata do not directly reveal the content of telephone calls, however, does not vitiate the privacy concerns arising out of the government's bulk collection of such data. Appellants and amici take pains to emphasize the startling amount of detailed information metadata can reveal—"information that could traditionally only be obtained by examining the contents of communications" and that is therefore "often a proxy for content." For example, a call to a single-purpose telephone number such as a "hotline" might reveal that an individual is: a victim of domestic violence or rape; a veteran; suffering from an addiction of one type or another; contemplating suicide; or reporting a crime. Metadata can reveal civil, political, or religious affiliations; they can also reveal an individual's social status, or whether and when he or she is involved in intimate relationships.

We recognize that metadata exist in more traditional formats, too, and that law enforcement and others have always been able to utilize metadata for investigative purposes. For example, just as telephone metadata may reveal the charitable organizations that an individual supports, observation of the outside of an envelope sent at the end of the year through the United States Postal Service to such an organization might well permit similar inferences, without requiring an examination of the envelope's contents. But the structured format of telephone and other technology-related metadata, and the vast new technological capacity for large-scale and automated review and analysis, distinguish the type of metadata at issue here from more traditional forms. The more metadata the government collects and analyzes, furthermore, the greater the capacity for such metadata to reveal ever more private and previously unascertainable information about individuals. Finally, as appellants and amici point out, in today's technologically based world, it is virtually impossible for an ordinary citizen to avoid creating metadata about himself on a regular basis simply by conducting his ordinary affairs.

The original version of Section 215, which pre-dated the PATRIOT Act, allowed the Director of the FBI or his designee to obtain orders from the FISC authorizing common carriers, among others, to provide to the government certain business records for the purpose of foreign intelligence and international terrorism investigations where there existed "specific and articulable facts giving reason to believe that the person to whom the records pertain was a foreign power or an agent of a foreign power." That provision was enacted in 1998 as an amendment to FISA. The PATRIOT Act substantially revised Section 215 to provide for the production not only of "business records" but also of "any tangible things," and to eliminate the restrictions on the types of businesses such orders can reach. As subsequently amended by successor bills to the PATRIOT Act, the current version of Section 215 allows the Director of the FBI or his designee to "make an application for an order requiring the production of any tangible things (including books, records, papers, documents, and other items) for an investigation to obtain foreign intelligence information not concerning a United States person or to protect against international terrorism or clandestine intelligence activities."

In its current form, the provision requires such an application to include "a statement of facts showing that there are reasonable grounds to believe that the tangible things sought are relevant to an authorized investigation (other than a threat assessment) conducted in accordance with subsection (a)(2) of this section to obtain foreign intelligence information not concerning a United States person or to protect against international terrorism or clandestine intelligence activities."

Such an order "may only require the production of a tangible thing if such thing can be obtained with a subpoena duces tecum issued by a court of the United States in aid of a grand jury investigation or with any other order issued by a court of the United States directing the production of records or tangible things." Finally, the statute requires the Attorney General to "adopt specific minimization procedures governing the retention and dissemination by the FBI of any tangible things, or information therein, received by the FBI in response to an order under this subchapter." Because Section 215 contained a "sunset" provision from its inception, originally terminating its authority on December 31, 2005, it has required subsequent renewal. Congress has renewed Section 215 seven times, most recently in 2011, at which time it was amended to expire on June 1, 2015.

II

THE BUSINESS OF ESPIONAGE

10

STRICTLY SURREPTITIOUS

Small, inconspicuous—and often highly sophisticated—bugging and wiretapping devices, such as hidden microphones and mini-cameras, have long been used by government agencies (and sometimes laymen) to listen in on others' conversations and monitor their movements without their knowledge.

The sales of certain of these electronic surreptitious surveillance devices—better known in the trade as "ESIDs"—are specifically banned by federal law unless sold to a law enforcement agency or destined for export. Three types of electronic surveillance are prevalent: wiretapping (intercepting telephone calls by physically penetrating the wire circuitry), bugging (placing a small microphone in one location to transmit conversations to a nearby receiver), and video surveillance (hidden cameras that transmit and record visual images).

Law enforcement agencies point out that these surveillance devices are often used to foster criminal activity. In Miami, for example, customs agents intercepted 500 kilograms of cocaine packaged to look like candy. When they inspected the cargo container and discovered its illicit contents, they also found two battery-operated, long-range transmitters the size of cigarette packs. Alerted to the fact that customs inspectors had discovered their cocaine shipment, the drug smugglers never claimed the package. These devices have also been used to carry out kidnaping and extortion plots by employing small transmitters in separate locations to coordinate their activities.

In an interesting piece of well-publicized litigation, four defendants—John Demeter, Eliezer Arce, Steve Alon, and John Biro—were convicted of a conspiracy to smuggle ESIDs into the United States for the purpose of selling them to the general public.

In late 1993, the U.S. Customs agency initiated an extensive investigation after receiving a tip that massive numbers of ESIDs were being imported into the states from Japan. The investigation focused on Spy Shops International, a business owned and operated by an individual named John Demeter, who the *Chicago Tribune* described as a "Bible-toting-quoting Yugoslavia-born Hungarian." Demeter proudly referred to his chain of stores as "the McDonald's of the electronics industry."

Spy Shops specialized in the sale of security equipment and electronic devices, and it operated three retail stores in south Florida. Many of these ESIDs were disguised as ordinary consumer goods such as three-prong plugs, pens, and pocket calculators, and Demeter derisively described the customers for these products as people who "have seen too many *Mission Impossible* movies." Besides wireless microphones and tape recorder detectors, the store sold telephone privacy scramblers, a phone that tells you if the conversation is tapped, and a lipstick-sized cylinder filled with a non-lethal biological spray that claimed to be instantly effective in subduing one's target.

The general manager of Spy Shops was Eliezer Arce, and his job was overseeing the stores. Along with Demeter, Arce was responsible for acquiring inventory to stock the stores. Sales personnel reported to Demeter and Arce, whose prior approval was required for the sale of all ESIDs. Demeter and Arce instructed the staff to vaguely describe sales of ESIDs as "security equipment" on receipts. Many of these devices were initially procured from a company called G.E.D. Electronics, which was owned by a businessman named Steve Alon.

While investigating Spy Shops and G.E.D. Electronics, U.S. Customs agents received word that Ken Taguchi, a sales representative for the Japanese company Micro Electronics, was arrested for smuggling illegal bugging and wiretapping devices. Pursuant to a plea agreement, Taguchi agreed to cooperate with the government in its investigation of Spy Shops and G.E.D. Taguchi had begun shipping ESIDs to Demeter from Japan for seven or eight years, and he provided customs agents with all of Micro's business correspondence with Demeter. Initially, the packages identified Micro as the shipper and Spy Shops as the addressee. Later, Demeter asked Taguchi to ship the ESIDs to another company he owned, and to use the name "Seibu," a Tokyo department store, as the shipper. Demeter requested that the products not be packaged in display boxes.

Taguchi also provided customs agents with Micro's correspondence concerning its business transactions with G.E.D. Electronics. These records reflected that Alon purchased approximately a hundred ESIDs disguised as pens. In April 1995, customs inspectors at Los Angeles International Airport discovered that two packages shipped by Micro to G.E.D., and pursuant to a search warrant, they seized the items. The customs officers also found invoices reflecting sales to Spy Shops. The agents did not find any purchase orders from law enforcement agencies or any documents authorizing G.E.D. to export ES-IDs to other countries.

To demonstrate that Spy Shops was selling ESIDs to the public, at trial the government presented the testimony of two customs agents who made undercover purchases. Customs agent Gary Lang went to the Fort Lauderdale store, and he falsely identified himself to manager John Biro as "Garrison Luhr," a businessman who wanted an ESID to eavesdrop on the conversations of a competitor. Biro showed agent Lang several ESIDs, which were retrieved from a back room. Biro told Lang that he had to sign a waiver stating that the devices were being bought for export and would not be used in the country.

Soon after, when Lang inquired about the range of the ESID disguised as a three-prong wall plug, Biro asked Lang for a business card and identification. Biro compared the two to make sure they matched. Biro then took Lang into an adjoining room and closed the door. Biro handled the ESIDs with a piece of paper, rather than use his bare hands.

Agent Lang purchased a scrambler designed to alter telephone conversations and an ESID disguised as a three-prong wall plug. Because Biro did not have the wall plug in stock, he asked Lang to return the following day. Lang paid a deposit for the purchase, but Biro refused to provide him with a receipt. Lang returned the following day and gave Biro the balance owed. Lang signed the waiver, and then confessed that he wasn't really planning to export the devices. Biro responded, "Right, don't worry about it," and completed the sale. When Lang mentioned needing another ESID for a friend, Biro told him not to call, but instead to come see him.

Customs agent Arkadis Karb went to the Spy Shops store in Miami. He posed as a European with a Russian accent. Karb explained to a salesperson that he wanted to purchase a device to record conversations surreptitiously. None of the ESIDs were on public display, but the salesperson produced from behind the counter two metal attaché cases which contained ESIDs disguised as pens and calculators. Karb returned the following day and told the salesperson he wanted to purchase an ESID. Karb inquired whether the devices would record conversations transmitted on telephones, and he was assured that they would. The salesperson informed Karb that the sale of ESIDs in the United States was illegal, but never asked Karb how he intended to use them.

Customs agents then searched the offices of both Spy Shops and G.E.D. pursuant to a search warrant. None of the defendants claimed that they were authorized to sell ESIDs because they had a contract with a governmental agency, or that they had been granted an export license by the Department of Commerce.

The defendants made two arguments in their defense. First, they contended that the statute prohibiting ESIDs was unconstitutionally vague; and second, Demeter contended that the district court lacked the jurisdiction to order his deportation.

The defendants contended that the applicable statute was unconstitutionally vague. They argued that the words "knowing, or having reason to know that the design of any electronic, mechanical, or other device renders it primarily useful for the purpose of the surreptitious interception of wire, oral, or electronic communications" failed to give adequate notice to the public of the prohibited conduct and did not contain sufficient guidelines to prevent arbitrary and discriminatory law enforcement.

The defendants also contended that the statute did not provide clear standards regarding the conduct Congress intended to prohibit. They argued that the failure of the statute to include examples of the specific types of prohibited devices violated the requirement that criminal statutes provide *notice* of what is forbidden.

The court remarked that it had previously upheld the constitutionality of similar ordinances, even though the challenged language did not clearly describe the nature or properties of the prohibited items. In this case, the court pointed out, the statutory language did expressly describe the nature of the prohibited items: those devices "primarily designed to function as surreptitious transmitters of communications." Therefore, the objective characteristics of the pens, wall plugs, and calculators containing concealed transmitters clearly came within the statutory prohibition.

The district court noted that the key word in the statute that clearly conveyed the intent of Congress to proscribe the sale of communication interception devices was *surreptitious*. In discussing the question of whether a device that deciphered scrambled satellite television signals fell within the plain meaning of the statute, the court in *United States v. Herring* had expounded:

Although the term "surreptitious" is not defined in the statute itself, its dictionary definition is well established: secret and unauthorized; clandestine; action by stealth or secretly. It is clear that this device operates surreptitiously, that is, without authority, secretly, and clandestinely. It is clear that the device was designed to intercept satellite television signals without detection by the programmers of pay-television.

The evidence introduced at trial demonstrated beyond a reasonable doubt that the pens, calculators, wall plugs, and other devices sold by the defendants were designed to conceal transmitters for the purpose of secretly intercepting oral communications. Moreover, the evidence and the defendants' theory of defense demonstrated that the statute provided clear and adequate notice regarding which devices were prohibited by the statute.

The defendants next contended that they believed they could legally possess and sell ESIDs to law enforcement officers or for export, and that the Spy Shops' policy of checking identification and obtaining written disclaimers was sufficient to comply with the law. This theory, and the evidence in support of it, were, the court pointed out, "patently inconsistent" with the defendants' assertion that the statute failed to give them notice as to what constituted a prohibited device.

As a result, the evidence was sufficient to show that each defendant had notice that the sale of ESIDs violated federal law. Demeter was responsible for purchasing the inventory, and he instructed Taguchi to ship the ESIDs to another company that he owned and to use the name "Seibu" in order to conceal the true identity of the buyer and seller. Demeter also requested that the ESIDs not be packaged in display boxes and that the value of the packages be misrepresented. Moreover, Demeter established the company's policy that he and Arce had to approve all sales of ESIDs.

Arce was also responsible for purchasing inventory. Sales personnel were required to obtain his approval before selling an ESID. Arce did not deny that Spy Shops sold ESIDs or that the sales were intentional. Rather, he argued that he thought the sales were perfectly legal because they were for export and to law enforcement agencies.

Biro claimed that he was merely a salesman selling a variety of security equipment that happened to include ESIDs. But the evidence clearly demonstrated to the contrary—Biro was well aware that the device he sold to agent Lang was prohibited by the statute.

No reasonable person, the court gently suggested, would pay over seven hundred dollars for a wall plug.

OPINION EXCERPT

Alarcon, Senior Circuit Judge.

[The defendant] Demeter focuses his vagueness challenge on the discriminatory law enforcement prong of the two-part vagueness test. First, Demeter argues that the vagueness of the statute is demonstrated by the fact that the officers "had to be tutored in what to look for in making undercover buys." We believe that the necessity to brief the officers regarding the deceptive appearance of the ESIDs is persuasive evidence that the ashtrays, light bulbs, phone jacks, beepers, calculators, pens, and wall plugs containing hidden transmitters were designed primarily for use in the surreptitious interception of oral communications.

Demeter also maintains that the statute is so vague that it results in discriminatory law enforcement. Demeter points to the fact that Radio Shack has not been prosecuted for selling a transmitter it advertises as being so tiny that "[i]f you could hollow out a sugar cube, this little baby would fit with room to spare." At trial, Biro offered evidence that his trial attorney went into a Radio Shack store and requested a transmitter that he could use to listen to a business competitor's conversations. The clerk sold him a wireless transmitter for $19.99.

The vagueness doctrine requires that legislation contain minimal guidelines to govern law enforcement in order to prevent arbitrary and discriminatory law enforcement. There is no requirement, however, that statutes define every factual situation that may arise. "That there may be marginal cases in which it is difficult to determine the side of the line on which a particular fact situation falls is no sufficient reason to hold the language too ambiguous to define a criminal offense."

We need not decide whether the Radio Shack device is an ESID in order to determine that Section 2512 provides minimal guidelines for law enforcement. The evidence demonstrates that there were significant differences between the devices sold by Demeter, Arce, Biro, and Alon and the transmitter sold by Radio Shack. While the sale of the Radio Shack transmitter may constitute a "marginal case" under Section 2512, requiring expert evidence, it is obvious from their structural characteristics that the devices sold by Spy Shops were designed to conceal a transmitter for the purpose of surreptitiously intercepting communications. No reasonable person would pay $720 for a wall plug that has the sole function of conducting electricity to a floor lamp. Radio Shack sold a small device that can transmit oral communications. Appellants failed to present any evidence establishing that it was the intent of the designer of the Radio Shack transmitter that it be used primarily for the surreptitious interception of oral communications. Tiny transmitters worn on lapels or clipped to clothing are used to amplify the voices of news readers, talk show guests, actors, and singers. The distinction between the tiny Radio Shack transmitter and the devices sold by Appellants is that their hidden transmitters were disguised as everyday objects that do not transmit oral communications.

Moreover, there are legitimate reasons why law enforcement might target certain vendors of ESIDs over others. The district court in *United States v. Spy Factory, Inc.*, an analogous case in which Section 2512 was challenged as unconstitutionally vague, stated as follows:

There is a perfectly understandable reason why officers and prosecutors seek convictions of defendants like the Spy Factory and not institutions like Radio Shack and Hammacher Schlemmer: because the Spy Factory, by its very name, and in countless other ways evidenced in the Government's papers, sets itself out as a place where one might be more likely to locate devices that can be used for illegal, rather than legal purposes. Therefore, even though Section 2512 might permit the prosecution of Radio Shack and Hammacher Schlemmer and other institutions selling similar devices, it is perfectly rational, and perhaps even prudent, for law enforcement officials to concentrate their efforts on the defendants who are not only most likely to be convicted, but also are most likely to serve a clientele bent on illegal practices.

The district court's rationale in *Spy Factory* is sound. The fact that law enforcement chose to target its efforts during its sting operation on the Spy Shops, and not Radio Shack, does not demonstrate that Section 2512 encourages arbitrary and discriminatory law enforcement. The district court did not err in rejecting each of Appellant's constitutional challenges.

11

THE "PUBLIC" SPY

In the espionage realm of the 1950s, a much-publicized lawsuit for libel involved an individual named Ilya Wolston, who sued the author and publisher of a book which flatly stated, without any reservation whatsoever, that Wolston was a Soviet spy.

It should be noted at the outset that libel cases are notoriously difficult to pursue. The plaintiff must prove that he is *not* a public figure (statements about whom the law gives considerably greater leeway for derogatory statements in order to encourage public debate), that the defamatory statement was made by the defendant with *malice*, and that the published untruth will do harm to the plaintiff's reputation by bringing ridicule, hatred, scorn, or contempt of others.

Wolston apparently did not take kindly to the unmitigated allegation that he was a Soviet spy. The pressing legal question before the court was whether this statement was true (the truth, after all, is a defense to a libel action) and whether Wolston was a public figure. The author and publisher were in the unenviable position of having to prove either that Wolston was a Soviet spy (to prove the truth of the statement that they had uttered) or that he was a public figure (about which they could say just about anything short of malicious).

There was certainly considerable circumstantial evidence that Wolston was a spy. He was the nephew of Jack and Myra Soble, who in April 1957 pled guilty to espionage in a well-publicized federal district court case and who six months later were sentenced to the penitentiary. Jack received a sentence of seven years, and Myra, four years. In this regard, Wolston himself was subpoenaed to testify before the grand jury in New York on several occasions concerning Russian espionage in the United States, and on July 1, 1958, Wolston failed to appear, leading some observers to come to the logical conclusion that Wolston did not want to testify because he too was a Soviet spy. As a result of his failure to appear before the grand jury, Wolston was charged with criminal contempt. After a plea of guilty, he was placed on probation for three years. The contempt proceeding generated a number of newspaper accounts in New York and in the District of Columbia, where Wolston lived.

The next year, Wolston's name appeared in a book entitled *My Ten Years as a Counterspy*, written by Boris Morros, a former colleague of the convicted spy Jack Soble, who later became a double agent for the FBI. (In 1960 the film *Man on a String* was released, loosely based as it was on Morros's account. Ernest Borgnine played the role of Morros.) According to this book, Soble himself claimed that his nephew Wolston was a Soviet agent. Wolston was an American citizen who entered the U.S. Army in World War II and became a military intelligence officer, and shortly thereafter, he began reporting to the Soviet intelligence under the code name "Slava." Wolston relayed to Soviet intelligence matters relating to the Army's intelligence school at Fort Ritchie, Maryland.

To add insult to injury, Wolston was also identified as a Soviet agent in an FBI report entitled "Expose of Soviet Espionage," published by the Senate Internal Security Subcommittee of the Committee on the Judiciary, which would seem to be a reputable source for a journalist.

The book at issue in the litigation—*KGB: The Secret Work of Soviet Secret Agents*—was authored by John Barron and first published in 1974, over sixteen years after the grand jury incident had occurred. The alleged libel appeared in the following passage, naming a long laundry list of Soviet spies, among which Wolston's name was one:

> Among Soviet agents identified in the United States were Elizabeth T. Bentley, Edward Joseph Fitzgerald, William Ludwig Ullmann, William Walter Remington, Franklin Victor Reno, Judith Coplon, Harry Gold, David Greenglass, Julius and Ethel Rosenberg, Morton Sobell, William Perl, Alfred Dean Slack, Jack Soble, Ilya Wolston, Alfred and Martha Stern.

It should be noted at this point that Barron said nothing further about Wolston in the book—only that he was "identified" as a Soviet agent in the United States.

Barron was a well-respected journalist who had graduated from the University of Missouri, studied Russian at the United States Naval Postgraduate School in Monterey, California, and served in Berlin as a naval intelligence officer. In 1957, he joined the *Washington Star* as an investigative reporter. In 1965, Barron joined the Washington bureau of *Reader's Digest*. There he wrote more than a hundred stories on a wide variety of subjects—notably a 1980 story concerning unanswered questions surrounding the drowning death of Mary Jo Kopechne at Chappaquiddick in a car driven by Ted Kennedy. After Barron published his 1974 book *KGB: The Secret World of Soviet Secret Agents*, the KGB attempted to discredit him by claiming that he was part of a Zionist conspiracy.

After Wolston sued the author and publisher for defamation, the defendants predictably moved for summary judgment on the grounds that there were no facts to be decided by the trial court. The court granted summary judgment for the defendants on the grounds (a) that Wolston was a public figure, and (b) there was no indication of malice on the part of the defendants. The D.C. Circuit Court of Appeals affirmed the district court, but its decision was eventually reversed by the U.S. Supreme Court.

Ilya Wolston was born in Russia in 1918, and he later lived in Lithuania, Germany, France, and England. In 1939 he emigrated to the United States, and in 1943 became a naturalized citizen. He was drafted into the United States Army, trained as a Russian interpreter, and served primarily in Alaska as a liaison to Soviet military personnel. After his discharge, he worked as an interpreter for the Department of State in Allied-occupied Berlin. On his return to the United States in 1951, Wolston first worked as a clerk, then enrolled in an undergraduate program, and in 1955 moved to Washington, DC, to work for the army map service and as a freelance translator.

On January 25, 1957, Wolston's aunt and uncle, Myra and Jack Soble, were arrested by the FBI on espionage charges. They were indicted on five counts of espionage, conspiracy, and violation of the registration acts. In April, Jack pled guilty to espionage and was sentenced to seven years.

On the same day that the Sobles were arrested, Wolston was interviewed at his home by the FBI. Shortly thereafter, he was subpoenaed to appear before a special grand jury convened to investigate the activities of Soviet intelligence agents. Wolston was interviewed by the FBI on at least three more occasions, and he made several trips to New York in response to subpoenas.

On July 1, 1958, Wolston failed to respond to a grand jury subpoena. Two weeks later, a federal district judge ordered that Wolston show cause why he should not be held in contempt. These events attracted a significant amount of media coverage. At least seven news articles were published in New York and Washington, DC, newspapers. The stories reported statements by the Assistant U.S. Attorney that Wolston had been in contact with the Sobles for a long time before their arrest. Three of these pieces reported a statement by the prosecution that Wolston was believed to have material information about the espionage matters under investigation.

On July 29, at least two newspapers reported that the judge commented that, "There is no question in my mind that there was a studied attempt by Wolston to avoid an appearance before this grand jury." Three newspaper stories noted that Wolston had repeatedly failed to appear to subpoenas, each time submitting a doctor's certificate the day before his scheduled appearance. On August 7, Wolston pled guilty to the charge of contempt of court, and his guilty plea was reported in two newspapers. Wolston received a one-year suspended sentence on his guilty plea, and he was placed on probation for three years provided he agree to appear before other grand juries. The following day, three newspapers reported the sentence and probation. Wolston was never asked to appear before another grand jury.

John Barron, the author of *KGB*, devoted four years to the book project. He was assisted by the Reader's Digest research staff, but it later appeared that the statements about Wolston were based primarily on the FBI report published in 1960, and to a lesser extent on the Morros book *My Ten Years As a Counterspy*, published in 1959. The FBI report, entitled "Expose of Soviet Espionage," was transmitted to the U.S. Senate's Subcommittee to Investigate the Administration of the Internal Security Act and Other Internal Security Laws, and it was published shortly thereafter. In a section entitled "Ilya Wolston," the report stated:

> On several occasions beginning May 7, 1950, Jack Soble furnished Boris Morros with information concerning an individual he described as a U.S. Army Colonel in Germany who furnished him information under the code name "Slava," which was very valuable to the Soviets. It is noted that from October, 1949, until July, 1951, Wolston was employed by the U.S. High Commissioner of Germany in Berlin. In January, 1955, Soble identified his nephew, Ilya Wolston as "Slava."
>
> In addition, Jack Soble, pleading guilty in April, 1957, furnished information identifying Wolston as a Soviet agent who provided him information for the Soviets on several occasions beginning when Wolston was in a military camp, about 1943. Soble said Wolston gave him information concerning his assignments and names of four persons at the camp whom he believed could be approached by the Soviets.

It was also apparent from the FBI report that Soble's statements were not the only basis for the agency's conclusion that Wolston was a Soviet agent. The report stated that "information concerning the probable identification of Wolston as a Soviet agent was furnished to the Department of State in 1951, together with data developed concerning his black market activities in Germany." In other words, the FBI report *independently* identified Wolston as a Soviet agent.

The report stated that the FBI's investigation of the case identified ten individuals as Soviet intelligence agents. Eight of these persons were indicted for espionage or perjury and pled guilty, were convicted, or became fugitives. The ninth, an attaché to the Soviet delegation to the United Nations, was declared *persona non grata* and left the country. The tenth was Wolston. Thus, the results demonstrated the validity of the agency's investigative conclusions. Furthermore, extensive research conducted by either Barron or his staff revealed no evidence that Wolston had ever objected to the statements about him in the agency report or in the Morros book.

In the book, Morros identified Wolston as a Soviet agent, but Morros added that he knew nothing about Wolston's activities except what Soble—"a confirmed liar"—told him. The book also stated that Wolston failed to respond to six subpoenas issued by a federal grand jury; that Wolston pled guilty to a contempt of court charge; and that he received a one-year suspended sentence. Approximately 12,500 copies of the hardcover edition of the Morros book were printed and 141,000 copies of the paperback edition.

Barron, the author of *KGB*, testified that he had read the Morros book identifying Wolston as a Soviet agent, but that for purposes of documentation, it was the Senate Report on which he primarily relied. In an affidavit he swore: "I was confident upon publication of *KGB* that the book as a whole and each and every statement in it were true, and I was aware of no fact that tended to make me doubt the truth of the book or of any statement in it. At no time have I been aware of any fact that would give me reason to doubt the truth of the FBI report or of any statement in it."

The district court noted:

> The record in this case fails to demonstrate clearly and convincingly that Barron or any of his co-defendants entertained serious doubts or, for that matter, any doubts about the truth of the statements in KGB that connect Wolston with espionage. Rather, Barron has stated under oath that he "was confident upon publication of *KGB* that the book as a whole and each and every statement in it were true, and was aware of no fact that tended to make him doubt the truth of the book or of any statement in it," and the record contains scarcely any evidence at all tending to impeach Barron's assertions.
>
> To be sure, sworn-to reliance on a report by the FBI might seem, in light of events in recent years, to be risky business. But reliance on an FBI report, absent an independent basis for entertaining serious doubts about its accuracy, falls far

short of the level of questionable activity necessary to raise a genuine issue with regard to actual malice. And Barron's knowledge of Soble's reputation as a liar is too slender a reed to support a judgment in Wolston's favor. Without reference to Soble the FBI's report categorically identifies Ilya Wolston on page 24 as a "Soviet intelligence agent;" at page 26 the report states that the Government had information supporting "the probable identification of Wolston as a Soviet agent" as early as 1951, well before Soble was arrested.

And in any case, even if Soble was directly or indirectly the Government's only source of information concerning Wolston, Barron knew that, after Soble was arrested, he provided information to the Government that proved "extremely useful and quite reliable in many cases." Moreover, and perhaps most important, despite the fact that Barron devoted over four years to researching and writing *KGB*, and did so with the assistance of a sizeable research staff, not a shred of evidence emerged suggesting that Wolston had ever objected to the assertions about him in Morros's book, published in 1959, or in the FBI's report, published in 1960. Under the circumstances, the court is satisfied not only that Barron did place his faith in the accuracy of the report, but also that he had ample reason to do so notwithstanding his awareness of the reputation for untrustworthiness which Soble had earned while acting as an undercover intelligence agent.

The district court noted that whether Wolston was a public figure was a question of law that had to be decided by the court, rather than a jury. Wolston contended that the complex factual question of whether he was a public figure was in fact one for the jury. The appellate court, however, agreed with the defendant, holding that it was for the trial judge—not the jury—to determine whether the proof showed Wolston to be a public figure.

Wolston also argued that there remained an issue of fact concerning the reasons for his failure to appear before the grand jury and to subject himself to a contempt proceeding. The issue, he said, was whether in so doing he intended to participate in the public debate concerning espionage investigations. The district court concluded that the undisputed facts demonstrated that he was a public figure, regardless of his subjective intent. The court of appeals concurred. By failing to appear before the grand jury Wolston invited public attention and comment. Until then, he enjoyed obscurity, but by subjecting himself to a citation for contempt, he voluntarily stepped into the spotlight. The reference to him in the book *KGB* related to those issues and did not intrude into his personal life or affairs.

The book *KGB* was published in 1974—sixteen years after Wolston's appearance on the public stage. Wolston argued that even if he once was a public figure for a limited period, the passage of time had restored him to the status of a private citizen. The district court remarked that, "Historical comment on the espionage-related activities of Wolston and others who became involved in the controversy during the 1950s requires just as much protection as did media coverage of the events as they occurred."

The D.C. Circuit Court of Appeals agreed. The issue of Soviet espionage in the '50s continued to be a legitimate topic of debate twenty-five years later, and the mere lapse of time was not decisive. Under the landmark case of *New York Times Co. v. Sullivan*, a plaintiff may not recover for a defamatory falsehood unless he can show that it was published with *actual malice*. In other words, the statement must be made with knowledge that the statement was false or with reckless disregard of whether it was false or not. This meant that the defendants were entitled to summary judgment unless Wolston could prove actual malice.

On further appeal, the U.S. Supreme Court disagreed with the lower courts' legal classification of Wolston as a public figure. First of all, the court did not believe that the facts justified the conclusion that Wolston *voluntarily* "injected" himself into discussion of Soviet espionage in the United States. The court said that it would be more accurate to say that Wolston was "dragged unwillingly" into the controversy, since the government pursued *him* in its investigation.

It was true that Wolston failed to respond to a grand jury subpoena, and that the subsequent citation for contempt attracted media attention. But the mere fact that Wolston voluntarily chose not to appear before the grand jury—knowing that his action might be attended by publicity—was *not*, in the court's view, decisive on the question of his status as a public figure.

OPINION EXCERPT

Rehnquist, J., delivered the opinion of the Court, in which Burger, Chief Justice, and Stewart, White, Powell, and Stevens, joined.

We do not agree with respondents and the lower courts that petitioner [Wolston] can be classed as such a limited-purpose public figure. First, the undisputed facts do not justify the conclusion of the District Court and Court of Appeals that petitioner [Wolston] "voluntarily thrust" or "injected" himself into the forefront of the public controversy surrounding the investigation of Soviet espionage in the United States. It would be more accurate to say that petitioner [Wolston] was dragged unwillingly into the controversy. The Government pursued him in its investigation. Petitioner [Wolston] did fail to respond to a grand jury subpoena, and this failure, as well as his subsequent citation for contempt, did attract media attention. But the mere fact that petitioner [Wolston] voluntarily chose not to appear before the grand jury, knowing that his action might be attended by publicity, is not decisive on the question of public figure status. In *Gertz,* we held that an attorney was not a public figure even though he voluntarily associated himself with a case that was certain to receive extensive media exposure.

We emphasized that a court must focus on the "nature and extent of an individual's participation in the particular controversy giving rise to the defamation." *Ibid.* In *Gertz,* the attorney took no part in the criminal prosecution, never discussed the litigation with the press, and limited his participation in the civil litigation solely to his representation of a private client. Similarly, petitioner [Wolston] never discussed this matter with the press, and limited his involvement to that necessary to defend himself against the contempt charge. It is clear that petitioner [Wolston] played only a minor role in whatever public controversy there may have been concerning the investigation of Soviet espionage. We decline to hold that his mere citation for contempt rendered him a public figure for purposes of comment on the investigation of Soviet espionage.

Petitioner's [Wolston's] failure to appear before the grand jury and citation for contempt no doubt were "newsworthy," but the simple fact that these events attracted media attention also is not conclusive of the public figure issue. A private individual is not automatically transformed into a public figure just by becoming involved in or associated with a matter that attracts public attention. To accept such reasoning would in effect reestablish the doctrine advanced by the plurality opinion in *Rosenbloom v. Metromedia, Inc.,* which concluded that the *New York Times* standard should extend to defamatory falsehoods relating to private persons if the statements involved matters of public or general concern. We repudiated this proposition in *Gertz* and in *Firestone,* however, and we reject it again today. A libel defendant must show more than mere newsworthiness to justify application of the demanding burden of *New York Times.*

Nor do we think that petitioner [Wolston] engaged the attention of the public in an attempt to influence the resolution of the issues involved. Petitioner [Wolston] assumed no "special prominence in the resolution of public questions." His failure to respond to the grand jury's subpoena was in no way calculated to draw attention to himself in order to invite public comment or influence the public with respect to any issue. He did not in any way seek to arouse public sentiment in his favor and against the investigation. Thus, this is not a case where a defendant invites a citation for contempt in order to use the contempt citation as a fulcrum to create public discussion about the methods being used in connection with an investigation or prosecution. To the contrary, petitioner's [Wolston's] failure to appear before the grand jury appears simply to have been the result of his poor health. He then promptly communicated his desire to testify and, when the offer was rejected, passively accepted his punishment. There is no evidence that petitioner's [Wolston's] failure to appear was intended to have, or did in fact have, any effect on any issue of public concern. In short, we find no basis whatsoever for concluding that petitioner [Wolston] relinquished, to any degree, his interest in the protection of his own name.

This reasoning leads us to reject the further contention of respondents that any person who engages in criminal conduct automatically becomes a public figure for purposes of comment on a limited range of issues relating to his conviction. We declined to accept a similar argument in *Time, Inc. v. Firestone*, where we said: "[W]hile participants in some litigation may be legitimate 'public figures,' either generally or for the limited purpose of that litigation, the majority will more likely resemble respondent, drawn into a public forum largely against their will in order to attempt to obtain the only redress available to them or to defend themselves against actions brought by the State or by others. There appears little reason why these individuals should substantially forfeit that degree of protection which the law of defamation would otherwise afford them simply by virtue of their being drawn into a courtroom. The public interest in accurate reports of judicial proceedings is substantially protected by *Cox Broadcasting Co. v. Cohn*. As to inaccurate and defamatory reports of facts, matters deserving no First Amendment protection . . . we think *Gertz* provides an adequate safeguard for the constitutionally protected interests of the press and affords it a tolerable margin for error by requiring some type of fault."

We think that these observations remain sound, and that they control the disposition of this case. To hold otherwise would create an "open season" for all who sought to defame persons convicted of a crime.

COVERT AGREEMENT

In this case, the plaintiffs—a husband-and-wife spy team—employed the fictitious names of John and Jane Doe for the purposes of this lawsuit. According to the court, the Does were former citizens of an "unnamed foreign country" that at the time was widely considered to be "an arch enemy" of the United States.

John Doe was a high-ranking diplomat, and he expressed an interest in defecting to the United States. The CIA, however, persuaded Mr. Doe to remain in his position and conduct espionage for the U.S. government, which promised in return that it would "ensure financial and personal security for life." After years of valuable and high-risk espionage the Does, with the aid of the U.S. government, assumed new names and identities and became American citizens. The CIA then began providing financial assistance and personal security.

John Doe, being an intelligent and resourceful individual, subsequently obtained gainful employment in the state of Washington. As his salary increased, the CIA began to decrease his stipend and eventually his benefits were discontinued. Years later, in 1997, he was laid off as a result of a corporate merger. He was unable to find new employment due to CIA restrictions on the types of jobs he could hold, and when he contacted the CIA for financial assistance, he was denied. Faced with the prospect of either returning to their home country (where the couple would no doubt face imprisonment) or remaining in the United States in their present circumstances, the Does filed suit against the CIA.

The Does contended, among other things, that the CIA violated their procedural and substantive due process rights by denying them support and by failing to provide them with an internal process for reviewing their claims. They sought injunctive relief ordering the CIA to resume monthly financial support pending further agency review.

The government moved to dismiss the complaint on the grounds that the landmark 1876 case of *Totten* v. *United States* barred the suit. In that case, the U.S. Supreme Court held that public policy forbid a Civil War spy from suing the government to enforce its obligations under a secret espionage agreement. In the present case, the district court and the court of appeals for the Ninth Circuit ruled that *Totten* did *not* bar the present suit, and that the case could proceed.

In *Totten,* the administrator of William A. Lloyd's estate brought suit against the United States to recover compensation for services that Lloyd rendered as a Union spy during the Civil War. Lloyd purportedly entered into a contract with President Lincoln in July 1861 to spy behind Confederate lines on troop placement and fort plans, for which he was to be paid $200 a month. The lower court found that Lloyd performed on the contract, but did not receive full compensation. After concluding that the President had the authority to bind the United States to contracts with secret agents, the Supreme Court observed that the very essence of the alleged contract between Lloyd and the government was its secrecy. Thus, the court maintained that the very nature of such a contract made it impossible for a former spy to enforce it.

In the instant suit, the district court went on to determine that the Does had properly stated both substantive and procedural due process claims, even apart from the existence of an alleged secret contract with the Agency. The district court found that "the Does may be able to base their entitlement to receipt of the CIA's monetary stipend on theories other than contract. For example, if plaintiffs are able to prove an entitlement to benefits based on a promissory or equitable estoppel theory, or if there is a regulatory or statutory basis for their entitlement, then they may be able to show a constitutionally protected property interest, regardless of *Totten.*" Furthermore, the trial court found that the Does had sufficiently stated due process claims on two separate theories—that the CIA had placed the Does in danger and that the CIA had created a special relationship with the Does.

On appeal to the Ninth Circuit Court of Appeals, the appellate court agreed with the district court that the Does could continue with their claim through the administrative process. The court explained:

> The national interest normally requires both protection of state secrets and the protection of fundamental constitutional rights. Here, the CIA has not invoked

the state secrets privilege nor has the district court had the opportunity independently to review the invocation of such a privilege. We should not precipitously close the courthouse doors to colorable claims of the denial of constitutional rights. The Does' case must therefore be remanded to the district court to provide the Agency the opportunity to formally invoke the state secrets privilege. If the Agency chooses to do so, the district court must then, after careful inquiry and consideration of alternative modes of adjudication, and with the utmost deference to the government's determination of national security interests, evaluate whether any aspect of the Does' case can go forward.

The government appealed the case to the U.S. Supreme Court, which concluded that the court of appeals was incorrect in holding that *Totten* did not require dismissal of the plaintiffs' claims when it reasoned that *Totten* prohibited breach-of-contract claims which sought to enforce the terms of espionage agreements, but did not bar claims based on due process or estoppel theories. The Supreme Court stated that the language of *Totten* was *not* so limited: "Public policy forbids the maintenance of *any suit* in a court of justice, the trial of which would inevitably lead to the disclosure of matters which the law itself regards as confidential."

The Supreme Court also held that the state secrets privilege in no way signaled a retreat from *Totten*'s broader holding that lawsuits premised on espionage agreements were completely forbidden. The court noted that there is an obvious difference between a suit brought by an acknowledged (though covert) employee of the CIA and one filed by an alleged former spy. Only in the latter scenario is Totten's core concern implicated—preventing even the existence of the plaintiff's relationship with the government from being revealed.

The court explained that the state secrets privilege and *in camera* judicial review simply could not provide the protection that is necessary in promoting the public policy behind the *Totten* rule. The possibility that an espionage arrangement might be revealed if the state secrets privilege was found not to apply was, in the court's view, completely unacceptable: "Even a small chance that some court will order disclosure of a source's identity could well impair intelligence gathering and cause sources to 'close up like a clam.'" Forcing the government to litigate these claims would also make it vulnerable to "graymail"—individual lawsuits brought to induce the CIA to settle a case (or prevent its filing) out of fear that litigating the action would reveal classified information that might undermine ongoing covert operations. Requiring the government to invoke the privilege on a case-by-case basis also risks the perception that it is either confirming or denying relationships with individual plaintiffs.

The judgment of the court of appeals was accordingly reversed, and Mr. and Mrs. Doe were left in a difficult situation with a spy-assistance agreement they could not enforce and a home country they could not return to.

OPINION EXCERPT

Chief Justice Rehnquist delivered the opinion of the Court.

In *Totten*, the administrator of William A. Lloyd's estate brought suit against the United States to recover compensation for services that Lloyd allegedly rendered as a spy during the Civil War. Lloyd purportedly entered into a contract with President Lincoln in July 1861 to spy behind Confederate lines on troop placement and fort plans, for which he was to be paid $200 a month. The lower court had found that Lloyd performed on the contract but did not receive full compensation. After concluding with "no difficulty," that the President had the authority to bind the United States to contracts with secret agents, we observed that the very essence of the alleged contract between Lloyd and the Government was that it was secret, and had to remain so:

> The service stipulated by the contract was a secret service; the information sought was to be obtained clandestinely, and was to be communicated privately; the employment and the service were to be equally concealed. Both employer and agent must have understood that the lips of the other were to be for ever sealed respecting the relation of either to the matter. This condition of the engagement was implied from the nature of the employment, and is implied in all secret employments of the government in time of war, or upon matters affecting our foreign relations, where a disclosure of the service might compromise or embarrass our government in its public duties, or endanger the person or injure the character of the agent.

Thus, we thought it entirely incompatible with the nature of such a contract that a former spy could bring suit to enforce it.

We think the Court of Appeals was quite wrong in holding that *Totten* does not require dismissal of respondents' claims. That court, and respondents here, reasoned first that *Totten* developed merely a contract rule, prohibiting breach-of-contract claims seeking to enforce the terms of espionage agreements but not barring claims based on due process or estoppel theories. In fact, *Totten* was not so limited: "[P]ublic policy forbids the maintenance of *any suit* in a court of justice, the trial of which would inevitably lead to the disclosure of matters which the law itself regards as confidential." No matter the clothing in which alleged spies dress their claims, *Totten* precludes judicial review in cases such as respondents' where success depends upon the existence of their secret espionage relationship with the Government.

Relying mainly on *United States v. Reynolds*, the Court of Appeals also claimed that *Totten* has been recast simply as an early expression of the evidentiary "state secrets" privilege, rather than a categorical bar to their claims. *Reynolds* involved a wrongful-death action brought under the Federal Tort Claims Act, by the widows of three civilians who died in the crash of a military B–29 aircraft. In the course of discovery, the plaintiffs sought certain investigation-related documents, which the Government said contained "highly secret," privileged military information. We recognized "the privilege against revealing military secrets, a privilege which is well established in the law of evidence," and we set out a balancing approach for courts to apply in resolving Government claims of privilege. We ultimately concluded that the Government was entitled to the privilege in that case.

When invoking the "well established" state secrets privilege, we indeed looked to *Totten*. But that in no way signaled our retreat from *Totten*'s broader holding that lawsuits premised on alleged espionage agreements are altogether forbidden. Indeed, our opinion in *Reynolds* refutes this very suggestion: Citing *Totten* as a case "where the very subject matter of the action, a contract to perform espionage, was a matter of state secret," we declared that such a case was to be "dismissed on the pleadings without ever reaching the question of evidence, since it was so obvious that the action should never prevail over the privilege."

In a later case, we again credited the more sweeping holding in *Totten*, thus confirming its continued validity. *Reynolds* therefore cannot plausibly be read to have replaced the categorical *Totten* bar with the balancing of the state secrets evidentiary privilege in the distinct class of cases that depend upon clandestine spy relationships.

Nor does *Webster v. Doe* support respondents' claim. There, we held that §102(c) of the National Security Act of 1947, may not be read to exclude judicial review of the constitutional claims made by a former CIA employee for alleged discrimination. In reaching that conclusion, we noted the "'serious constitutional question' that would arise if a federal statute were construed to deny any judicial forum for a colorable constitutional claim." But there is an obvious difference, for purposes of *Totten*, between a suit brought by an acknowledged (though covert) employee of the CIA and one filed by an alleged former spy. Only in the latter scenario is *Totten*'s core concern implicated: preventing the existence of the plaintiff's relationship with the Government from being revealed. That is why the CIA regularly entertains Title VII claims concerning the hiring and promotion of its employees, as we noted in Webster, supra, at 604, yet Totten has long barred suits such as respondents'.

There is, in short, no basis for respondents' and the Court of Appeals' view that the *Totten* bar has been reduced to an example of the state secrets privilege. In a far closer case than this, we observed that if the "precedent of this Court has direct application in a case, yet appears to rest on reasons rejected in some other line of decisions, the Court of Appeals should follow the case which directly controls, leaving to this Court the prerogative of overruling its own decisions."

13

TRAVEL RESTRICTIONS

This lawsuit involved the validity of a passport restriction imposed on a former CIA agent.

Philip Agee, who had previously worked for the CIA, travelled extensively abroad on a U.S. passport. He had become disillusioned with the work of the agency, and he wrote and spoke widely, often attacking U.S. intelligence efforts and revealing names of CIA agents and operatives. His controversial book, *Inside the Company: CIA Diary*, published in 1975, identified hundreds of individuals and companies working undercover around the world for the agency.

The Department of State believed that Agee's activities were particularly significant—and harmful—in light of the recent Iranian crisis. The department notified Agee that his passport was revoked and should be surrendered immediately. The Secretary of State explained that Agee's actions abroad were causing damage to the national security of the United States. Agee filed suit in the district court, which elaborated:

> On December 23, 1979, the Department notified Agee by letter that his passport was immediately revoked and should be surrendered. As grounds for this action, the Secretary of State relied on the provisions of 22 C.F.R. §§ 51.70(b) (4) and 51.71, asserting specifically his conclusion that Agee's activities abroad "are causing or are likely to cause serious damage to the national security or the foreign policy of the United States." Agee was provided with a statement of reasons supporting the Department's determination, and was informed of his right to an administrative appeal which was subsequently offered on an expedited basis. He rejected this option, and instead by appropriate papers seeks declaratory and injunctive relief from the Court.

Agee alleges that the revocation of his passport is invalid because it rests on a regulation which has not been authorized by Congress. In addition, he attacks the constitutionality of the regulation on its face, claiming that it conflicts impermissibly with rights guaranteed under the First and Fifth Amendments to the Constitution.

The matter presented a pure question of law since, for purposes of the motion, Agee conceded that he was causing, and likely to cause, serious damage to the national security or foreign policy of the United States.

In reviewing the case, the district court noted that the right to travel is constitutionally protected. The Secretary of State's power to revoke or limit a passport flows from Congress, but the law does not confer "unbridled discretion" to grant, revoke, or otherwise restrict passports. The Supreme Court had previously held that the authority to revoke passports was to be *narrowly* construed, especially when concerning the passport of a single individual. In this case, the Secretary of State argued that he acted pursuant to an explicit delegation from Congress, and that he followed consistent administrative practice to warrant the implied approval of Congress.

The issue was then whether congressional approval could be established. The Secretary of State urged that there existed a long-standing practice allowing passport denials. The district court responded that all of these powers were delegated to meet exigent circumstances for a *limited* purpose. The congressional actions taken were not, the court made clear, persuasive on the issue of *implicit* authorization to invoke national security in peacetime when no national emergency had been declared and no criminal conduct charged.

The Secretary of State also pointed to State Department testimony during a series of congressional hearings concerning passport legislation in 1957 and 1958. The Secretary argued that because the department had already asserted the power to regulate passports, the failure of Congress to reject this executive interpretation conveyed implicit approval. This argument, the court countered, could not withstand scrutiny. Arguments made during the 1957 hearings had to be read in light of *Kent v. Dulles*, which seriously limited the Secretary's power to deny passports in similar circumstances.

After the *Kent* decision, the administration introduced a bill that would have given the Secretary the precise authority sought in this case. But Congress failed to act, and legislative silence cannot be read as implicit adoption of an obscure regulation. The court therefore concluded that the Secretary's promulgation of the challenged regulation was without congressional authorization.

This holding, the court said, was in no way intended to affect the President's authority to limit Agee's travel by other means. While it was obvious that the national security may be endangered when a former government official travels to foreign countries denouncing the U.S. intelligence service and revealing the names of government agents, the issue was whether the regulation was legally authorized. If Agee was indicted for a violation of the law, his passport could be cancelled. If his activities were detrimental to the hostages in Iran, a special statute gave the President extraordinary authority to act, and so on.

Because the regulation at issue was invalid, the court granted Mr. Agee's motion for summary judgment, and his beloved passport was at long last restored. The D.C. Circuit Court of Appeals affirmed the district court holding, but the U.S. Supreme court eventually reversed it.

The Supreme Court began its analysis with the language of The Passport Act of 1926, which states that, "The Secretary of State may grant and issue passports, and cause passports to be granted, issued, and verified in foreign countries by diplomatic representatives of the United States under such rules as the President shall designate and prescribe for and on behalf of the United States, and no other person shall grant, issue, or verify such passports." While the act does not explicitly confer upon the Secretary a power to revoke a passport, the Supreme Court held that it is beyond dispute that the Secretary has the power to *deny* a passport for reasons not specified in the statutes. Agee conceded that, if the Secretary may deny a passport application for a certain reason, he may revoke a passport on the same ground. The court reasoned that this is so in light of the broad rulemaking authority of the executive branch, especially in the important areas of foreign policy and national security.

The court noted that a passport is, in a sense, a letter of introduction in which the issuing sovereign vouches for the bearer and requests other sovereigns to aid the bearer. A passport is virtually the only means by which an American can lawfully leave the country or return to it. From the outset, Congress endorsed not only the underlying premise of Executive authority in the areas of foreign policy and national security, but also its specific application to the subject of passports. Early Congresses enacted statutes expressly recognizing the executive authority with respect to passports, and Congress made clear its expectation that the executive would curtail or prevent international travel by American citizens if it was contrary to the national security.

Agee attacked the Secretary's action on three constitutional grounds: (1) that the revocation of his passport impermissibly burdens his freedom to travel, (2) that the action was intended to penalize his exercise of free speech and deter his criticism of Government policies and practices, (3) and that failure to accord him a pre-revocation hearing violated his Fifth Amendment right to procedural due process.

The Supreme Court responded that in light of the express language of the passport regulations—which permits their application only in cases involving likelihood of "serious damage" to national security or foreign policy—Agee's claims were without merit. The court noted that the freedom to travel outside the United States must be distinguished from the right to travel within the United States, and that no governmental interest is more compelling than the security of the nation.

The court stated that not only had Agee jeopardized the security of the United States, but he had also endangered the interests of countries other than the United States, thus creating serious problems for American foreign relations and foreign policy. Restricting Agee's foreign travel was in effect the only means open to the government to limit these activities.

Furthermore, the court found that Agee's First Amendment claim had no foundation. Agee's repeated disclosures of intelligence operations and names of intelligence personnel, which had the declared purpose of obstructing intelligence operations and the recruiting of intelligence personnel, were clearly not protected by the Constitution. To the extent the revocation of his passport operated to inhibit Agee, it was an inhibition of action, rather than of speech, the court said. The court therefore reversed the judgment of the Court of Appeals.

The activities of Agee and others eventually prompted Congress to pass the Intelligence Identities Protection Act of 1982, making it a crime to intentionally reveal the identity of a covert intelligence officer. Agee was blamed for endangering the lives of those doing intelligence work and disrupting intelligence efforts. At a ceremony honoring the fiftieth anniversary of the CIA in 1997, former president and CIA director George Bush stated that he considered Agee a traitor to the country.

In Agee's obituary, *The New York Times* reported: "Deprived of his American passport and expelled from several countries at the request of the United States, he had lived for the most part in Germany and Cuba, where he operated a travel Web site, cubalinda.com." Agee died of peritonitis in Havana on January 10, 2018, at the age of 72.

OPINION EXCERPT

Chief Justice Burger delivered the opinion of the Court.

The question presented is whether the President, acting through the Secretary of State, has authority to revoke a passport on the ground that the holder's activities in foreign countries are causing or are likely to cause serious damage to the national security or foreign policy of the United States.

Philip Agee, an American citizen, currently resides in West Germany. From 1957 to 1968, he was employed by the Central Intelligence Agency. He held key positions in the division of the Agency that is responsible for covert intelligence gathering in foreign countries. In the course of his duties at the Agency, Agee received training in clandestine operations, including the methods used to protect the identities of intelligence employees and sources of the United States overseas. He served in undercover assignments abroad and came to know many Government employees and other persons supplying information to the United States. The relationships of many of these people to our Government are highly confidential; many are still engaged in intelligence gathering.

In 1974, Agee called a press conference in London to announce his "campaign to fight the United States CIA wherever it is operating." He declared his intent "to expose CIA officers and agents and to take the measures necessary to drive them out of the countries where they are operating."

Since 1974, Agee has, by his own assertion, devoted consistent effort to that program, and he has traveled extensively in other countries in order to carry it out. To identify CIA personnel in a particular country, Agee goes to the target country and consults sources in local diplomatic circles whom he knows from his prior service in the United States Government. He recruits collaborators and trains them in clandestine techniques designed to expose the "cover" of CIA employees and sources. Agee and his collaborators have repeatedly and publicly identified individuals and organizations located in foreign countries as undercover CIA agents, employees, or sources. The record reveals that the identifications divulge classified information, violate Agee's express contract not to make any public statements about Agency matters without prior clearance by the Agency, have prejudiced the ability of the United States to obtain intelligence, and have been followed by episodes of violence against the persons and organizations identified.

In December, 1979, the Secretary of State revoked Agee's passport and delivered an explanatory notice to Agee in West Germany. The notice states in part:

"The Department's action is predicated upon a determination made by the Secretary under the provisions of [22 CFR] Section 51.70(b) (4) that your activities abroad are causing or are likely to cause serious damage to the national security or the foreign policy of the United States. The reasons for the Secretary's determination are, in summary, as follows: Since the early 1970's, it has been your stated intention to conduct a continuous campaign to disrupt the intelligence operations of the United States. In carrying out that campaign you have traveled in various countries (including, among others, Mexico, the United Kingdom, Denmark, Jamaica, Cuba, and Germany), and your activities in those countries have caused serious damage to the national security and foreign policy of the United States. Your stated intention to continue such activities threatens additional damage of the same kind."

The notice also advised Agee of his right to an administrative hearing and offered to hold such a hearing in West Germany on 5 days' notice.

Agee at once filed suit against the Secretary. He alleged that the regulation invoked by the Secretary, 22 CFR § 51.70(b)(4) (1980), has not been authorized by Congress and is invalid; that the regulation is impermissibly overbroad; that the revocation prior to a hearing violated his Fifth Amendment right to procedural due process; and that the revocation violated a Fifth Amendment liberty interest in a right to travel and a First Amendment right to criticize Government policies. He sought declaratory and injunctive relief, and he moved for summary judgment on the question of the authority to promulgate the regulation and on the constitutional claims. For purposes of that motion, Agee conceded the Secretary's factual averments and his claim that Agee's activities were causing or were likely to cause serious damage to the national security or foreign policy of the United States. The District Court held that the regulation exceeded the statutory powers of the Secretary under the Passport Act of 1926, 22 U.S.C. § 211a, granted summary judgment for Agee, and ordered the Secretary to restore his passport.

A divided panel of the Court of Appeals affirmed. It held that the Secretary was required to show that Congress had authorized the regulation either by an express delegation or by implied approval of a "substantial and consistent" administrative practice. The court found no express statutory authority for the revocation. It perceived only one other case of actual passport revocation under the regulation since it was promulgated, and only five other instances prior to that in which passports were actually denied "even arguably for national security or foreign policy reasons." The Court of Appeals took note of the Secretary's reliance on "a series of statutes, regulations, proclamations, orders and advisory opinions dating back to 1856," but declined to consider those authorities, reasoning that "the criterion for establishing congressional assent by inaction is the actual imposition of sanctions, and not the mere assertion of power."

The Court of Appeals held that it was not sufficient that "Agee's conduct may be considered by some to border on treason," since "we are bound by the law as we find it." The court also regarded it as material that most of the Secretary's authorities dealt with powers of the Executive Branch "during time of war or national emergency."

14

CIA CENSORSHIP

Ralph McGehee was a former CIA officer who, like all CIA agents, was required to sign an agreement with the agency that barred him from revealing classified information without prior approval.

After the CIA censored portions of a manuscript he wrote, McGehee sought a declaratory judgment concluding that the CIA classification and censorship scheme violated the First Amendment; or in the alternative, that his article contained no properly classified material. The district court not only rejected McGehee's First Amendment challenge but found that the CIA had properly classified the censored materials.

When he joined the CIA in 1952, McGehee signed an agreement in which he promised not to divulge "classified information" obtained by virtue of his employment unless specifically authorized in writing by the CIA to do so. Pursuant to this contract, he submitted an article to the CIA in March 1981 for pre-publication review. The article asserted that the CIA had mounted a campaign of deceit to convince the world that the "revolt of the poor natives against a ruthless U.S.-backed oligarchy" in El Salvador was really "a Soviet/Cuban/Bulgarian/Vietnamese/PLO/Ethiopian/Nicaraguan/ International Terrorism challenge to the United States." To lend credibility to his assertion, McGehee's article proceeded to review a few examples of CIA disinformation programs in Iran, Vietnam, Chile, and Indonesia. Four days later, the CIA notified McGehee that portions of his article contained secret information, and the agency accordingly withheld permission to publish those portions.

The CIA, it turned out, employs three classification levels. The most sensitive is labeled *Top Secret*, and it includes information that reasonably could be expected to cause "exceptionally grave" damage to the national security. The least restricted, but still sensitive, is labeled *Confidential*, and it includes information that reasonably could be expected to cause "identifiable damage" to the national security. The classification of *Secret* is the middle level between *Top Secret* and *Confidential*, and it applies to information which reasonably could be expected to cause "serious damage" to the national security.

The CIA classified the censored portions of McGehee's article as "Secret." The CIA reasoned that McGehee's identification of countries where the CIA had established bases would damage U.S. relations with those countries, and that his discussion of a CIA operation in Indonesia would disclose secret intelligence methods and sources. The CIA concluded that McGehee's article threatened to cause "serious damage" to the national security.

The next month *The Nation* magazine published McGehee's article with the censored portions deleted. McGehee then sought judicial review in the district court of the District of Columbia, challenging (1) the constitutionality of the CIA's classification and censorship scheme, and (2) the propriety of classifying portions of his article "secret." The district court summarily rejected McGehee's constitutional challenge. The court found that the CIA had properly classified the documents and was justified in its censorship.

On appeal to the D.C. Court of Appeals, McGehee renewed his claim that the CIA classification and censorship scheme violated the First Amendment, and that even if the scheme was constitutional, the CIA improperly classified portions of his article. The appellate court affirmed, holding that:

> (1) when balanced against the First amendment interests in public disclosure of former agents' writings, the CIA scheme of classifying and censoring secret information was constitutional because (a) the government has a substantial interest in assuring secrecy in the conduct of foreign intelligence operations, and (b) the criteria for what constitutes "secret" information were neither overbroad,
>
> (2) in reviewing whether specified information reasonably could be expected to cause actual serious harm if divulged, courts should accord deference to the CIA's reasoned explanation of its classification decision, and (3) in this case, the CIA properly classified the censored portions of McGehee's article.

In the 1980 case of *Snepp v. United States*, the Supreme Court had held that the CIA could, consistent with the First Amendment, recover damages for breach of a secrecy agreement in which a former agent promised to submit CIA-related writings to the CIA for pre-publication clearance. The court found the secrecy agreement to be a reasonable means of protecting the information important to national security and the appearance of confidentiality essential to the effective operation of the country's foreign intelligence service.

In *Snepp*, the former agent published CIA-related information without submitting his manuscript for pre-publication review. The government's action in *Snepp*, therefore, did not depend upon whether Snepp's book actually contained classified information. The government simply claimed that Snepp should have given the CIA an opportunity to determine whether the material would compromise classified information or sources.

The court in *Snepp* explained:

> Snepp's employment with the CIA involved an extremely high degree of trust. In the opening sentence of the agreement that he signed, Snepp explicitly recognized that he was entering a trust relationship. The trust agreement specifically imposed the obligation not to publish any information relating to the Agency without submitting the information for clearance. Snepp stipulated at trial that— after undertaking this obligation—he had been "assigned to various positions of trust" and that he had been granted "frequent access to classified information, including information regarding intelligence sources and methods." Snepp published his book about CIA activities on the basis of this background and exposure. He deliberately and surreptitiously violated his obligation to submit all material for prepublication review. Thus, he exposed the classified information with which he had been entrusted to the risk of disclosure.
>
> Whether Snepp violated his trust does not depend upon whether his book actually contained classified information. The Government does not deny—as a general principle—Snepp's right to publish unclassified information. Nor does it contend—at this stage of the litigation—that Snepp's book contains classified material. The Government simply claims that, in light of the special trust reposed in him and the agreement that he signed, Snepp should have given the CIA an opportunity to determine whether the material he proposed to publish would compromise classified information or sources. Neither of the Government's concessions undercuts its claim that Snepp's failure to submit to prepublication review was a breach of his trust.

But in the present case, McGehee complied with the agreement. He submitted his manuscript for pre-publication review, and he deleted portions of it accordingly. At issue was the constitutionality of the CIA policy concerning how to classify, and thereby censor, writings of former agents.

The appellate court noted that McGehee's secrecy agreement applied only when he sought to publish classified information that he acquired by virtue of his connection with the CIA. The agreement did *not* extend to unclassified materials or information obtained from public sources, which the government may not censor. The CIA required all of its employees to enter into the agreement as a condition of employment, and this fact was critical to the court's First Amendment analysis.

The court held that it must apply a balancing test in determining whether the CIA's censorship of ex-agents' writings violated the First Amendment. A review of relevant cases revealed that the precise standard for balancing was not well settled. The appellate court discerned two themes from previous cases. First, the restrictions must protect a substantial government interest unrelated to the suppression of free speech. Second, the restriction must be narrowly drawn to restrict speech no more than is necessary to protect the governmental interest.

The CIA classified portions of McGehee's articles as "Secret," believing that disclosure could reasonably be expected to cause "serious damage to the national security." The appellate court held that the CIA censorship of such information did not violate the First Amendment. The censorship protected a substantial governmental interest unrelated to the suppression of free expression. In fact, the court stated that the government has a *compelling* interest in protecting the secrecy of information important to national security.

Furthermore, the court said, the classification criteria reasonably confined the resulting censorship to cases in which a substantial governmental interest was served. The criteria did not sweep too broadly because it limited disclosure only when it posed a reasonable probability of "serious" harm. In addition, the classification criteria were not excessively vague. The term national security was defined for classification purposes as "the national defense and foreign relations of the United States." So defined, the term is inherently vague, but in this case, the governing executive order added specificity by enumerating the types of information that may be considered for classification:

Information may not be considered for classification unless it concerns:

(a) military plans, weapons, or operations
(b) foreign government information
(c) intelligence activities, sources or methods
(d) foreign relations or foreign activities of the United States
(e) scientific, technological, or economic matters relating to the national security
(f) United States Government programs for safeguarding nuclear materials or facilities

(g) other categories of information which are related to national security and which require protection against unauthorized disclosure as determined by the president, by a person designated by the president, or by an agency head.

Item (d), the court pointed out, refers broadly to "foreign relations or foreign activities of the United States." Standing alone, such a classification standard might be excessively vague. The CIA, however, had articulated narrower standards, and the guidelines pertinent to this case were sufficiently precise to withstand a constitutional challenge.

In this case, the executive order, by establishing a pre-clearance procedure, engendered less of a chilling effect on free speech. This was not to say, of course, that imprecise standards might not still present an intolerable burden by allowing the censor unwarranted discretion in vetoing material, but the appellate court did not find the standards unconstitutionally vague. As the court noted, the agent may always seek judicial review of the CIA's decision.

The court of appeals concluded that the classification scheme, taken as a whole, did not result in real or substantial deterrence of protected speech. The "Secret" and "Top Secret" classifications place constitutional burdens on the speech of former CIA agents. The court was not prepared to hold that the burdens placed on such speech by the "Confidential" classification are sufficiently heavy or widespread to render the entire classification scheme substantially overbroad and therefore invalid on its face. As the court noted, the CIA classification and censorship scheme reduces deterrence, because prepublication review alleviates a former agent's fear that his disclosure of non-sensitive information might result in liability. Thus the CIA's scheme reduces the chilling effect on the agent's freedom of speech.

This case, the court pointed out, was significantly different from a request of CIA documents under the Freedom of Information Act (FOIA). In a FOIA case, an individual seeks to compel release of documents in the government's possession. By contrast, McGehee wished to disclose information that he already possessed, and the government determined that an agreement forbid disclosure.

The court remarked that judicial review of CIA classification decisions, by reasonable necessity, cannot second guess CIA judgments on matters in which the judiciary lacks the requisite expertise: "Due to the mosaic-like nature of intelligence gathering, what may seem trivial to the uninformed may appear of great moment to one who has a broad view of the scene and may put the questioned item of information in context."

After conducting an *in camera* review of the parties' affidavits, the district court concluded that disclosure of the censored portions of McGehee's article could reasonably be expected to cause damage to the national security. The affidavits offered convincing and detailed evidence of a serious risk that intelligence sources and methods would be compromised. These risks identified in the CIA affidavits did not rise to the level of certainty, but the court found them reliable enough to justify the classification decision.

To Mr. McGehee's consternation, the trial court's judgment in favor of the CIA was thus affirmed.

OPINION EXCERPT

WALD, Circuit Judge.

The district court found that the CIA "properly classified the relevant documents and was warranted in their censorship" of portions of McGehee's article. We agree, although we take this opportunity to clarify the standard of judicial review appropriate to a case such as this one.

This case arises in a posture significantly different from a request for release of CIA documents under the Freedom of Information Act (FOIA). In a FOIA case, an individual seeks to compel release of documents in the government's possession. Here, by contrast, McGehee wishes publicly to disclose information that he already possesses, and the government has ruled that his secrecy agreement forbids disclosure.

This difference between seeking to obtain information and seeking to disclose information already obtained raises McGehee's constitutional interests in this case above the constitutional interests held by a FOIA claimant.

As a general rule, citizens have no first amendment right of access to traditionally nonpublic government information. A litigant seeking release of government information under FOIA, therefore, relies upon a statutory entitlement—as narrowed by statutory exceptions—and not upon his constitutional right to free expression.

In this case, however, McGehee wishes to publish information he possesses, and the CIA wishes to silence him. Although neither the CIA's administrative determination nor any court order in this case constitutes a prior restraint in the traditional sense upon McGehee or any other party, the entire scheme of prepublication review is designed for the purpose of preventing publication of classified information. McGehee therefore has a strong first amendment interest in ensuring that CIA censorship of his article results from a proper classification of the censored portions.

Our ruling today merely upholds the CIA secrecy agreement and determines that the CIA properly classified the deleted items in McGehee's article. The CIA has not sought an injunction against publication of the censored items. If the CIA did seek judicial action to restrain publication, it would bear a much heavier burden. The Supreme Court has long observed that "the chief purpose of the first amendment's guaranty is to prevent previous restraints upon publication."

We must accordingly establish a standard for judicial review of the CIA classification decision that affords proper respect to the individual rights at stake while recognizing the CIA's technical expertise and practical familiarity with the ramifications of sensitive information. We conclude that reviewing courts should conduct a *de novo* review of the classification decision, while giving deference to reasoned and detailed CIA explanations of that classification decision.

We begin with an examination of the standard employed in the review of FOIA requests for classified information, because the scope of judicial review in this case should be at least that broad. The FOIA calls for de novo judicial review of an agency decision, and places the burden on the agency to justify its claim of exemption. At the same time, courts are to "accord substantial weight to an agency's affidavit concerning the details of the classified status of the disputed record" because "the Executive departments responsible for national defense and foreign policy matters have unique insights into what adverse affects [sic] might occur as a result of a particular classified record."

This circuit has on many occasions reviewed whether the denial of a FOIA request properly fell within the FOIA exemption for classified documents. In these cases, we have established that CIA explanations for its classification decisions should be neither "conclusory, merely reciting statutory standards, [nor] too vague [n]or sweeping." At the same time, "once satisfied that the proper procedures have been followed and that the information logically falls into the exemption claimed, the courts 'need not go further to test the expertise of the agency, or to question its veracity when nothing appears to raise the issue of good faith.'" Similarly, in Alfred A. Knopf, Inc. v. Colby, the Fourth Circuit, after invoking the FOIA standard, announced a "presumption of regularity" for CIA classification decisions.

Because the present case implicates first amendment rights, however, we feel compelled to go beyond the FOIA standard of review for cases reviewing CIA censorship pursuant to secrecy agreements. While we believe courts in securing such determinations should defer to CIA judgment as to the harmful results of publication, they must nevertheless satisfy themselves from the record, in camera or otherwise, that the CIA in fact had good reason to classify, and therefore censor, the materials at issue. Accordingly, the courts should require that CIA explanations justify censorship with reasonable specificity, demonstrating a logical connection between the deleted information and the reasons for classification. These should not rely on a "presumption of regularity" if such rational explanations are missing. We anticipate that in camera review of affidavits, followed if necessary by further judicial inquiry, will be the norm. Moreover, unlike FOIA cases, in cases such as this both parties know the nature of the information in question. Courts should therefore strive to benefit from "criticism and illumination by the party with the actual interest in forcing disclosure." This was, in fact, the procedure employed by the district court here.

This circuit has devised a system that employs "detailed public justifications" by the CIA and rebuttal by the FOIA claimant, in an attempt to create some semblance of adversarial process.

We accordingly reject McGehee's claim that the district court improperly gave "conclusive deference" to the CIA in this case.

We are, of course, well aware that judicial review of CIA classification decisions, by reasonable necessity, cannot second-guess CIA judgments on matters in which the judiciary lacks the requisite expertise. Due to the "mosaic-like nature of intelligence gathering," for example, "what may seem trivial to the uninformed may appear of great moment to one who has a broad view of the scene and may put the questioned item of information in context." But while the CIA's tasks include the protection of the national security and the maintenance of the secrecy of sensitive information, the judiciary's tasks include the protection of individual rights. Considering that "speech concerning public affairs is more than self-expression; it is the essence of self-government," and that the line between information threatening to foreign policy and matters of legitimate public concern is often very fine, courts must assure themselves that the reasons for classification are rational and plausible ones.

We have made such a judgment in this case, and, after examining the detailed in camera affidavits of the parties, we conclude that the CIA properly classified the information at issue. The CIA affidavits give us reason to believe that disclosure of the censored portions of McGehee's article could reasonably be expected to cause serious damage to the national security. The affidavit offers reasonably convincing and detailed evidence of a serious risk that intelligence sources and methods would be compromised by disclosures proposed by McGehee. We also believe, on the basis of plausible scenarios put forward in the CIA affidavit, that the United States could suffer significant strategic and diplomatic setbacks as a result of the disclosure of the deleted information. These risks identified in the CIA affidavits do not, of course, rise to the level of certainty, but we believe they are real and serious enough to justify the classification decision in this case.

⓯

FREEDOM TO KNOW

etween 1953 and 1966, the Central Intelligence Agency (CIA) financed a massive project—code-named MKULTRA—funding the research and development of "chemical, biological, and radiological materials capable of employment in clandestine operations to control human behavior." MKULTRA was established to counter what was then perceived as Soviet and Chinese advances in sophisticated brainwashing and interrogation techniques.

The wide-ranging program consisted of some 149 subprojects which the CIA consigned to various universities and research foundations. At least 80 institutions and 185 private researchers participated. Because the CIA funded MKULTRA indirectly, many of those participating were not even aware that they were dealing with the CIA.

Over the years, the program included various medical and psychological experiments, some of which led to, as the court described, "untoward results." These controversial aspects of MKULTRA were publicized during the 1970s and quickly became the subject of executive and congressional investigations.

In August of 1977, John C. Sims, an attorney, and Sidney M. Wolfe, MD, the director of the Public Citizen Health Research Group, filed a request with the CIA through the Freedom of Information Act (FOIA) in order to obtain further information about MKULTRA. Specifically, Sims and Wolfe requested the grant proposals and contracts awarded under the MKULTRA program and the names of the institutions and individuals that had performed research.

In response to this request, the CIA made available all of the MKULTRA grant proposals and contracts. But the CIA *declined* to disclose the names of all individual researchers and 21 institutions, citing Exemption 3 of the FOIA for its refusal to do so.

Exemption 3 of the FOIA provides that an agency need not disclose "matters that are specifically exempted from disclosure by statute, provided that such statute refers to particular types of matters to be withheld." For the applicable statute, the CIA relied on 102(d)(3) of the National Security Act of 1947, which provides that "the Director of Central Intelligence shall be responsible for protecting intelligence sources and methods from unauthorized disclosure."

Dissatisfied with the CIA's limited disclosure Sims and Wolfe filed suit under the FOIA in the U.S. district court for the District of Columbia. The court ultimately ordered disclosure of the names of the participants, holding that the MKULTRA researchers and affiliated institutions were *not* "intelligence sources" within the meaning of 102(d)(3).

The government appealed the decision. On appeal, the D.C. Circuit Court of Appeals concluded, as had the district court, that 102(d)(3) qualifies as a withholding statute under Exemption 3 of the FOIA, but that the district court's analysis of that statute under the FOIA lacked a coherent definition of "intelligence sources." The court then remanded the case for reconsideration in light of the following definition: "An 'intelligence source' is a person or institution that provides, has provided, or has been engaged to provide the CIA with information of a kind the Agency needs to perform its intelligence function effectively, yet could not reasonably expect to obtain without guaranteeing the confidentiality of those who provide it."

On remand, the district court applied this definition, and it then ordered the CIA to disclose the names of 47 researchers and their affiliated institutions. The district court rejected the government's contention that the MKULTRA research was not needed to perform the CIA's intelligence function, explaining that "in view of the agency's concern that potential foreign enemies could be engaged in similar research and the desire to take effective counter-measures, the CIA could reasonably determine that this research was needed for its intelligence function."

The district court then turned to the question whether the CIA could show, as the appellate court's definition required, that it could not reasonably have expected to obtain the information supplied by the MKULTRA sources without guaranteeing confidentiality to them. The district court concluded that the CIA's policy of considering its relationships with MKULTRA researchers as confidential was *not* sufficient to satisfy the appellate court's definition because "the chief desire for confidentiality was on the part of the CIA."

The district court recognized that some of the researchers had sought—and received—express guarantees of confidentiality from the CIA, and as to those, the court held that their identities need not be disclosed. The district court also exempted other researchers from disclosure on the ground that their work for the CIA, apart from MKULTRA, required that their identities remain secret in order not to compromise the CIA's intelligence networks in foreign countries.

Finally, the district court held that there was no need to disclose the institutional affiliations of the individual researchers whose identities were exempt from disclosure. This withholding was justified by the need to eliminate the unnecessary risk that such intelligence sources would be identified indirectly.

Both the CIA and the plaintiffs appealed the district court's decision. The court of appeals affirmed that part of the district court's judgment exempting from disclosure the institutional affiliations of individual researchers found to be intelligence sources. However, it reversed the district court's ruling with respect to which individual researchers satisfied "the need-for-confidentiality" aspect of its formulation of exempt "intelligence sources."

At the outset, the appellate court rejected the suggestion that it reconsider the definition of "intelligence sources." The court then criticized the district court for focusing its inquiry on whether the CIA had in fact promised confidentiality to individual researchers. The court held that the district court's decision to automatically exempt from disclosure those researchers to whom confidentiality had been promised was erroneous.

The court directed the district court on remand to focus its inquiry on whether the CIA offered sufficient proof that it needed to cloak its efforts in confidentiality in order to obtain the type of information provided by the researcher. Only upon such a showing would the individual qualify as an "intelligence source" exempt from disclosure under the FOIA.

On appeal to the U.S. Supreme Court, it was recognized that the mandate of the FOIA calls for broad disclosure of government records. Congress recognized, however, that public disclosure is not always in the public interest and thus provided that agency records may be withheld from disclosure under any of the nine exemptions defined in 5 U.S.C. 552(b). Under Exemption 3 disclosure need not be made as to information "specifically exempted from disclosure by statute."

The questions the court considered were: (1) does 102(d)(3) of the National Security Act of 1947 constitute a statutory exemption to disclosure within the meaning of Exemption 3, and (2) are the MKULTRA researchers included within 102(d)(3)'s protection of "intelligence sources."

The court noted that Congress made the director of the CIA "responsible for protecting intelligence sources and methods from unauthorized disclosure." As part of its postwar reorganization of the national defense system, Congress chartered the CIA with the responsibility of coordinating intelligence activities relating to national security. In order to carry out its mission, the CIA was expressly entrusted with protecting the heart of all intelligence operations— "sources and methods."

Section 102(d)(3) of the National Security Act of 1947, which calls for the director of Central Intelligence to protect "intelligence sources and methods," clearly "refers to particular types of matters," and thus qualifies as a withholding statute under Exemption 3. The plain meaning of the relevant statutory provisions was therefore sufficient to resolve the question. Moreover, the legislative history of the FOIA confirmed that Congress intended 102(d)(3) to be a withholding statute under Exemption 3. Indeed, this is the uniform view among other federal courts.

The Supreme Court's conclusion that 102(d)(3) qualifies as a withholding statute under Exemption 3 was only the first step of the inquiry. CIA records are protected under 102(d)(3) only to the extent they contain "intelligence sources and methods" or if disclosure would reveal otherwise protected information.

Sims and Wolfe contended that the appellate court's definition of "intelligence sources"—focusing on the need to guarantee confidentiality in order to obtain the type of information desired—drew the proper line regarding intelligence sources deserving exemption from the FOIA. But the Supreme Court held that the plain meaning of the statutory language, as well as the legislative history of the National Security Act, indicated that Congress vested in the CIA director very *broad* authority to protect *all* sources of intelligence information from disclosure. The appellate court's narrowing of this authority not only contravened the express intention of Congress, but overlooked the practical necessities of modern intelligence gathering—the very reason Congress entrusted the CIA with such sweeping power to protect its intelligence sources and methods.

The Supreme Court pointed out that Section 102(d)(3) did not state that the CIA director is authorized to protect intelligence sources *only* if such protection is needed to obtain information that otherwise could not be acquired. Nor did the statute provide that *only* confidential or nonpublic intelligence sources are protected. Congress protected *all* sources of intelligence that provide, or are engaged to provide, information the CIA needs to perform its statutory duties with respect to foreign intelligence. The plain statutory language could not be ignored.

The legislative history of 102(d)(3) also made clear that Congress intended to give the CIA director broad power to protect the secrecy and integrity of the intelligence process. Without such protections, the agency would be virtually impotent. Congress knew the CIA would gather intelligence from an array of diverse sources. Indeed, one of the primary reasons for creating the CIA was Congress' recognition that the government would have to collect and analyze massive amounts of information in order to safeguard national security. Against this background, Congress expressly made the director responsible for "protecting intelligence sources and methods from unauthorized disclosure." Congress therefore gave the CIA broad power to control the disclosure of intelligence sources.

Applying the definition of intelligence sources fashioned by the Congress in Section 102(d)(3), the Supreme Court held that the CIA director was well within his statutory authority to withhold the names of the MKULTRA researchers from disclosure under the FOIA. The district court specifically ruled that the CIA "could reasonably determine that this research was needed for its intelligence function," and the appellate court did not question this ruling. Indeed, the record revealed that the MKULTRA research was related to the CIA's intelligence-gathering function in part because it revealed information about the ability of foreign governments to use drugs and other biological, chemical, or physical agents in warfare or intelligence operations against adversaries.

Consistent with its responsibility to maintain national security, the CIA reasonably determined that major research efforts were necessary in order to keep informed of our potential adversaries' perceived threat. The court thus concluded that MKULTRA researchers were "intelligence sources" within the broad meaning of the statute because they provided information the CIA needed to fulfill its statutory obligations with respect to foreign intelligence.

The court of appeals narrowed the CIA director's authority under Section 102(d)(3) to withhold only those intelligence sources who supplied the agency with information unattainable without guaranteeing confidentiality. This interpretation of the statute contravened its express language, the statute's legislative history, and the harsh realities of modern times. The dangerous consequences of that narrowing of the statute, the Supreme Court said, is why Congress chose to vest the director of the CIA with broad discretion to safeguard the agency's sources and methods of operation.

The Supreme Court reasoned that the appellate court had underestimated the importance of providing intelligence sources with an assurance of confidentiality that is as absolute as possible. Under that approach, the CIA would be forced to disclose a source whenever a court determined, after the fact, that the

CIA could have obtained the kind of information supplied without promising confidentiality. This forced disclosure of the identities of its intelligence sources would have a devastating impact on the CIA's ability to carry out its mission.

The Supreme Court also noted that the court of appeals failed to recognize that when Congress protected intelligence sources from disclosure, it was not simply protecting sources of secret intelligence information. Under that approach, the CIA could not withhold the identity of a source of intelligence if that information was publicly available. This analysis ignored the realities of intelligence work, which often involves seemingly innocuous sources who provide valuable intelligence information.

The court pointed out that disclosure of the subject matter of the CIA's research efforts and inquiries may compromise its ability to gather intelligence as much as disclosure of the identities of intelligence sources. A foreign government can learn a great deal about the CIA's activities by knowing the public sources of information that interest the agency. If foreign governments knew the CIA had ongoing research projects concerning brainwashing and possible countermeasures, they might have been able to infer the general nature and scope of the CIA's inquiry.

The court held that the statutory mandate of Section 102(d)(3) was therefore clear: Congress gave the director wide-ranging authority to "protect intelligence sources and methods from unauthorized disclosure." An intelligence source provides information the CIA needs to fulfill its statutory obligations, and the record established that the MKULTRA researchers provided the agency with information related to its intelligence function. Therefore, the director was authorized to withhold the identities of these researchers from disclosure under the FOIA.

The cross-petition called for a decision on whether the district court and the appellate court correctly ruled that the CIA director need not disclose the institutional affiliations of the MKULTRA researchers previously held to be "intelligence sources." The district court, in a ruling affirmed by the Court of Appeals, permitted the director to withhold the institutional affiliations of the researchers whose identities were exempt from disclosure on the ground that disclosure of "the identities of the institutions might lead to the indirect disclosure of" individual researchers. This conclusion is supported by the record. The director reasonably concluded that an observer who was knowledgeable about a particular intelligence research project, like MKULTRA, could, upon learning that research was performed at a certain institution, determine the identities of the individual researchers who are protected "intelligence sources." The court held that FOIA does not require disclosure under such circumstances.

The court remarked that the national interest sometimes makes it advisable, or even imperative, to disclose information that may lead to the identity of intelligence sources. And it is the responsibility of the CIA director, not the judiciary, to determine whether disclosure of information may lead to an unacceptable risk of compromising the CIA's intelligence-gathering process. The Supreme Court therefore held that the CIA director properly invoked Section 102(d)(3) of the National Security Act of 1947 to withhold disclosure of the identities of the individual MKULTRA researchers as protected "intelligence sources." The court also held the FOIA does not require the director to disclose the institutional affiliations of the exempt researchers in light of the record which supports the Agency's determination that such disclosure would lead to an unacceptable risk of disclosing the sources' identities.

As a result, the Supreme Court reversed that part of the judgment of the Court of Appeals regarding the disclosure of the individual researchers and affirmed that part of the judgment pertaining to disclosure of the researchers' institutional affiliations.

OPINION EXCERPT

Chief Justice Burger delivered the opinion of the Court.

Respondents' belated effort to question the [Central Intelligence] Agency's authority to engage scientists and academic researchers as intelligence sources must fail. The legislative history of 102(d)(3) indicates that Congress was well aware that the Agency would call on a wide range and variety of sources to provide intelligence. Moreover, the record developed in this case confirms the obvious importance of scientists and other researchers as American intelligence sources. Notable examples include those scientists and researchers who pioneered the use of radar during World War II as well as the group which took part in the secret development of nuclear weapons in the Manhattan Project.

The Court of Appeals narrowed the Director's authority under 102(d)(3) to withhold only those "intelligence sources" who supplied the Agency with information unattainable without guaranteeing confidentiality. That crabbed reading of the statute contravenes the express language of 102(d)(3), the statute's legislative history, and the harsh realities of the present day. The dangerous consequences of that narrowing of the statute suggest why Congress chose to vest the Director of Central Intelligence with the broad discretion to safeguard the Agency's sources and methods of operation.

The Court of Appeals underestimated the importance of providing intelligence sources with an assurance of confidentiality that is as absolute as possible. Under the court's approach, the Agency would be forced to disclose a source whenever a court determines, after the fact, that the Agency could have obtained the kind of information supplied without promising confidentiality. This forced disclosure of the identities of its intelligence sources could well have a devastating impact on the Agency's ability to carry out its mission. "The Government has a compelling interest in protecting both the secrecy of information important to our national security and the appearance of confidentiality so essential to the effective operation of our foreign intelligence service." If potentially valuable intelligence sources come to think that the Agency will be unable to maintain the confidentiality of its relationship to them, many could well refuse to supply information to the Agency in the first place.

Even a small chance that some court will order disclosure of a source's identity could well impair intelligence gathering and cause sources to "close up like a clam." To induce some sources to cooperate, the Government must tender as absolute an assurance of confidentiality as it possibly can. "The continued availability of intelligence sources depends upon the CIA's ability to guarantee the security of information that might compromise them and even endanger their personal safety."

We seriously doubt whether a potential intelligence source will rest assured knowing that judges, who have little or no background in the delicate business of intelligence gathering, will order his identity revealed only after examining the facts of the case to determine whether the Agency actually needed to promise confidentiality in order to obtain the information. An intelligence source will "not be concerned with the underlying rationale for disclosure of" his cooperation if it was secured "under assurances of confidentiality." Moreover, a court's decision whether an intelligence source will be harmed if his identity is revealed will often require complex political, historical, and psychological judgments. There is no reason for a potential intelligence source, whose welfare and safety may be at stake, to have great confidence in the ability of judges to make those judgments correctly.

The Court of Appeals also failed to recognize that when Congress protected "intelligence sources" from disclosure, it was not simply protecting sources of secret intelligence information. As noted above, Congress was well aware that secret agents as depicted in novels and the media are not the typical intelligence source; many important sources provide intelligence information that members of the public could also obtain. Under the Court of Appeals' approach, the Agency could not withhold the identity of a source of intelligence if that information is also publicly available. This analysis ignores the realities of intelligence work, which often involves seemingly innocuous sources as well as unsuspecting individuals who provide valuable intelligence information.

Disclosure of the subject matter of the Agency's research efforts and inquiries may compromise the Agency's ability to gather intelligence as much as disclosure of the identities of intelligence sources. A foreign government can learn a great deal about the Agency's activities by knowing the public sources of information that interest the Agency. The inquiries pursued by the Agency can often tell our adversaries something that is of value to them. For example, disclosure of the fact that the Agency subscribes to an obscure but publicly available Eastern European technical journal could thwart the Agency's efforts to exploit its value as a source of intelligence information. Similarly, had foreign governments learned the Agency was using certain public journals and ongoing open research projects in its MKULTRA research of "brainwashing" and possible countermeasures, they might have been able to infer both the general nature of the project and the general scope that the Agency's inquiry was taking.

The "statutory mandate" of 102(d)(3) was clear: Congress gave the Director wide-ranging authority to "protect intelligence sources and methods from unauthorized disclosure." An intelligence source provides, or is engaged to provide, information the Agency needs to fulfill its statutory obligations. The record established that the MKULTRA researchers did in fact provide the Agency with information related to the Agency's intelligence function. We therefore hold that the Director was authorized to withhold the identities of these researchers from disclosure under the FOIA.

OPINION EXCERPT

Justice Marshall, with whom Justice Brennan joins, concurring in the result.

Today's decision enables the [Central Intelligence] Agency to avoid making the showing required under the carefully crafted balance embodied in Exemption 1 [information that is classified to protect national security] and thereby thwarts Congress' effort to limit the Agency's discretion. The Court identifies two categories of information—the identity of individuals or entities, whether or not confidential, that contribute material related to Agency information gathering, and material that might enable an observer to discover the identity of such a "source"—and rules that all such information is per se subject to withholding as long as it is related to the Agency's "intelligence function." The Agency need not even assert that disclosure will conceivably affect national security, much less that it reasonably could be expected to cause at least identifiable damage. It need not classify the information, much less demonstrate that it has properly been classified. Similarly, no court may review whether the source had, or would have had, any interest in confidentiality, or whether disclosure of the information would have any effect on national security. No court may consider whether the information is properly classified, or whether it fits the categories of the Executive Order. By choosing to litigate under Exemption 3 [information that is prohibited from disclosure by another federal law], and by receiving this Court's blessing, the Agency has cleverly evaded all these carefully imposed congressional requirements.

If the class thus freed from judicial review were carefully defined, this result conceivably could make sense. It could mean that Congress had decided to slice out from all the Agency's possible documents a class of material that may always be protected, no matter what the scope of the existing executive order. But the class that the Court defines is boundless. It is difficult to conceive of anything the Central Intelligence Agency might have within its many files that might not disclose or enable an observer to discover something about where the Agency gathers information. Indeed, even newspapers and public libraries, road maps and telephone books appear to fall within the definition adopted by the Court today. The result is to cast an irrebuttable presumption of secrecy over an expansive array of information in Agency files, whether or not disclosure would be detrimental to national security, and to rid the Agency of the burden of making individualized showings of compliance with an executive order. Perhaps the Court believes all Agency documents should be susceptible to withholding in this way. But Congress, it must be recalled, expressed strong disagreement by passing, and then amending, Exemption 1. In light of the Court's ruling, the Agency may nonetheless circumvent the procedure Congress has developed and thereby undermine this explicit effort to keep from the Agency broad and unreviewable discretion over an expansive class of information.

The Court today reads its own concerns into the single phrase, "intelligence source." To justify its expansive reading of these two words in the National Security Act the Court explains that the Agency must be wary, protect itself, and not allow observers to learn either of its information resources or of the topics of its interest. "Disclosure of the subject matter of the Agency's research efforts and inquiries may compromise the Agency's ability to gather intelligence as much as disclosure of the identities of intelligence sources," the Court observes, and the "intelligence source" exemption must bear the weight of that concern as well. That the Court points to no legislator or witness before Congress who expressed a concern for protecting such information through this provision is irrelevant to the Court. That each of the examples the Court offers of material that might disclose a topic of interest, and that should not be disclosed, could be protected through other existing statutory provisions, is of no moment. That the public already knows all about the MKULTRA project at issue in this case, except for the names of the researchers, and therefore that the Court's concern about disclosure of the Agency's "topics of interest" argument is not appropriate to this case, is of no consequence. And finally, that the Agency now has virtually unlimited discretion to label certain information "secret," in contravention of Congress' explicit efforts to confine the Agency's discretion both substantively and procedurally, is of no importance. Instead, simply because the Court can think of information that it believes should not be disclosed, and that might otherwise not fall within this exemption, the Court undertakes the task of interpreting the exemption to cover that information. I cannot imagine the canon of statutory construction upon which this reasoning is based.

Congress gave to the Agency considerable discretion to decide for itself whether the topics of its interest should remain secret, and through Exemption 1 it provided the Executive with the means to protect such information. If the Agency decides to classify the identities of nonconfidential contributors of information so as not to reveal the subject matter or kinds of interests it is pursuing, it may seek an Exemption 1 right to withhold. Under Congress' scheme, that is properly a decision for the Executive. It is not a decision for this Court. Congress has elsewhere identified particular types of information that it believes may be withheld regardless of the existence of an executive order, such as the identities of Agency employees, or, recently, the contents of Agency operational files. Each of these categorical exemptions reflects a congressional judgment that as to certain information, the public interest will always tip in favor of nondisclosure. In these cases, we have absolutely no indication that Congress has ever determined that the broad range of information that will hereinafter be enshrouded in secrecy should be inherently and necessarily confidential. Nevertheless, today the Court reaches out to substitute its own policy judgments for those of Congress.

To my mind, the language and legislative history of 102(d)(3), along with the policy concerns expressed by the Agency, support only an exemption for sources who provide information based on an implicit or explicit promise of confidentiality and information leading to disclosure of such sources. That reading of the "intelligence source" exemption poses no threat that sources will "clam up" for fear of exposure, while at the same time it avoids an injection into the statutory scheme of the additional concerns of the Members of this Court. The Court of Appeals, however, ordered the release of even more material than I believe should be disclosed. Accordingly, I would reverse and remand this case for reconsideration in light of what I deem to be the proper definition of the term "intelligence source."

16

SEED MONEY

This case involved a Californian named Andrew Daulton Lee who stole classified military documents from Christopher Bryce, a longtime friend. Boyce was a code clerk employed with TRW, a large U.S. defense contractor. The classified documents revealed important information—how to decrypt secure U.S. government message traffic, and the specifications of the latest U.S. spy satellites. Lee delivered the data to agents of the Soviet Union.

With Boyce's stolen documents in hand, Lee would travel to Mexico City, where he would deliver them to Soviet embassy officials. Lee would also use these trips as an opportunity to engage in drug deals, when not busy with espionage. The espionage money thus became the seed money for Lee's drug deals. Lee would hide drugs inside the restroom of a commercial airliner, and then purchase a ticket on another airline to the same destination where he would recover the drugs on arrival.

Lee and Boyce made an agreement to evenly split the profits from the espionage ring. Boyce used his profits for personal use, while Lee financed his burgeoning drug business, purchasing even more expensive drugs, such as heroin.

On January 6, 1977, Lee was arrested by Mexican police, in front of the Soviet embassy in Mexico City, for littering. Lee was taken to Mexican police headquarters for questioning. When asked to empty his pockets, Lee removed an envelope which contained ten to fifteen strips of photographic film negatives. Pictures made from these negatives were of documents marked "Pyramider" and "Top Secret." Lee was extradited to the United States, where he was indicted for espionage:

- Count One of the indictment charged Lee with a conspiracy to knowingly and willfully deliver to the USSR information relating to the national defense of the United States.
- Count Two charged Lee with intent and reason to believe that the information would be used to the advantage of the USSR.
- Count Three charged Lee with a conspiracy for the purpose of obtaining information respecting the national defense of the United States and delivering it to the USSR.
- Count Four charged Lee with the substantive offense underlying Count Three
- Count Five charged Lee with receiving from Boyce the top-secret Pyramider documents.
- Count Seven charged Lee with having "unauthorized possession" of the various documents relating to the national defense and delivering them to the USSR.
- Count Ten charged Lee with knowingly and willfully act(ing) as an agent of the USSR without prior notification to the Secretary of State.
- Count Twelve charged Lee with knowingly and willfully receiving for his own use stolen records exceeding in value the sum of $100.00.

The evidence introduced at trial revealed that Boyce worked for TRW, Inc., which performed special studies for secret projects of the U.S. intelligence community. One such study for the CIA was the "Pyramider" project. While Boyce was given a "Top Secret" security clearance by the CIA for other work with TRW, he was never authorized access or clearance to the Pyramider project documents. The FBI found 25 of Boyce's fingerprints on Pyramider documents, and one of Lee's fingerprints was discovered on a piece of equipment in the communications vault at TRW. The assistant director of security at TRW testified that neither Boyce nor Lee had authorization to handle the files or the equipment.

Lee and Boyce apparently made many trips together to Mexico City, and Lee often traveled alone to Mexico City under an alias. On one such trip a man named Cameron Adams traveled to Mexico City with Lee. While there, Lee took tape and placed an "X" on certain poles. When Adams asked him why he did this, Lee told him that he was just "involved with a spy thing here" and that the marker on the poles was "to inform his people that he was in town."

On another occasion, Lee showed an individual named Sabel Shields a Minox camera that he owned; and Lee told Shields that "he was a Russian spy and that this was his espionage camera and that this is what he used to film top secret documents." Testimony at trial noted that this type of camera was widely used for photographing book pages and documents. Lee's camera was seized during a search of his residence. An FBI special agent and photographic expert testified that the film negatives of the Pyramider project taken from Lee in Mexico City came from Lee's camera.

Lee, according to the evidence at trial, would return from these trips to Mexico with "stacks" and "bundles" of money. He would then often proceed directly to Boyce's residence to split the proceeds.

Lee's improbable defense was that he was actually an agent of the CIA when he sold the classified information to Russian agents. Evidence of Lee's defense was always speculative at best, and it was later confirmed to be false.

On appeal to the Ninth Circuit Court of Appeals, Lee alleged (1) that the trial court did not adequately instruct the jury on his theory of defense, (2) that the admission into evidence of three affidavits prepared by CIA officials denied him his right to confrontation and were inadmissible hearsay, (3) that denial of his discovery motions was prejudicial to the preparation of his defense, (4) that the trial court improperly limited his expert's testimony, and (5) that the trial court should have held an evidentiary hearing regarding a possible conflict of interest among attorneys.

Lee contended that the trial court erred when it refused to give a requested jury instruction regarding his employment with the government. The rejected instruction read: "Unless you are convinced beyond a reasonable doubt that Andrew Daulton Lee was neither working for the U.S. government, nor had a reasonable belief he was working for the U.S. government with regard to the allegations of the indictment, you must find him not guilty. You may only convict Andrew Daulton Lee if you are convinced beyond a reasonable doubt that Andrew Daulton Lee was not working for the U.S. government and that he had no reasonable belief he was working for the U.S. government with regard to the allegations of the indictment. Otherwise you must find him not guilty."

The appellate court held that the instructions given to the jury adequately covered Lee's theory of defense. The court noted that if the jury had found that Lee had delivered the information as part of his employment by the CIA, then they could not have found that he had the necessary intent as explained in the court's instructions. The trial judge repeatedly explained what intent the jury must find to support a guilty verdict under each one of the counts of the indictment. Additionally, the indictment was read to the jury during the course of the instructions and a copy setting forth the different charges against Lee was given to the jury during their deliberations.

The trial judge instructed the jury that the crimes Lee was charged with "require proof of specific intent," which required the government to prove "that the defendant knowingly did an act which the law forbids, purposely intending to violate the law." Had the jury believed that Lee was acting for the CIA or had a reasonable belief that he was acting for the CIA, the appellate court reasoned that the government could not have found that he had the specific intent as the judge had instructed them.

Counts One, Two, Three, and Four all contained requirements that Lee must have acted with an intent that such actions would be to the advantage of the USSR. If the jury had chosen to believe the defense theory, then Lee could not have been convicted on those counts.

To refute any claim by Lee that he was employed by the CIA, the government introduced certified affidavits from three CIA officials to show that a search of the respective records in their departments had failed to disclose any entry containing Lee's name or either of his two aliases prior to the date of his arrest on January 6, 1977.

In other words, these affidavits were introduced by the government so that the jury could draw the inference that Lee had never been in the employment of the CIA. Lee contended that the admission of these affidavits into evidence was error because his Sixth Amendment confrontation right was violated and because the affidavits were inadmissible hearsay. The appellate court thought otherwise.

The government had to prove that the information gathered or transmitted by Lee related to the "national defense." Lee contended on appeal that the Pyramider project did not relate to the "national defense." The appellate court explained that there was no requirement in these statutes that the documents be marked "Top Secret," or for that matter, that they be marked secret at all. It was sufficient that the documents be related to the national defense and that they were transmitted with the intent to advantage a foreign nation or injure the United States. There was no question from the evidence produced at trial, the appellate court reiterated, that the Pyramider documents did in fact relate to "national defense."

As a result, the appellate court affirmed the guilty verdict of the trial court, which sentenced Lee to life in prison and Boyce to 40 years in prison.

OPINION EXCERPT

J. Blaine Anderson, Circuit Judge:

To refute any claim by Lee that he was employed by the CIA, the government introduced certified affidavits from three CIA officials, Robert W. Gambino, Director of the Office of Security, Robert A. Barteaux, Chief of the Information Processing Group, Information Services Staff, Directorate for Operations, and F.W.M. Janney, Director of Personnel, to show that a search of the respective records in their departments had failed to disclose any entry containing Lee's name or either of his two aliases prior to the date of his arrest on January 6, 1977. In other words, these affidavits were introduced by the government so that the jury could draw the inference that Lee had never been in the employment of the CIA. Lee contends that the admission of these affidavits into evidence was error because his Sixth Amendment confrontation right was violated and because the affidavits were inadmissible hearsay.

Although the right of confrontation and the hearsay rule protect similar interests of a defendant, they do not have identical applications. Evidence may be admissible under an exception to the hearsay rule and still violate the Confrontation Clause. Or, it may not violate the Confrontation Clause, but still be inadmissible hearsay.

The affidavits in question were admitted under a well-established exception to the hearsay rule. The absence of any record, or a negative record, is generally admissible into evidence over a hearsay objection. Rule 27 of the Federal Rules of Criminal Procedure provides that "an official record or an entry therein or the lack of such a record or entry may be proved in the same manner as in civil actions." Rule 44 of the Federal Rules of Civil Procedure provides that: "(b) written statement that after a diligent search no record or entry of a specified tenor is found to exist in the records (of his office,) designated by the statement, is admissible as evidence that the records contain no such record or entry."

And finally, the Federal Rules of Evidence specifically allow the admission of these negative records: "The following are not excluded by the hearsay rule, even though the declarant is available as a witness . . . *(10) Absence of public record or entry*. To prove the absence of a record, report, statement, or data compilation, in any form, or the nonoccurrence or nonexistence of a matter of which a record, report, statement, or data compilation, in any form, was regularly made and preserved by a public office or agency, evidence in the form of a certification in accordance with rule 902, or testimony, that diligent search failed to disclose the record, report, statement, or data compilation, or entry."

The Advisory Committee to the Federal Rules of Evidence said that the absence of any record is "probably not hearsay as defined in Rule 801." The exceptions to the hearsay rule which provide for the admissibility of negative records in the Federal Rules were designed to resolve any doubts about such evidence in favor of admissibility. When confronted with hearsay objections to evidence of the absence of any record, most courts have held such evidence admissible. Therefore, we find that the district court did not err in admitting the CIA affidavits over Lee's hearsay objection.

Dutton v. Evans is the leading Supreme Court case on the Sixth Amendment confrontation right when evidence has been admitted pursuant to a well-recognized exception to the hearsay rule. The court gave four reasons in support of its conclusion that the hearsay evidence had not violated the defendant's right of confrontation:

- The statement contained no express assertion about past facts.
- The declarant was in a position to have personal knowledge of the matters in the statement.
- The possibility that the declarant's statement was founded on faulty recollection is extremely remote.
- The circumstances surrounding the making of the statement were such that the possibility of misrepresentation was unlikely.

After applying these factors to the present case, we conclude that the admission of the CIA affidavits did not deprive Lee of his Sixth Amendment right of confrontation.

The first factor is the only one which may support Lee's position. Assuming, as we do, that the affidavits contained statements about past facts, the other factors strongly support our holding. All three of the CIA officials were in a position to know what their files contained. Lee did not challenge the foundation for the receipt of the affidavits. Robert W. Gambino personally examined the files of the Office of Security and found no previous record of Lee. Robert A. Barteaux and F. W. M. Janney, as custodians of the records in their respective departments, supervised searches of the records by personnel in their departments. These CIA officials were in positions to have personal knowledge of whether there was any record of Lee. It is doubtful that the statements were based on faulty recollection. As indicated by the affidavits, all three of the officials were in positions of superior responsibility. The rationale which underlies all of the public document exceptions to the hearsay rules is that statements made by public officials in the discharge of their duties are generally trustworthy. The fact that the CIA is the public agency involved is not a sufficient reason in itself to doubt the veracity of its officials. And finally, the circumstances surrounding the making of the affidavits also give credence to them. They were prepared on May 9, 1977, during the trial in this case. The CIA officials knew that they were to be used in this action. Presumably, these officials are aware of the consequences of swearing to the absence of any record in a court proceeding if in fact a record had existed.

Guided by these indicia of reliability, we are convinced that the admission of the CIA affidavits did not violate Lee's Sixth Amendment confrontation right. We find additional support for our holding in that the majority of the courts, by far, which have considered the admission of negative records against the Sixth Amendment challenge have arrived at the same conclusion.

APPENDIX 1

Espionage Act

THE ESPIONAGE ACT OF 1917 PROVIDES IN PART:

Section 1

That: (a) whoever, for the purpose of obtaining information respecting the national defense with intent or reason to believe that the information to be obtained is to be used to the injury of the United States, or to the advantage of any foreign nation, goes upon, enters, flies over, or otherwise obtains information, concerning any vessel, aircraft, work of defense, navy yard, naval station, submarine base, coaling station, fort, battery, torpedo station, dockyard, canal, railroad, arsenal, camp, factory, mine, telegraph, telephone, wireless, or signal station, building, office, or other place connected with the national defense, owned or constructed, or in progress of construction by the United States or under the control of the United States, or of any of its officers or agents, or within the exclusive jurisdiction of the United States, or any place in which any vessel, aircraft, arms, munitions, or other materials or instruments for use in time of war are being made, prepared, repaired. or stored, under any contract or agreement with the United States, or with any person on behalf of the United States, or otherwise on behalf of the United States, or any prohibited place within the meaning of section six of this title; or

(b) whoever for the purpose aforesaid, and with like intent or reason to believe, copies, takes, makes, or obtains, or attempts, or induces or aids another to copy, take, make, or obtain, any sketch, photograph, photographic negative, blue print, plan, map, model, instrument, appliance, document, writing or note of anything connected with the national defense; or

(c) whoever, for the purpose aforesaid, receives or obtains or agrees or attempts or induces or aids another to receive or obtain from any other person, or from any source whatever, any document, writing, code book, signal book, sketch, photograph, photographic negative, blue print, plan, map, model, instrument, appliance, or note, of anything connected with the national defense, knowing or having reason to believe, at the time he receives or obtains, or agrees or attempts or induces or aids another to receive or obtain it, that it has been or will be obtained, taken, made or disposed of by any person contrary to the provisions of this title; or

(d) whoever, lawfully or unlawfully having possession of, access to, control over, or being entrusted with any document, writing, code book, signal book, sketch, photograph, photographic negative, blue print, plan, map, model, instrument, appliance, or note relating to the national defense, willfully communicates or transmits or attempts to communicate or transmit the same and fails to deliver it on demand to the officer or employee of the United States entitled to receive it; or

(e) whoever, being entrusted with or having lawful possession or control of any document, writing, code book, signal book, sketch, photograph, photographic negative, blue print, plan, map, model, note, or information, relating to the national defense, through gross negligence permits the same to be removed from its proper place of custody or delivered to anyone in violation of his trust, or to be list, stolen, abstracted, or destroyed, shall be punished by a fine of not more than $10,000, or by imprisonment for not more than two years, or both.

Section 2

Whoever, with intent or reason to believe that it is to be used to the injury of the United States or to the advantage of a foreign nation, communicated, delivers, or transmits, or attempts to, or aids, or induces another to, communicate, deliver or transmit, to any foreign government, or to any faction or party or military or naval force within a foreign country, whether recognized or unrecognized by the United States, or to any representative, officer, agent, employee, subject, or citizen thereof, either directly or indirectly and document, writing, code book, signal book, sketch, photograph, photographic negative, blue print, plan, map, model, note, instrument, appliance, or information relating to the national defense, shall be punished by imprisonment for not more than twenty years: Provided, that whoever shall violate the provisions of subsection:

(a) of this section in time of war shall be punished by death or by imprisonment for not more than thirty years; and

(b) whoever, in time of war, with intent that the same shall be communicated to the enemy, shall collect, record, publish or communicate, or attempt to elicit any information with respect to the movement, numbers, description, condition, or disposition of any of the armed forces, ships, aircraft, or war materials of the United States, or with respect to the plans or conduct, or supposed plans or conduct of any naval or military operations, or with respect to any works or measures undertaken for or connected with, or intended for the fortification of any place, or any other information relating to the public defense, which might be useful to the enemy, shall be punished by death or by imprisonment for not more than thirty years.

Section 3

Whoever, when the United States is at war, shall willfully make or convey false reports or false statements with intent to interfere with the operation or success of the military or naval forces of the United States or to promote the success of its enemies and whoever when the United States is at war, shall willfully cause or attempt to cause insubordination, disloyalty, mutiny, refusal of duty, in the military or naval forces of the United States, or shall willfully obstruct the recruiting or enlistment service of the United States, to the injury of the service or of the United States, shall be punished by a fine of not more than $10,000 or imprisonment for not more than twenty years, or both.

Section 4

If two or more persons conspire to violate the provisions of section two or three of this title, and one or more of such persons does any act to effect the object of the conspiracy, each of the parties to such conspiracy shall be punished as in said sections provided in the case of the doing of the act the accomplishment of which is the object of such conspiracy.

Section 5

Whoever harbors or conceals any person who he knows, or has reasonable grounds to believe or suspect, has committed, or is about to commit, an offense under this title shall be punished by a fine of not more than $10,000 or by imprisonment for not more than two years, or both.

APPENDIX 2

National Security Act

THE NATIONAL SECURITY ACT OF 1947 PROVIDES IN PART:

Central Intelligence Agency

Sec. 104. [50 U.S.C. §403-4]

(a) Central Intelligence Agency—There is a Central Intelligence Agency.

(b) Function—The function of the Central Intelligence Agency is to assist the Director of the Central Intelligence Agency in carrying out the responsibilities specified in section 104A(c).

Director of the Central Intelligence Agency

Sec. 104A. [50 U.S.C. §403-4a]

(a) Director of Central Intelligence Agency—There is a Director of the Central Intelligence Agency who shall be appointed by the President, by and with the advice and consent of the Senate.

(b) Supervision—The Director of the Central Intelligence Agency shall report to the Director of National Intelligence regarding the activities of the Central Intelligence Agency.

(c) Duties—The Director of the Central Intelligence Agency shall—

(1) serve as the head of the Central Intelligence Agency; and

(2) carry out the responsibilities specified in subsection (d).

(d) Responsibilities—The Director of the Central Intelligence Agency shall—

(1) collect intelligence through human sources and by other appropriate means, except that the Director of the Central Intelligence Agency shall have no police, subpoena, or law enforcement powers or internal security functions;

(2) correlate and evaluate intelligence related to the national security and provide appropriate dissemination of such intelligence;

(3) provide overall direction for and coordination of the collection of national intelligence outside the United States through human sources by elements of the intelligence community authorized to undertake such collection and, in coordination with other departments, agencies, or elements of the United States Government which are authorized to undertake such collection, ensure that the most effective use is made of resources and that appropriate account is taken of the risks to the United States and those involved in such collection; and

(4) perform such other functions and duties related to intelligence affecting the national security as the President or the Director of National Intelligence may direct.

(e) Termination of Employment of CIA Employees—

(1) Notwithstanding the provisions of any other law, the Director of the Central Intelligence Agency may, in the discretion of the Director, terminate the employment of any officer or employee of the Central Intelligence Agency whenever the Director deems the termination of employment of such officer or employee necessary or advisable in the interests of the United States.

(2) Any termination of employment of an officer or employee under paragraph (1) shall not affect the right of the officer or employee to seek or accept employment in any other department, agency, or element of the United States Government if declared eligible for such employment by the Office of Personnel Management.

(f) Coordination with Foreign Governments—Under the direction of the Director of National Intelligence and in a manner consistent with section 207 of the Foreign Service Act of 1980 (22 U.S.C. §3927), the Director of the Central Intelligence Agency shall coordinate the relationships between elements of the intelligence community and the intelligence or security services of foreign governments or international organizations on all matters involving intelligence related to the national security or involving intelligence acquired through clandestine means.

(g) Foreign Language Proficiency for Certain Senior Level Positions in Central Intelligence Agency—

(1) Except as provided pursuant to paragraph (2), an individual in the Directorate of Intelligence career service or the National Clandestine Service career service may not be appointed or promoted to a position in the Senior

Intelligence Service in the Directorate of Intelligence or the National Clandestine Service of the Central Intelligence Agency unless the Director of the Central Intelligence Agency determines that the individual has been certified as having a professional speaking and reading proficiency in a foreign language, such proficiency being at least level 3 on the Interagency Language Roundtable Language Skills Level or commensurate proficiency level using such other indicator of proficiency as the Director of the Central Intelligence Agency considers appropriate.

(2) The Director of the Central Intelligence Agency may, in the discretion of the Director, waive the application of paragraph (1) to any position, category of positions, or occupation otherwise covered by that paragraph if the Director determines that foreign language proficiency is not necessary for the successful performance of the duties and responsibilities of such position, category of positions, or occupation.

[...]

PROTECTION OF IDENTITIES OF CERTAIN UNITED STATES UNDERCOVER INTELLIGENCE OFFICERS, AGENTS, INFORMANTS, AND SOURCES

Sec. 601. [50 U.S.C. §421]

(a) Whoever, having or having had authorized access to classified information that identifies a covert agent, intentionally discloses any information identifying such covert agent to any individual not authorized to receive classified information, knowing that the information disclosed so identifies such covert agent and that the United States is taking affirmative measures to conceal such covert agent's intelligence relationship to the United States, shall be fined under title 18, United States Code, or imprisoned not more than 15 years, or both.

(b) Whoever, as a result of having authorized access to classified information, learns the identity of a covert agent and intentionally discloses any information identifying such covert agent to any individual not authorized to receive classified information, knowing that the information disclosed so identifies such covert agent and that the United States is taking affirmative measures to conceal such covert agent's intelligence relationship to the United States, shall be fined under title 18, United States Code, or imprisoned not more than 10 years, or both.

(c) Whoever, in the course of a pattern of activities intended to identify and expose covert agents and with reason to believe that such activities would impair or impede the foreign intelligence activities of the United States, discloses any information that identifies an individual as a covert agent to any individual not authorized to receive classified information, knowing that the information disclosed so identifies such individual and that the United States is taking affirmative measures to conceal such individual's classified intelligence relationship to the United States, shall be fined under title 18, United States Code, or imprisoned not more than three years, or both.

(d) A term of imprisonment imposed under this section shall be consecutive to any other sentence of imprisonment.

APPENDIX 3

Foreign Intelligence Surveillance Act

THE FOREIGN INTELLIGENCE SURVEILLANCE ACT OF 1978 PROVIDES IN PART:

Application for an Order

Sec. 104. [50 U.S.C. §1804]

(a) Each application for an order approving electronic surveillance under this title shall be made by a Federal officer in writing upon oath or affirmation to a judge having jurisdiction under section 103. Each application shall require the approval of the Attorney General based upon his finding that it satisfies the criteria and requirements of such application as set forth in this title. It shall include—

(1) the identity of the Federal officer making the application;

(2) the identity, if known, or a description of the specific target of the electronic surveillance;

(3) a statement of the facts and circumstances relied upon by the applicant to justify his belief that—

(A) the target of the electronic surveillance is a foreign power or an agent of a foreign power; and

(B) each of the facilities or places at which the electronic surveillance is directed is being used, or is about to be used, by a foreign power or an agent of a foreign power;

(4) a statement of the proposed minimization procedures;

(5) a description of the nature of the information sought and the type of communications or activities to be subjected to the surveillance;

(6) a certification or certifications by the Assistant to the President for National Security Affairs, an executive branch official or officials designated by the President from among those executive officers employed in the area of national security or defense and appointed by the President with the advice and consent of the Senate, or the Deputy Director of the Federal Bureau of Investigation, if designated by the President as a certifying official—

(A) that the certifying official deems the information sought to be foreign intelligence information;

(B) that a significant purpose of the surveillance is to obtain foreign intelligence information;

(C) that such information cannot reasonably be obtained by normal investigative techniques;

(D) that designates the type of foreign intelligence information being sought according to the categories described in section 101(e); and

(E) including a statement of the basis for the certification that—

(i) the information sought is the type of foreign intelligence information designated; and

(ii) such information cannot reasonably be obtained by normal investigative techniques;

(7) a summary statement of the means by which the surveillance will be effected and a statement whether physical entry is required to effect the surveillance;

(8) a statement of the facts concerning all previous applications that have been made to any judge under this title involving any of the persons, facilities, or places specified in the application, and the action taken on each previous application; and

(9) a statement of the period of time for which the electronic surveillance is required to be maintained, and if the nature of the intelligence gathering is such that the approval of the use of electronic surveillance under this title should not automatically terminate when the described type of information has first been obtained, a description of facts supporting the belief that additional information of the same type will be obtained thereafter.

(b) The Attorney General may require any other affidavit or certification from any other officer in connection with the application.

(c) The judge may require the applicant to furnish such other information as may be necessary to make the determinations required by section 105.

(d) (1)(A) Upon written request of the Director of the Federal Bureau of Investigation, the Secretary of Defense, the Secretary of State, or the Director of National Intelligence, or the Director of the Central Intelligence Agency, the Attorney General shall personally review under subsection (a) an application under that subsection for a target described in section 101(b)(2).

(B) Except when disabled or otherwise unavailable to make a request referred to in subparagraph (A), an official referred to in that subparagraph may not delegate the authority to make a request referred to in that subparagraph.

(C) Each official referred to in subparagraph (A) with authority to make a request under that subparagraph shall take appropriate actions in advance to ensure that delegation of such authority is clearly established in the event such official is disabled or otherwise unavailable to make such request.

(2)(A) If as a result of a request under paragraph (1) the Attorney General determines not to approve an application under the second sentence of subsection (a) for purposes of making the application under this section, the Attorney General shall provide written notice of the determination to the official making the request for the review of the application under that paragraph. Except when disabled or otherwise unavailable to make a determination under the preceding sentence, the Attorney General may not delegate the responsibility to make a determination under that sentence. The Attorney General shall take appropriate actions in advance to ensure that delegation of such responsibility is clearly established in the event the Attorney General is disabled or otherwise unavailable to make such determination.

(B) Notice with respect to an application under subparagraph (A) shall set forth the modifications, if any, of the application that are necessary in order for the Attorney General to approve the application under the second sentence of subsection (a) for purposes of making the application under this section.

(C) Upon review of any modifications of an application set forth under subparagraph (B), the official notified of the modifications under this paragraph shall modify the application if such official determines that such modification is warranted. Such official shall supervise the making of any modification under this subparagraph. Except when disabled or otherwise unavailable to supervise the making of any modification under the preceding sentence, such official may not delegate the responsibility to supervise the making of any modification under that preceding sentence. Each such official shall take appropriate actions in advance to ensure that delegation of such responsibility is clearly established in the event such official is disabled or otherwise unavailable to supervise the making of such modification.

Issuance of an Order

Sec. 105. [50 U.S.C. §1805]

(a) Upon an application made pursuant to section 104, the judge shall enter an ex parte order as requested or as modified approving the electronic surveillance if he finds that—

(1) the application has been made by a Federal officer and approved by the Attorney General;

(2) on the basis of the facts submitted by the applicant there is probable cause to believe that—

(A) the target of the electronic surveillance is a foreign power or an agent of a foreign power: Provided, That no United States person may be considered a foreign power or an agent of a foreign power solely upon the basis of activities protected by the first amendment to the Constitution of the United States; and

(B) each of the facilities or places at which the electronic surveillance is directed is being used, or is about to be used, by a foreign power or an agent of a foreign power;

(3) the proposed minimization procedures meet the definition of minimization procedures under section 101(h); and

(4) the application which has been filed contains all statements and certifications required by section 104 and, if the target is a United States person, the certification or certifications are not clearly erroneous on the basis of the statement made under section 104(a)(7)(E) and any other information furnished under section 104(d).

(b) In determining whether or not probable cause exists for purposes of an order under subsection (a)(2), a judge may consider past activities of the target, as well as facts and circumstances relating to current or future activities of the target.

(c)(1) Specifications—An order approving an electronic surveillance under this section shall specify—

(A) the identity, if known, or a description of the specific target of the electronic surveillance identified or described in the application pursuant to section 104(a)(3) of this Act;

(B) the nature and location of each of the facilities or places at which the electronic surveillance will be directed, if known;

(C) the type of information sought to be acquired and the type of communications or activities to be subjected to the surveillance;

(D) the means by which the electronic surveillance will be effected and whether physical entry will be used to effect the surveillance; and

(E) the period of time during which the electronic surveillance is approved.

(2) Directions—An order approving an electronic surveillance under this section shall direct—

(A) that the minimization procedures be followed;

(B) that, upon the request of the applicant, a specified communication or other common carrier, landlord, custodian, or other specified person, or in circumstances where the Court finds, based upon specific facts provided in the application, that the actions of the target of the application may have the effect of thwarting the identification of a specified person, such other persons, furnish the applicant forthwith all information, facilities, or technical assistance necessary to accomplish the electronic surveillance in such a manner as will protect its secrecy and produce a minimum of interference with the services that such carrier, landlord, custodian, or other person is providing that target of electronic surveillance;

(C) that such carrier, landlord, custodian, or other person maintain under security procedures approved by the Attorney General and the Director of National Intelligence any records concerning the surveillance or the aid furnished that such person wishes to retain; and

(D) that the applicant compensate, at the prevailing rate, such carrier, landlord, custodian, or other person for furnishing such aid.

(3) Special directions for certain orders—An order approving an electronic surveillance under this section in circumstances where the nature and location of each of the facilities or places at which the surveillance will be directed is unknown shall direct the applicant to provide notice to the court within ten days after the date on which surveillance begins to be directed at any new facility or place, unless the court finds good cause to justify a longer period of up to 60 days, of—

(A) the nature and location of each new facility or place at which the electronic surveillance is directed;

(B) the facts and circumstances relied upon by the applicant to justify the applicant's belief that each new facility or place at which the electronic surveillance is directed is or was being used, or is about to be used, by the target of the surveillance;

(C) a statement of any proposed minimization procedures that differ from those contained in the original application or order, that may be necessitated by a change in the facility or place at which the electronic surveillance is directed; and

(D) the total number of electronic surveillances that have been or are being conducted under the authority of the order.

(d)(1) An order issued under this section may approve an electronic surveillance for the period necessary to achieve its purpose, or for ninety days, whichever is less, except that

(A) (1) an order under this section shall approve an electronic surveillance targeted against a foreign power, as defined in section 101(a), (1), (2), or (3), for the period specified in the application or for one year, whichever is less, and

(B) an order under this Act for a surveillance targeted against an agent of a foreign power, who is not a United States person may be for the period specified in the application or for 120 days, whichever is less.

(2) Extensions of an order issued under this title may be granted on the same basis as an original order upon an application for an extension and new findings made in the same manner as required for an original order, except that

(A) an extension of an order under this Act for a surveillance targeted against a foreign power, as defined in paragraph (5), (6), or (7) of section 101(a), or against a foreign power as defined in section 101(a)(4) that is not a United States person, may be for a period not to exceed one year if the judge finds probable cause to believe that no communication of any individual United States person will be acquired during the period, and

(B) an extension of an order under this Act for a surveillance targeted against an agent of a foreign power who is not a United States person may be for a period not to exceed 1 year.

(3) At or before the end of the period of time for which electronic surveillance is approved by an order or an extension, the judge may assess compliance with the minimization procedures by reviewing the circumstances under which information concerning United States persons was acquired, retained, or disseminated.

(e)(1) Notwithstanding any other provision of this title, the Attorney General may authorize the emergency employment of electronic surveillance if the Attorney General—

(A) reasonably determines that an emergency situation exists with respect to the employment of electronic surveillance to obtain foreign intelligence information before an order authorizing such surveillance can with due diligence be obtained;

(B) reasonably determines that the factual basis for the issuance of an order under this title to approve such electronic surveillance exists;

(C) informs, either personally or through a designee, a judge having jurisdiction under section 103 at the time of such authorization that the decision has been made to employ emergency electronic surveillance; and

(D) makes an application in accordance with this title to a judge having jurisdiction under section 103 as soon as practicable, but not later than 7 days after the Attorney General authorizes such surveillance.

(2) If the Attorney General authorizes the emergency employment of electronic surveillance under paragraph (1), the Attorney General shall require that the minimization procedures required by this title for the issuance of a judicial order be followed.

(3) In the absence of a judicial order approving such electronic surveillance, the surveillance shall terminate when the information sought is obtained, when the application for the order is denied, or after the expiration of 7 days from the time of authorization by the Attorney General, whichever is earliest.

(4) A denial of the application made under this subsection may be reviewed as provided in section 103.

(5) In the event that such application for approval is denied, or in any other case where the electronic surveillance is terminated and no order is issued approving the surveillance, no information obtained or evidence derived from such surveillance shall be received in evidence or otherwise disclosed in any trial, hearing, or other proceeding in or before any court, grand jury, department, office, agency, regulatory body, legislative committee, or other authority of the United States, a State, or political subdivision thereof, and no information concerning any United States person acquired from such surveillance shall subsequently be used or disclosed in any other manner by Federal officers or employees without the consent of such person, except with the approval of the Attorney General if the information indicates a threat of death or serious bodily harm to any person.

(6) The Attorney General shall assess compliance with the requirements of paragraph (5).

(f) Notwithstanding any other provision of this Act, officers, employees, or agents of the United States are authorized in the normal course of their official duties to conduct electronic surveillance not targeted against the communications of any particular person or persons, under procedures approved by the Attorney General, solely to—

(1) test the capability of electronic equipment, if—

(A) it is not reasonable to obtain the consent of the persons incidentally subjected to the surveillance;

(B) the test is limited in extent and duration to that necessary to determine the capability of the equipment;

(C) the contents of any communication acquired are retained and used only for the purpose of determining the capability of the equipment, are disclosed only to test personnel, and are destroyed before or immediately upon completion of the test; and

(D) Provided, That the test may exceed ninety days only with the prior approval of the Attorney General;

(2) determine the existence and capability of electronic surveillance equipment being used by persons not authorized to conduct electronic surveillance, if—

(A) it is not reasonable to obtain the consent of persons incidentally subjected to the surveillance;

(B) such electronic surveillance is limited in extent and duration to that necessary to determine the existence and capability of such equipment; and

(C) any information acquired by such surveillance is used only to enforce chapter 119 of title 18, United States Code, or section 705 of the Communications Act of 1934, or to protect information from unauthorized surveillance; or

(3) train intelligence personnel in the use of electronic surveillance equipment, if—

(A) it is not reasonable to—

(i) obtain the consent of the persons incidentally subjected to the surveillance;

(ii) train persons in the course of surveillances otherwise authorized by this title; or

(iii) train persons in the use of such equipment without engaging in electronic surveillance;

(B) such electronic surveillance is limited in extent and duration to that necessary to train the personnel in the use of the equipment; and

(C) no contents of any communication acquired are retained or disseminated for any purpose, but are destroyed as soon as reasonably possible.

(g) Certifications made by the Attorney General pursuant to section 102(a) and applications made and orders granted under this title shall be retained for a period of at least ten years from the date of the certification or application.

(h) No cause of action shall lie in any court against any provider of a wire or electronic communication service, landlord, custodian, or other person (including any officer, employee, agent, or other specified person thereof) that furnishes any information, facilities, or technical assistance in accordance with a court order or request for emergency assistance under this Act for electronic surveillance or physical search.

(i) In any case in which the Government makes an application to a judge under this title to conduct electronic surveillance involving communications and the judge grants such application, upon the request of the applicant, the judge shall also authorize the installation and use of pen registers and trap and trace devices, and direct the disclosure of the information set forth in section 402(d)(2).

Use of Information

Sec. 106. [50 U.S.C. §1806]

(a) Information acquired from an electronic surveillance conducted pursuant to this title concerning any United States person may be used and disclosed by Federal officers and employees without the consent of the United States person only in accordance with the minimization procedures required by this title. No otherwise privileged communication obtained in accordance with, or in violation of, the provisions of this Act shall lose its privileged character. No information acquired from an electronic surveillance pursuant to this title may be used or disclosed by Federal officers or employees except for lawful purposes.

(b) No information acquired pursuant to this title shall be disclosed for law enforcement purposes unless such disclosure is accompanied by a statement that such information, or any information derived therefrom, may only be used in a criminal proceeding with the advance authorization of the Attorney General.

(c) Whenever the Government intends to enter into evidence or otherwise use or disclose in any trial, hearing, or other proceeding in or before any court, department, officer, agency, regulatory body, or other authority of the United States, against an aggrieved person, any information obtained or derived from an electronic surveillance of that aggrieved person pursuant to the authority of this Act, the Government shall, prior to the trial, hearing, or other proceeding or at a reasonable time prior to an effort to so disclose or so use that information or submit it in evidence, notify the aggrieved person and the court or other authority in which the information is to be disclosed or used that the Government intends to so disclose or so use such information.

(d) Whenever any State or political subdivision thereof intends to enter into evidence or otherwise use or disclose in any trial, hearing, or other proceeding in or before any court, department, officer, agency, regulatory body, or other authority of a State or a political subdivision thereof, against an aggrieved person any information obtained or derived from an electronic surveillance of that aggrieved person pursuant to the authority of this Act, the State or political subdivision thereof shall notify the aggrieved person, the court or other authority in which the information is to be disclosed or used, and the Attorney General that the State or political subdivision thereof intends to so disclose or so use such information.

(e) Any person against whom evidence obtained or derived from an electronic surveillance to which he is an aggrieved person is to be, or has been, introduced or otherwise used or disclosed in any trial, hearing, or other proceeding in or before any court, department, officer, agency, regulatory body, or other authority of the United States, a State, or a political subdivision thereof, may move to suppress the evidence obtained or derived from such electronic surveillance on the grounds that—

(1) the information was unlawfully acquired; or

(2) the surveillance was not made in conformity with an order of authorization or approval. Such a motion shall be made before the trial, hearing, or other proceeding unless there was no opportunity to make such a motion or the person was not aware of the grounds of the motion.

(f) [*In Camera and Ex Parte Review by District Court.*] Whenever a court or other authority is notified pursuant to subsection (c) or (d), or whenever a motion is made pursuant to subsection (e), or whenever any motion or request is made by an aggrieved person pursuant to any other statute or rule of the United States or any State before any court or other authority of the United States or any State to discover or obtain applications or orders or other materials relating to electronic surveillance or to discover, obtain, or suppress evidence or information obtained or derived from electronic surveillance under this Act, the United States district court or, where the motion is made before another authority, the United States district court in the same district as the authority, shall, notwithstanding any other law, if the Attorney General files an affidavit under oath that disclosure or an adversary hearing would harm the national security of the United States, review in camera and ex parte the application, order, and such other materials relating to the surveillance as may be necessary to determine whether the surveillance of the aggrieved person was lawfully authorized and conducted. In making this determination, the court may disclose to the aggrieved person, under appropriate security procedures and protective orders, portions of the application, order, or other materials relating to the surveillance only where such disclosure is necessary to make an accurate determination of the legality of the surveillance.

(g) If the United States district court pursuant to subsection (f) determines that the surveillance was not lawfully authorized or conducted, it shall, in accordance with the requirements of law, suppress the evidence which was unlawfully obtained or derived from electronic surveillance of the aggrieved person or otherwise grant the motion of the aggrieved person. If the court determines that the surveillance was lawfully authorized and conducted, it shall deny the motion of the aggrieved person except to the extent that due process requires discovery or disclosure.

(h) Orders granting motions or requests under subsection (g), decisions under this section that electronic surveillance was not lawfully authorized or conducted, and orders of the United States district court requiring review or granting disclosure of applications, orders, or other materials relating to a surveillance shall be final orders and binding upon all courts of the United States and the several States except a United States court of appeals and the Supreme Court.

(i) In circumstances involving the unintentional acquisition by an electronic, mechanical, or other surveillance device of the contents of any communication, under circumstances in which a person has a reasonable expectation of privacy and a warrant would be required for law enforcement purposes, and if both the sender and all intended recipients are located within the United States, such contents shall be destroyed upon recognition, unless the Attorney General determines that the contents indicates a threat of death or serious bodily harm to any person.

(j) If an emergency employment of electronic surveillance is authorized under section 105(e) and a subsequent order approving the surveillance is not obtained, the judge shall cause to be served on any United States person named in the application and on such other United States persons subject to electronic surveillance as the judge may determine in his discretion it is in the interest of justice to serve, notice of—

(1) the fact of the application;

(2) the period of the surveillance; and

(3) the fact that during the period information was or was not obtained.

On an ex parte showing of good cause to the judge the serving of the notice required by this subsection may be postponed or suspended for a period not to exceed ninety days. Thereafter, on a further ex parte showing of good cause, the court shall forego ordering the serving of the notice required under this subsection.

(k)(1) Federal officers who conduct electronic surveillance to acquire foreign intelligence information under this title may consult with Federal law enforcement officers or law enforcement personnel of a State or political subdivision of a State (including the chief executive officer of that State or political subdivision who has the authority to appoint or direct the chief law enforcement officer of that State or political subdivision) to coordinate efforts to investigate or protect against—

(A) actual or potential attack or other grave hostile acts of a foreign power or an agent of a foreign power;

(B) sabotage, international terrorism, or the international proliferation of weapons of mass destruction by a foreign power or an agent of a foreign power; or

(C) clandestine intelligence activities by an intelligence service or network of a foreign power or by an agent of a foreign power.

(2) Coordination authorized under paragraph (1) shall not preclude the certification required by section 104(a)(7)(B) or the entry of an order under section 105.

APPENDIX 4

Economic Espionage Act

THE ECONOMIC ESPIONAGE ACT OF 1996 PROVIDES IN PART:

§ 1831. Economic Espionage

(a) In General—Whoever, intending or knowing that the offense will benefit any foreign government, foreign instrumentality, or foreign agent, knowingly—

(1) steals, or without authorization appropriates, takes, carries away, or conceals, or by fraud, artifice, or deception obtains a trade secret;

(2) without authorization copies, duplicates, sketches, draws, photographs, downloads, uploads, alters, destroys, photocopies, replicates, transmits, delivers, sends, mails, communicates, or conveys a trade secret;

(3) receives, buys, or possesses a trade secret, knowing the same to have been stolen or appropriated, obtained, or converted without authorization;

(4) attempts to commit any offense described in any of paragraphs (1) through (3); or

(5) conspires with one or more other persons to commit any offense described in any of paragraphs (1) through (3), and one or more of such persons do any act to effect the object of the conspiracy, shall, except as provided in subsection (b), be fined not more than $5,000,000 or imprisoned not more than 15 years, or both.

(b) Organizations—Any organization that commits any offense described in subsection (a) shall be fined not more than the greater of $10,000,000 or 3 times the value of the stolen trade secret to the organization, including expenses for research and design and other costs of reproducing the trade secret that the organization has thereby avoided.

(a) Whoever, with intent to convert a trade secret, that is related to a product or service used in or intended for use in interstate or foreign commerce, to the economic benefit of anyone other than the owner thereof, and intending or knowing that the offense will, injure any owner of that trade secret, knowingly—

(1) steals, or without authorization appropriates, takes, carries away, or conceals, or by fraud, artifice, or deception obtains such information;

(2) without authorization copies, duplicates, sketches, draws, photographs, downloads, uploads, alters, destroys, photocopies, replicates, transmits, delivers, sends, mails, communicates, or conveys such information;

(3) receives, buys, or possesses such information, knowing the same to have been stolen or appropriated, obtained, or converted without authorization;

(4) attempts to commit any offense described in paragraphs (1) through (3); or

(5) conspires with one or more other persons to commit any offense described in paragraphs (1) through (3), and one or more of such persons do any act to effect the object of the conspiracy, shall, except as provided in subsection (b), be fined under this title or imprisoned not more than 10 years, or both.

(b) Any organization that commits any offense described in subsection (a) shall be fined not more than the greater of $5,000,000 or 3 times the value of the stolen trade secret to the organization, including expenses for research and design and other costs of reproducing the trade secret that the organization has thereby avoided.

APPENDIX 5

Freedom of Information Act

THE FREEDOM OF INFORMATION ACT PROVIDES IN PART:

a) Each agency shall make available to the public information as follows:

[. . .]

(3)

(A) Except with respect to the records made available under paragraphs (1) and (2) of this subsection, and except as provided in subparagraph (E), each agency, upon any request for records which (i) reasonably describes such records and (ii) is made in accordance with published rules stating the time, place, fees (if any), and procedures to be followed, shall make the records promptly available to any person.

(B) In making any record available to a person under this paragraph, an agency shall provide the record in any form or format requested by the person if the record is readily reproducible by the agency in that form or format. Each agency shall make reasonable efforts to maintain its records in forms or formats that are reproducible for purposes of this section.

(C) In responding under this paragraph to a request for records, an agency shall make reasonable efforts to search for the records in electronic form or format, except when such efforts would significantly interfere with the operation of the agency's automated information system.

(D) For purposes of this paragraph, the term "search" means to review, manually or by automated means, agency records for the purpose of locating those records which are responsive to a request.

(E) An agency, or part of an agency, that is an element of the intelligence community (as that term is defined in section 3(4) of the National Security Act of 1947 (50 U.S.C. 401a(4))) [1] shall not make any record available under this paragraph to—

(i) any government entity, other than a State, territory, commonwealth, or district of the United States, or any subdivision thereof; or

(ii) a representative of a government entity described in clause (i).

[. . .]

(8)

(A) An agency shall—

(i) withhold information under this section only if—

(I) the agency reasonably foresees that disclosure would harm an interest protected by an exemption described in subsection (b); or

(II) disclosure is prohibited by law; and

(ii)

(I) consider whether partial disclosure of information is possible whenever the agency determines that a full disclosure of a requested record is not possible; and

(II) take reasonable steps necessary to segregate and release nonexempt information; and

(B) Nothing in this paragraph requires disclosure of information that is otherwise prohibited from disclosure by law, or otherwise exempted from disclosure under subsection (b)(3).

(b) This section does not apply to matters that are—

(1)

(A) specifically authorized under criteria established by an Executive order to be kept secret in the interest of national defense or foreign policy and (B) are in fact properly classified pursuant to such Executive order;

(2) related solely to the internal personnel rules and practices of an agency;

(3) specifically exempted from disclosure by statute (other than section 552b of this title), if that statute—

(A)

(i) requires that the matters be withheld from the public in such a manner as to leave no discretion on the issue; or

(ii) establishes particular criteria for withholding or refers to particular types of matters to be withheld; and

(B) if enacted after the date of enactment of the OPEN FOIA Act of 2009, specifically cites to this paragraph.

(4) trade secrets and commercial or financial information obtained from a person and privileged or confidential;

(5) inter-agency or intra-agency memorandums or letters that would not be available by law to a party other than an agency in litigation with the agency, provided that the deliberative process privilege shall not apply to records created 25 years or more before the date on which the records were requested;

(6) personnel and medical files and similar files the disclosure of which would constitute a clearly unwarranted invasion of personal privacy;

(7) records or information compiled for law enforcement purposes, but only to the extent that the production of such law enforcement records or information (A) could reasonably be expected to interfere with enforcement proceedings, (B) would deprive a person of a right to a fair trial or an impartial adjudication, (C) could reasonably be expected to constitute an unwarranted invasion of personal privacy, (D) could reasonably be expected to disclose the identity of a confidential source, including a State, local, or foreign agency or authority or any private institution which furnished information on a confidential basis, and, in the case of a record or information compiled by criminal law enforcement authority in the course of a criminal investigation or by an agency conducting a lawful national security intelligence investigation, information furnished by a confidential source, (E) would disclose techniques and procedures for law enforcement investigations or prosecutions, or would disclose guidelines for law enforcement investigations or prosecutions if such disclosure could reasonably be expected to risk circumvention of the law, or (F) could reasonably be expected to endanger the life or physical safety of any individual[.]

APPENDIX 6

A Brief Diversion: Hollywood Spies

A true cultural phenomenon—and one of the greatest commercial successes of the modern film industry—was the suave and handsome British Secret Intelligence Service agent James Bond, who adroitly utilized fast cars, an ever-present handgun, and disguised gadgets to accomplish his lofty mission to save the free world from nefarious villains.

Known to millions of readers and cinema goers as Agent 007, James Bond was, it turns out, the subject of a complicated stream of litigation that arose out of an almost forty-year dispute over the origins and ownership of the literary and movie character. The courts were faced with the competing claims to the rights of the James Bond character and two vigorously opposing arguments over the source from which the revered spy sprang.

One of the most important players in this litigation was Kevin McClory, an Irish screenwriter and producer who contended that he transformed the more violent and alcoholic James Bond of the Ian Fleming novels into the congenial and debonair movie character that became so wildly popular. McClory claimed infringement of his rights in eight James Bond movies that the defendants produced—*Dr. No*; *From Russia with Love*; *Goldfinger*; *Thunderball*; *You Only Live Twice*; *Diamonds Are Forever*; *The Spy Who Loved Me*; and *The World Is Not Enough*.

The defendant, a company named Danjaq, LLC, was in the business of making and distributing James Bond films, and it strongly countered the accusations of the plaintiff with the defense that James Bond was largely the creation of its original author Ian Fleming. Danjaq claimed that with one narrow exception, it owned the rights to the Bond character, rights which were transferred to it over the years by Fleming himself and by producers Harry Saltzman and Albert "Cubby" Broccoli. As a result of these diametrically competing claims, the court was asked to determine primarily whether the plaintiff McClory waited too long to claim his piece of the pie, whatever share of the pie that might be.

The beginnings of the Bond dispute could be traced back to the late 1950s, when efforts were made to bring the literary character James Bond to the screen. Ian Fleming had written seven books featuring Bond, but he had had little success in transforming the books into a screenplay, a more difficult job than it might first appear. So Fleming sought assistance and collaborated with McClory and a screenwriter named Jack Whittingham in an effort to produce a suitable movie script for the dashing secret agent. Together, the three of them composed various materials that were the precursor to the film *Thunderball* (originally called *Longitude 78 West*), which by all accounts differed significantly from Fleming's books. In particular, the screenplay deliberately modified the James Bond character created by Fleming. McClory (who, interestingly enough, had been engaged to Elizabeth Taylor before she broke it off for another man) claimed that the screenplay was the source of the "cinematic James Bond," as opposed to the literary character created by Fleming. Moreover, according to McClory, the script materials introduced the uber-evil organization SPEC-TRE (an acronym for Special Executive for Counter-intelligence, Terrorism, Revenge, and Extortion); the cat-stroking villain Ernst Stavro Blofeld; and the overarching theme of nuclear blackmail.

In 1961, unbeknownst to McClory, Fleming wrote his next book, which was also entitled *Thunderball*. It was published the same year, and it credited Fleming as the author, with no mention of either McClory or Whittingham. They were clearly offended by the slight, and they brought suit against Fleming in England, alleging that the *Thunderball* book infringed upon the rights to their screenplay.

At this same time, Danjaq was quickly moving forward with plans to make James Bond movies. It had commissioned another writer, Richard Maibaum, to write a *Thunderball* screenplay. The film followed Bond in his critical mission to find two NATO atomic bombs stolen by SPECTRE, which held the world ransom for £100 million in diamonds. The search eventually led Bond to the Bahamas, where he encountered Emilio Largo, the card-playing, eye patch-wearing SPECTRE Number Two. Backed by CIA agent Felix Leiter and Largo's mistress Domino Derval, Bond's search culminated in a riveting underwater battle with Largo's thugs.

According to McClory, this screenplay was the origin of Danjaq's various infringing acts. McClory claimed that Maibaum's screenplay was based on the earlier *Thunderball* scripts and the allegedly infringing *Thunderball* book, and

that Maibaum's screenplay lifted from them the cinematic James Bond character; SPECTRE; and the theme of nuclear blackmail. This contention was hotly
disputed by the defendants; Danjaq's president testified in his deposition that
screenwriter Maibaum did not even have access to the McClory scripts.

In order to avoid the legal disputes over the *Thunderball* script, producers
Saltzman and Broccoli decided that they would instead make *Dr. No* as the first
Bond movie. Maibaum was hired as the screenwriter. In the film, James Bond
is sent to Jamaica to investigate the disappearance of a fellow British agent. The
trail leads him to the underground base of Dr. No, who is plotting to disrupt an
early American-manned space launch with a radio beam weapon. According to
McClory, Maibaum again incorporated elements from the earlier *Thunderball*
scripts. The movie *Dr. No* was released in 1962; and after Fleming transferred
to Danjaq the film and television rights to his novels, Danjaq teamed up with
United Artists to produce other Bond films.

At this same time, the litigation over the book *Thunderball* was continuing
in Britain. In late 1963, Fleming finally admitted that the novel reproduced "a
substantial part" of the copyright material in the film scripts. The suit quickly
settled, and Fleming assigned most of his rights in *Thunderball* to McClory.
Accordingly, future versions of the book credited McClory, Whittingham, and
Fleming as the authors. The next significant event occurred in 1965, when Mc-
Clory granted Danjaq a ten-year license to make a movie based on *Thunderball*.
The movie was released later that year.

In the mid-1970s, McClory began writing a new James Bond script, together
with Sean Connery. This too led to a flurry of litigation. In 1976, McClory and
Connery sued Broccoli, United Artists, and Danjaq, claiming that the forth-
coming movie *The Spy Who Loved Me* infringed upon the script that they were
preparing (entitled either *James Bond of the Secret Service* or *Warhead*), and
they sought to enjoin the defendants from infringing upon McClory's rights in
the novel *Thunderball*. Two months later, McClory and Connery abandoned
their attempt to enjoin the release of *The Spy Who Loved Me*.

Although the 1976 case was the end of litigation relevant to this case, it
was not the end of the dispute between the parties. Between 1978 and 1983,
United Artists and the trustees of Fleming's estate sought to prevent McClory
from releasing *Never Say Never Again*, a remake of *Thunderball*. Even after
that litigation finally ended, the dispute raged on. In 1986, McClory contacted
MGM/UA to inform them that their Bond movies infringed upon his rights in
Thunderball. In 1987, he filed a correction registration with the U.S. Copyright
Office regarding the book *Thunderball*, listing himself and Whittingham as co-
authors of the book.

Fast forward ten years to 1997. By that time Danjaq had produced numerous James Bond movies, all of which turned out to be huge box office successes. In October of 1997, Sony acquired McClory's rights (whatever they were) to make Bond movies, and the company announced its plans to do so. In January 1998, Danjaq filed suit, alleging thirteen separate causes of action against Sony, Columbia Pictures, and McClory. Sony and Columbia fought back with nine counterclaims of their own.

Later that same year, Sony was enjoined from making James Bond movies. That injunction was affirmed by the Ninth Circuit Court of Appeals. In March 1999, Sony and Columbia entered into a stipulated dismissal with Danjaq. The only claim that remained was Sony's third cause of action against Danjaq for damages arising from copyright infringement. This claim was assigned back to McClory.

The last lawsuit among the parties over the James Bond character pitted McClory against Danjaq, and the gist of McClory's claim was that certain of the Bond movies released over the past thirty-six years infringed on McClory's copyrights. McClory argued that he possessed the rights to both the novel *Thunderball* and the materials developed during the preparation of the initial *Thunderball* script, and that he owned the rights to certain plot elements that first appeared in those works: namely, the "cinematic" James Bond character; SPECTRE; the villain Blofeld; and the theme of nuclear blackmail. According to Danjaq, this was the first time he was aware of such a claim.

The court eventually ruled that McClory's claims were barred by the legal doctrine of laches, concluding that McClory had known of the alleged infringement since at least 1961. McClory's suit to enforce any rights against Danjaq was filed in 1976, and it was unrelated to the claims in the present case. Thus, there had been a delay of at least 21 years—and more likely, 36 years—between McClory's knowledge of the potential claims and the initiation of litigation. The court also noted that Danjaq had presented overwhelming evidence of substantial prejudice due to McClory's delay.

The court also found *no* evidence of deliberate infringement that would excuse the delay in bringing suit. To the contrary, Danjaq had formerly acknowledged McClory's limited rights in *Thunderball* and obtained a license for these rights. The court therefore dismissed McClory's case with prejudice. McClory appealed the ruling.

The primary issue before the court was Danjaq's contention that McClory's claim was barred by laches, a little-used legal theory that prevents a plaintiff, who with full knowledge of the facts, acquiesces in a transaction and then rests on his rights. To demonstrate laches, the defendant must prove both an unreasonable delay by the plaintiff and resulting prejudice to the defendant. The relevant period of delay in laches generally spans the period from when the plaintiff knew (or should have known) of the allegedly infringing conduct until the initiation of the lawsuit. For seven of the eight allegedly infringing movies in the present case, the calculation was simple, and from the time the films were released (between 1962 and 1977) until McClory filed his counterclaim in this suit (1998), McClory took no legal action to stop or seek redress for the alleged infringements. The period of delay therefore ranged from 36 years (*Dr. No*) to 19 years (*The Spy Who Loved Me*). By any measure, the delay was clearly sufficient to constitute laches in the court's view.

McClory urged the court to calculate the delay a little differently. He contended that various actions on his behalf should actually stop the clock. He first referred to his 1961 lawsuit as such an event, but the court pointed out that this suit was against Fleming—not Danjaq. Second, McClory urged the court to stop the clock with the filing of his 1976 lawsuit in which he sought to enjoin Danjaq from infringing his rights in *Thunderball*. That litigation, however, was dismissed the same year. To the extent the suit tolled laches, it was only momentary, and the clock soon began running again—some twenty-two years before McClory brought the instant claims.

The court also dealt with the plaintiff's claims of infringement stemming from re-releases of Bond movies on DVD that were "delayed" for purposes of laches. Where infringement of the DVD was identical to the infringement in the underlying movie, the court felt that the two should be treated identically for purposes of laches. It would be incongruous, the court said, to hold the contrary and say that McClory's claim for infringement on a re-release survives despite dismissal on the original work. This exception, the court said, would effectively swallow the rule of laches and render it a useless defense.

For similar reasons, the court rejected McClory's argument that laches cannot bar a claim for infringement brought within the statute of limitations. Although such an application of laches may be unusual, it was appropriate here. The court concluded that McClory's extraordinary delay and the resulting prejudice to Danjaq rendered laches appropriate in spite of the statute of limitations.

The next question was whether McClory's delay was reasonable. The court held that it was not. Delay is permissible when it is necessitated by the exhaustion of administrative remedies, when it is used to evaluate and prepare a complicated claim, and when its purpose is to determine whether the scope of proposed infringement will justify the cost of litigation. But such a delay is inexcusable when its purpose is to capitalize on the alleged infringer's labor after it becomes clear that the infringing product is profitable.

In the instant case, McClory explained that he did not know of the extent of the infringement until recently. The court was unsympathetic, and it admonished the plaintiff, remarking that this was not a case of secret computer code but of widely distributed movies that were first released some forty years earlier. The very purpose of laches as an *equitable* doctrine—and the reason it differs from a statute of limitations—is that the claim is barred because the plaintiff's delay caused the defendant's prejudice. Courts have recognized two forms of prejudice in the laches context—evidentiary and expectations-based. Evidentiary prejudice includes such matters as lost, stale, or degraded evidence, or witnesses whose memories have faded or who have died. A defendant may also demonstrate prejudice by showing that it took actions or suffered consequences that it would not have had the plaintiff promptly brought suit.

The trial court concluded that Danjaq established both forms of prejudice. It was uncontested that many of the key figures in the creation of the James Bond movies had died in the intervening forty years. These included Ian Fleming, Harry Saltzman, and Cubby Broccoli (the producers); Terence Young (the director of *Dr. No*; *From Russia with Love*; and *Thunderball*); Richard Maibaum (the screenwriter who wrote seven of the allegedly infringing films); and Richard Whittingham (the screenwriter hired by McClory to work on *Thunderball*).

The president of Danjaq presented testimony that many of the relevant records were missing, and that he did not know where the remaining documents were. The Maibaum scripts for *Thunderball* were gone, as were all but the final draft of the *Dr. No* shooting script. McClory responded that there were still some witnesses who could testify, and that the case primarily depended upon a comparison of written materials rather than live testimony. But neither argument was sufficient to alleviate the obvious evidentiary prejudice to Danjaq. The proper inquiry was not, the court pointed out, whether *some* witnesses might be available, but whether the absence of *other* witnesses (who were unavailable because of McClory's delay) would prejudice Danjaq.

It appeared clear that Danjaq would be harmed by the absence of key witnesses. Maibaum wrote the allegedly infringing *Thunderball* shooting script, as well as the allegedly infringing *Dr. No* script. He was surely the person most familiar with the composition of those scripts (as well as the ones that followed), and he would be the best source if Danjaq were to advance a defense of "independent creation" to the infringement claim. Likewise, the producers were integral to the background of the case. The fact that there were still a few survivors to tell part of the story did little to reduce the prejudice caused by the unavailability of most of the key players.

McClory next argued that the equitable defense of laches was nonetheless inapplicable because Danjaq *willfully* infringed his intellectual property rights. Rather than imposing new standards on this already complex area of law, the court accepted the parties' agreement to adopt the definition of willful infringement used elsewhere in the Copyright Act.

The court recounted the record before it. In the early 1960s, McClory and Fleming were embroiled in a dispute over the rights to the *Thunderball* novel and script materials. Danjaq was aware of this dispute and took care not to infringe McClory's rights. In the negotiation of the film rights to Fleming's books, *Thunderball* was expressly excluded from the deal pending the outcome of the litigation between Fleming and McClory. When the litigation dragged on, Danjaq abandoned its plans to make *Thunderball*, and instead it proceeded with *Dr. No*.

Despite McClory's struggles with Fleming over the rights to *Thunderball,* McClory did not file suit against Danjaq for purported infringements in *Dr. No* or *From Russia with Love,* nor did he complain about it. Indeed, not only did he fail to sue Danjaq, he went into business with them. In 1965, McClory and Danjaq negotiated a ten-year license in which Danjaq released *Thunderball.* This fact, too, suggested an absence of bad faith on Danjaq's part, and it further indicated that Danjaq had no notice of any copyright claims by McClory regarding Danjaq projects. When McClory sued Danjaq in 1976, alleging, among other things, that the soon-to-be released movie *The Spy Who Loved Me* infringed upon his rights in *Thunderball,* Danjaq responded by removing the allegedly infringing material. The suit settled, and although Danjaq had released nine other Bond films by that time, McClory never claimed that it had pirated the Bond character.

This was not to say that Danjaq's conduct was beyond reproach. According to McClory, certain elements that were first developed in McClory's materials made their way into Maibaum's script for *Dr. No*. In particular, McClory claimed that he originated the "cinematic" James Bond character, one who was witty and dashing rather than brooding and alcoholic.

But even assuming his allegations to be true, McClory could only show infringement—not *willful* infringement. McClory produced no direct evidence of willful infringement, nor did the circumstantial evidence support this claim. Indeed, Danjaq was not on notice that McClory claimed a right in the cinematic

James Bond character. The Bond character had been developed by Fleming over the course of six years and seven books before McClory came into the picture. Even assuming that McClory reinvented the Bond character in the *Thunderball* script materials, there was no way for Danjaq to know that McClory was laying claim to such a property. The complexity of the chain of title to the various stories further precluded a jury finding of willful infringement. Both *Dr. No* and *Thunderball* were produced under color of title, an arrangement that defeated the willfulness claim. Danjaq was simply *not* on notice as to the rights now claimed by McClory, nor was there any evidence that Danjaq decided to gamble on the ultimate determination of rights.

McClory argued that laches did not bar *all* of his claims. In particular, McClory argued that even if laches applied, it did not bar a prospective injunction against future infringement. But in this case, any future infringements would be *identical* to the alleged past infringements. Sequels and re-releases presented this issue most directly. McClory contended that each of the objectionable James Bond movies—past, present, and future—infringed upon his rights in the same way, stemming from Maibaum's access to the *Thunderball* script materials. The court held that in a situation like this one, laches may bar *prospective* injunctive relief as well.

In the end, Danjaq had clearly established its laches defense, and because McClory was unable to show willful infringement, his claims were banned in their entirety. A dozen years after this litigation ended, MGM and Danjaq announced that they had acquired all rights to James Bond from the estate of Kevin McClory, finally bringing to an end a dispute about the famed British spy that had spanned almost half a century.

NOTES

CHAPTER ONE

Gorin v. U.S., 111 F.2d 712 (9th Cir. 1940)
Gorin v. U.S., 312 U.S. 19 (1941)

CHAPTER TWO

Rosenberg v. U.S., 195 F.2d 583 (2d Cir. 1952)
Rosenberg v. U.S., 346 U.S. 273 (1953)
Rosenberg v. U.S., 346 U.S. 324 (1953)
Rosenberg v. U.S., 360 U.S. 367 (1959)

CHAPTER THREE

U.S. v. Abel, 155 F.Supp. 8 (E.D. N.Y. 1957)
U.S. v. Abel, 258 F.2d 485 (2d Cir. 1958)
U.S. v. Abel, 362 U.S. 217 (1960)

CHAPTER FIVE

U.S. v. Campa, 459 F.3d 1121 (11th Cir. 2006)
U.S. v. Campa, 529 F.3d 980 (11th Cir. 2008) (en banc)

CHAPTER SIX

U.S. v. Truong, 629 F.2d 908 (4th Cir. 1980)

CHAPTER SEVEN

U.S. v. Duran, 596 F.3d 1283 (11th Cir. 2010)

CHAPTER EIGHT

U.S. v. Chung, 659 F.3d 815 (9th Cir. 2011)

CHAPTER NINE

American Civil Liberties Union v. Clapper, 785 F.3d 787 (2d Cir. 2015)
U.S. v. Miller, 874 F.2d 1255 (9th Cir. 1989)

CHAPTER TEN

U.S. v. Biro, 143 F.3d 1421 (11th Cir. 1998)

CHAPTER ELEVEN

Wolston v. Reader's Digest Association, Inc., 429 F.Supp. 167 (D.D.C. 1977)
Wolston v. Reader's Digest Association, Inc., 578 F.2d 427 (D.C. Cir. 1978)
Wolston v. Reader's Digest Association, Inc., 433 U.S. 157 (1979)

CHAPTER TWELVE

Tenet v. Doe, 329 F.3d 1135 (9th Cir. 2003)
Tenet v. Doe, 544 U.S. 1 (2005)

CHAPTER THIRTEEN

Agee v. Vance, 483 F. Supp. 729 (D.D.C. 1980)
Agee v. Muskie, 629 F.2d 80 (D.C. Cir. 1980)
Haig v. Agee, 453 U.S. 280 (1981)

CHAPTER FOURTEEN

McGehee v. Casey, 718 F.2d 1137 (D.C. Cir. 1983)

CHAPTER FIFTEEN

CIA v. Sims, 642 F.2d 562 (D.C. Cir. 1980)
CIA v. Sims, 709 F.2d. 95 (D.C. Cir. 1983)
CIA v. Sims, 471 U.S. 159 (1985)

CHAPTER SIXTEEN

U.S. v. Dalton, 589 F.2d 980 (9th Cir. 1979)

APPENDIX 1

Pub.L. 65–24, 40 Stat. 217

APPENDIX 2

Pub.L. 80-253, 61 Stat. 495, 50 U.S.C. ch. 15 § 401

APPENDIX 3

92 Stat. 1783, 50 U.S.C. ch. 36 § 1801 et seq

APPENDIX 4

Pub. L. 104–294, 110 Stat. 3488

APPENDIX 5

Pub. L. 89–487, 80 Stat. 250, 5 U.S.C. ch. 5, subch. II § 552

APPENDIX 6

Danjaq LLC v. Sony Corporation, 263 F.3d 942 (9th Cir. 2001)

Note: For the sake of clarity, the judicial opinion excerpts do not include references to legal citations.

INDEX

ABOUT THE AUTHOR

Cecil C. Kuhne III is a litigator in the Dallas office of Norton Rose Fulbright and the author of eighteen books on litigation published by the American Bar Association. He reluctantly confesses that the closest he has ever come to the world of espionage is a shelf full of John le Carré spy novels—though he does readily admit to a certain penchant for the well-worn trench coat.